1

*All recent photos included in **You Too Can Mow the Grass** were taken by Laura Beth Wheeler of lbwphotography in Flowery Branch, Georgia.*

All other photos are personal snap shots from family.

December 2010

ISBN-13: 978-1468073317
ISBN-10: 1468073311

This book is dedicated to my great-grandmother, my grandmother, my mother, my daughters, and all of the friends in my life who have made their own share of mistakes and burdens to carry on their journey to find real love and happiness; divorce happens to some of us, death comes to us all in time, and so does real love, and real loves lasts forever...

Acknowledgements

Even if you feel alone, you are not alone. There are people who will go out of their way to extend kindness. Over the years, many have helped me make it through the tragedy of the moment and many have celebrated the triumphs beside me. Some are mentioned in this book, and when you read their names, you should know that I will always be eternally grateful for the ways in which blessings came to me through their words and actions. I want to acknowledge directly the people who supported me since my divorce and through the writing of this book. To my parents who have been right there for every bump in the road, and even when they disagreed with my opinions or disapproved of my actions, they never failed me. To my daughters who had to make difficult transitions when their lives should have been more stable; I am so proud of you for your strength and your resilience and your goodness. To Dr. Brent Archer of Northeast Georgia Diagnostic, Dr. Eddie Allen of Gastroenterology Associates, Dr. Wendell Turner of Gainesville Gynecology, Dr. Tom Brosky of Foot & Ankle Clinic of Oakwood, and especially to my friend, Dr. Kent G. Miller of Kent G. Miller Gynecology, for above and beyond medical care. To all of my friends who bring joy and hope and fun to my life; I don't have space to name every friend, but the following hold a special place in my heart: Debbie, Beth, Sharon, Thomas, Elizabeth, Charles, Noel, Misti, Yvette, Celena, my bbf Dana, Alexa, and Ellie. You may not remember the exact moment you made me feel loved; but I do. And so, I thank you. *Merci, bonnes amies*, forever and always.

Prologue – Welcome to my Life

After having been married for over 14 years, I had no idea how to start over. Getting a divorce was not part of my life plan. I still tell my daughters that when you marry you make a promise for a lifetime to stay committed. And yet, I am divorced now. I am divorced for the second time. That's right; a woman who believes in monogamy and lifetime commitment to her husband has been divorced twice. Sometimes life just doesn't happen the way you expect. I decided to write this book over the second year to share with you how I learned to have a positive attitude about the life I actually have. The events of each day led me to reflect on the events of my entire life from childhood to now. As you read my journal, you'll become acquainted with the emotional pain of domestic abuse, loss of a child, death, divorce, failure and the wonderful discovery of happiness in the midst of it all. No doubt you have experienced something similar in your life and if you're struggling with depression, fear, anxiety, self disregard, and more, then I hope these stories of my life will help you find what you need to be happy. Please share my life story with your friends who are hurting and starting over after a failed relationship. I ask many questions throughout my journal in my search to find myself, and I pose these questions to you. I encourage you to start your own journal and write down your responses. I encourage you to look for the beauty in nature and the good in every situation. And then I encourage you to take care of yourself, stand up for yourself, and begin today creating a new life full of joy and laughter and love.

You too can mow the grass

A Journal about finding Happiness after Divorce

by

Allison Joy Ainsworth

Monday, November 15, 2010

A year ago today I came home to Georgia from a business trip in Chicago to a dark and empty house. My second husband, Stuart, of 14 plus years had moved out. The children were sleeping over at the grandparents, because my flight was getting in so late. I knew when I boarded the plane I would be all alone that night at my house. I just dropped my suitcases in the middle of the floor and crawled into the bed. I cried until I fell asleep. My mother dropped the kids off in the morning. I sent them to school, and I went to work the next morning just like it was any other day. But it wasn't like any other day.

And this was not the first time I entered a dark and empty house, or to be more accurate, a dark and empty apartment. Or at least, I thought it was empty. But across the room I could see the faint glow of the end of a cigarette. It was the middle of a normal hot Louisiana afternoon in 1990; I had just come home from working at the restaurant where I waited tables. My baby was sleeping in his crib. My first husband, Roger, was smoking a cigarette in the dark. The blinds were closed, and the lights were turned off. By the time my eyes adjusted to the darkness, he was already across the room and standing in front of me. And then he hit me so hard I fell down. It was not the first time he had hit me. And then he kicked me in the ribs. I think I took too long driving home from work. I don't know how many times he struck me before he picked me up and threw me out the front door of the apartment onto the sidewalk. I was screaming at him. He was cursing at me. Our neighbor, his friend, came running out with his shotgun. I remember him standing in front of me facing my first husband. I remember him saying "don't touch her" and holding the shotgun firmly. It was if time froze. I don't know how long we all stood there. The deputy arrived. What was going on

8

was obvious, but he asked the question anyway. My neighbor answered for me. "Yes, he was beating her". The deputy asked if I was stabbed or shot. I said shook my head no. "Well", he said, "if there's no blood, then I think you can just go back inside and settle this for yourselves". My neighbor answered for me again. "My wife's a nurse. The only place Allison is going is to the hospital."

And then I realized what was happening. My baby was sleeping in his crib in the apartment, my first husband was standing in the doorway of the apartment, and I was standing on the sidewalk outside. I squeaked out, "What about Matthew? Can I go get my baby?" Roger shook his head no. The deputy said "he didn't know whose baby he was, so he wasn't going to worry about that". That day I learned possession is 9/10 of the law, and I could choose to go in and stay, or I could go to the hospital. My neighbor answered for me again. Hospital. In the ER, the doctor examined all of my injuries. No stab wounds. No bullet holes. Bruises, bruises, and more bruises. Cracked ribs. I don't know if you've ever been examined in the ER for something like this, but this is what the doctors do. On what looks like a child's coloring sheet of the human body, the doctor makes an identical mark on the page like the mark on your body. My paper body was colored on quite a bit. Eventually I was released from the ER, and I stayed with family. About two weeks later, I got the judge to allow me to see my baby. One of my waitress friends from work went with me. He cursed at me the entire time I was there. About two months later, I moved back in. I just couldn't stand being away from my baby. This wasn't the first time I was beaten. And it wasn't the last time I was beaten. It took me a couple of years to get the courage to leave, because Roger had learned the secret to make me stay. My son Matthew.

After the flood which totally destroyed our apartment complex, we moved to another apartment with two entrances, a regular living room front door which faced the pool, and a back door which entered through the master bedroom. In the almost three years we were married, we lived three different places. Roger's drinking got worse. The abuse got worse. Sometimes I would go days without eating, because I wasn't allowed to eat. I read my Bible in secret, because that too was a punishable offense. I started tucking a few dollars of my tip money inside my sock before I came home, so that I'd have money to buy milk and diapers. Most of my tip money purchased Crown Royal, cigarettes, and I don't know what else. I managed to stay in college although my grades were horrible.

I can honestly say, divine intervention, got me out of my first marriage alive. I hadn't spoken with my family in months, because that too was a punishable offense. In fact, everything was a punishable offense. I had to ask permission to go to the bathroom, to eat, to do anything. Most of the time, I just did what he said. It was easier. But sometimes I would stand up to him if it was really important. Like the time when we picked my son up from day care and my first husband didn't want to take the time for me to buckle him into the car seat. But I buckled him in anyway. He slammed my head into the top of the car door. I got a cut on my forehead, but I got my way. My son rode home safely in the car seat. And when we were around friends, he would put his arm around me and whisper in my ear. Friends used to think he was being romantic, but really he was informing me how I had messed up, and how he would punish me later. In detail, he would describe the torture I would receive. And if I didn't smile, or if I let on that I was anything but happy, then the punishment would be worse. And sometimes that meant my son would be denied a bottle and locked in a separate room from me, so I'd be forced to listen to him wailing in hunger in between the beatings or the threats of something worse. That's how it was the last night I lived with my first husband listening to Matthew cry in the other room while Roger threatened to do things to me that would make Jeffrey Dahmer look like a saint.

And with a lot of help from people God put into my path – my supervising teacher, Mrs. Guyton, at the middle school where I did my student teaching, her husband Mr. Guyton - the chief of police, my attorney Mr. Foley – a good Christian man who let me tutor his children to pay off my legal bills, a few friends, and my parents and grandparents – I escaped two months before I graduated with my college degree in education. Many things happened between 1992 and 1995, but I'll share some of those details later. The most important thing that happened was I was safe. And I chose a safe relationship. I married my second husband, Stuart, because I loved him, of course. But also, he was kind to me and to my son. I knew he would never hit me. In 14 years, he never raised his voice that I can remember. I also married him, because I thought he'd be a good provider. So that's what I thought I was getting, safety and security. I thought the best I could hope for was to not live in an abusive marriage.

I don't think I really knew what to expect from my second marriage. I thought if I had a husband who didn't hit me, I'd be happy. And I was. Stuart and I had a good marriage, better than most. At least, that's what I told myself when I cried myself to sleep that night, November 15, 2009. I really didn't know why we were getting a divorce. Our marriage fell apart over time; it wasn't like it was a surprise. But being alone in my house was a shock. I never really thought he would leave. I never really thought that my safety and security could evaporate just like that. A week later, the day before Thanksgiving, Stuart served me with divorce papers. He left them on the dining room table while my children, my mother, and I were eating lunch out. My second marriage was over, and the next day, I put a Thanksgiving feast on the table like it was just another Thanksgiving. But it wasn't like any other Thanksgiving. I just didn't know what else to do except to pretend for my daughters Isabel and Grace that everything was normal even though Daddy no longer lived at home.

Thursday, November 18, 2010

It's been an entire year. I just returned from a business trip in San Francisco. Every night I attended parties hosted by various business colleagues, publishers, and friends. The past year, I published a small textbook, and so I was chatting with the different ladies who helped me with that project. My friend, Noel, also a spectacular, professional woman, said "Wow, you look great!" To which I replied, "I'm single now, so you never know who you will meet at one of these things". All three of them hollered "Update!" Well, they aren't Southern woman, so they didn't holler, but they really wanted to know what I meant, because when they had seen me a year earlier, I was married. Except for two of my friends at the conference in Chicago who happened to be sitting next to me when I got the message about the moving van in my driveway, no one knew I came home to an empty house a year earlier. "Okay, well, since I saw you last, my husband left me, I finished my dissertation, received a promotion at work, and I learned to mow the grass". Yes, I went to Home Depot and bought a lawn mower. You should have seen me at the Home Depot; the poor sales guy was forced to answer my litany of questions about the operation and maintenance of lawn mowers for over an hour.

Ironically, Stuart and I had a lawn service. But my reduced household income couldn't afford a lawn service and shoes and legal bills. At first, I felt like this was a necessary evil. Someone had to mow the grass. I didn't really want that someone to be me. And then, I started mowing the grass. Yes, I actually mowed the grass for the first time in my life at 41 years of age. I thought to myself, I'm a woman! A smart, capable woman! I almost have a doctorate degree. I read the instruction manual, and I mixed the additive with the gasoline like I was supposed to, and I knew how to check the oil. I don't need a man to mow the grass! Who knew that mowing grass could be so empowering. Did you know that something as simple as mowing the grass can make you feel invincible and ready to tackle any bad things that happen in your life? Well, it can. In this past year, I've learned a lot of things about myself. I've learned how to do a lot of things. I've done things I never thought I could do, things I wanted to do, but just never have, and I've done them without a husband.

Standing there in the sexy red dress I borrowed from my friend, I told them about my neighbor Jenn whose husband recently left her for another woman. They have three small children together. She is a nurse who moved down to Georgia from New Jersey. I remember the night she called me. She told me, because she knew I'd understand how she was feeling. After all, I was a divorced, professional woman, with children. And as she blurted out all the details, I replied when she took a breath, "He left the lawn mower?" "Yes, he left everything." "Well, don't worry, because if I can do it, you can too. You too can mow the grass!" Either everyone laughed because the way I told the story was funny or because there was an open bar; Noel said, "Allison, you should write a book, and the title is obvious." *You too can mow the grass.*

And what else can a woman do in addition to mowing the grass? I looked back at my life and for the first time I saw the woman I had become in the past twenty years. And I like her. And I think you'll like her too. So today, I started writing down stories of the things which happened to me over my lifetime and after my divorce(s) to inspire women to have a happy and positive attitude about life. I don't want to be one of those women that spend the rest of their life being bitter and angry. I know too many women who are miserable and victimized. I wasn't going to be like that. I set out trying to figure out how to be happy, and I want to share what I learned with you, because I don't want you to be bitter and angry about your failed relationships either. Whether your divorce happened recently or many years ago, whether you're a child of divorce who hasn't healed from the pain of your parents' divorce, or whether you're just afraid to make the wrong choice in a life partner, I hope one of my stories will inspire you to be happy, to love, to have a renewed spirit, and to believe that good things will happen in your life.

Friday, November 19, 2010

Friends are great! I don't know if I could have survived the year after my divorce if it weren't for my friends. They have kept me on the party invitation list, even though I come alone. When a long time married couple divorces, friends struggle with knowing what to do and with whom to be friends. And whether you ask them to or not, friends tend to take sides. Friends will decide which one of the couple is the one to keep and which one is the one to divorce from the friend circle. Sometimes they stick with the one they were friends with before the marriage. Sometimes they go with the one they believe got screwed. Sometimes they go with the one they just like better. And friends do not care what your divorce agreement says or whether or not your ex likes the post-divorce friend shakeup. My friends were mean, where I couldn't be. My friends said and did stuff in the interest of having my back that I had to ask them to stop doing. No matter how someone hurts me, if I love him, I cannot intentionally hurt him or take revenge. But I can laugh at the crazy game plans they thought of, but then I would beg them not to follow through. I have children, after all. And friends, of course, want you to start dating immediately. They will try to talk you into on-line dating. They will secretly try to introduce you to someone at a party without being too obvious.

But until you are ready to date, just don't worry about dating. Some women are content to live a single life and avoid serious relationships out of fear. Some women live vicariously through their children. Some women let themselves go and stay home in front of the TV every night. Some women go through a series of short-lived romances that burn fast and flame out quickly. I don't want any of those choices. I'm willing to date to get to know men and to find the man with whom I enjoy being a companion, who satisfies me completely in every way, and who loves me for me. And if I have to date for a long time, or if I never find such a man, then that's okay. I'm not willing to settle for anything less than the complete package. After all, I've been married twice, and if I ever do get married again, it will be for life. And I want to have no doubts about that before I commit. Are you ready to start dating again? Are you ready to start over? Or are you just trying to survive today without losing your mind? Are you afraid that you're going to make the same mistakes over and over again?

I'd like to think that I've learned from my past mistakes and bad judgment. I married at 19 honestly because I was going to have a baby. I didn't want to get married, but everyone said I should. Roger didn't want to marry me, but everyone said he should. We really weren't even that serious of a couple, and if God hadn't blessed us with a baby boy, we wouldn't have been a couple. I wish I could say that I was a good girl who never committed any sins. I never committed any crimes, and I have a really good heart. But when it came to men, I was naïve and I was pretty. And that is not a good combination for a 17 year old girl who moves off to college. But I have an independent streak, and I'm somewhat impulsive. And quite often, more often than not, I said no to a man's advances. I should have said no to Roger – when I met him at a party, when I started sleeping with him, and when I got pregnant and he asked me to marry him. However, I said yes, and six months later I was married, pregnant, and alone on my wedding night. I have yet to have a glorious honeymoon experience. When I married my first husband, Roger wouldn't tell anyone, not even me, where he was taking me for our honeymoon. We drove all the way to Kansas to his mother's house. She didn't come to our wedding, because she was older and not in good health. On our wedding night, I became acquainted with my new mother-in-law while he went out partying with his brothers and friends. I woke up and found him at 2:30 in the morning sleeping off his drunken stupor on the couch in the basement. I guess that's what happens to a girl already pregnant on her wedding night when she marries a man who didn't really want to marry her; no reason to have romance.

My second honeymoon wasn't much better. At least Stuart and I had a wedding night in a quaint bed and breakfast in Natchez, Mississippi on the way to Georgia for his job interview. This time we stayed with my family, my

16

grandfather, instead of in-laws. Other women receive these fabulous honeymoon vacations in Hawaii or Paris. I got Leavenworth, Kansas, and Conyers, Georgia. Lucky me. I really need to exercise better judgment in the future. But to have a third chance to get that romantic getaway, I guess I'm going to have to be willing to take some risks and date.

So in the past year, I learned to put myself out there -- hello, I am single! I stopped wearing my wedding ring the day my divorce was final. I wrote a new life story that didn't begin with "Well, my husband and I moved..." to a personal life story that started "My goals in life are..." or "What is going on with me today is so much more interesting than what happened ten years ago, so may I tell you about that..." It really is a turn off when you talk about your ex when you are on a date; save those conversations for when you are with girlfriends. So let's talk about today. Today, I decided to get a massage. If you've never had a massage, I definitely recommend you get one. And then go get a manicure and pedicure. And whatever other beauty treatment you've been making excuses not to do. I have always wondered what massage therapists think about while giving massages. I guess she thought about me and my divorce and my dating life while she was giving me a massage. I guess I tempted her when I said I needed a massage from having too much sex. Because after I got dressed, and she gave me some water, she said, "You know, it's been a long time since I got divorced too, and I've been thinking I should put myself out there. I've just been hesitant, basically that means frozen in fear, but you seem to really be enjoying yourself." Sometimes I say things just to be funny. But wouldn't that be a nice problem to have – too sore to walk from having too much great sex? Oh yes, girl, put yourself out there. And don't stress out about trying to find the perfect man, just have a good time. You'll never meet anyone sitting at home in front of the

TV. It's okay to go on just one or two dates with one person and then another date with someone else. But it's not a good idea to have sex with multiple partners; sex really complicates your ability to make a good decision about a new life partner, so it's really best to wait until you're sure.

For months I've been telling my friends, if you know a smart, attractive, available male in my age bracket in my city, introduce me, please. I'm having fun meeting men. Each one is different. And some you realize you don't like at all within 5 minutes. Sometimes they don't follow through; you talk on the phone a few times, email or text, and then you just never meet face2face. The entire time I was in San Francisco, my friend kept texting and calling me, can I give out your phone number to a doctor friend of mine who is divorced? Finally I acquiesced, and said yes, but said please tell him not to call until I return from my trip. By the way, that was yesterday, and the Doctor called. I was so busy in San Fran. I had several presentations to give; I was meeting with publishers trying to negotiate another book, I was hosting a party at the Aquarium for 100 friends, and I was hoping to meet a nice, attractive, compatible man on the West Coast while I was there for no other reason than to just have a companion for dinner.

At this very moment, I'm waiting for a blind date now, what I like to call a coffee date. You don't have to drink coffee. A coffee date is just a casual, relaxed, I just want to see what the person with whom I talked on the phone or emailed looks like in person. Why commit to dinner and a movie with someone you don't enjoy being around for 15 minutes of communicating? You know, it's somewhat difficult dating again after 20 years. Not difficult as in you can't do it, but difficult in the rules have changed. Direct communication is a must, and no one wants to waste time. If there's no "click" - there's no second date. And I'm good with that. So if you're dating, and you're a little nervous, that's okay. You'll make a lot of new friends - smart, attractive, nice men - in the process of waiting for the "click". And believe it or not, the men you don't click with will try to find you a blind date too. When you are older, and you're a professional, you will date older, professional men. And just like we network for business contacts, dating is kind of the same thing. I can go on a date with someone, and then if we don't go out again, I remember his goals, and if I get a tip about a job or something in his best interest, I'll send him a message about it. So don't approach every date worrying about if he's the one. Think about dating as a way to make new friends, and along the way, you may find the one. Enjoy the process. Right now, I'm sitting at my desk waiting. My blind date called, and his appointment ran over, he's running late, and I'm trying to decide if I am willing to wait 15 minutes for a 15 minute date.

Sunday, November 21, 2010

Finding happiness post-divorce is not all about dating. I had to learn to love myself for myself. I had to learn how to let go of what I thought was wrong with me, of rehashing my failures, and to embrace my life just the way it is today. I had to embrace my post-divorce life with joy. Yes, I was a good wife. I didn't want to be divorced, but here I am. No one is perfect, and if you've been disappointed, hurt, or frustrated because you've been trying to be the person you think someone else wants you to be. Stop trying so hard. Just be yourself. Start doing things for yourself. Date yourself. Wear a sexy dress and heels. Get your hair done. Have a makeover. Then look in the mirror at yourself, and love you for being you.

This morning in church, the minister said that God doesn't see what we see. We see our inadequacies; God sees our heart. After my divorce, I learned to love myself for who I am. I get dressed up for myself, not for anyone else. It makes me feel good to look pretty. And even though it sounds a little corny, when I look pretty, I feel happier, and I smile more. And when I smile more, I speak nicely to strangers. Think of dating kind of like interviewing. You dress nice and focus on making a good impression. But interview conversation requires communication skills. Dating also requires communication skills. The more interviews you do while searching for a job, the better of an interviewee you become. You learn what to say and what not to say. The more dates you go on, the better you become at dating. You learn what to say and what not to say. Flirting is a learned skill. And it takes practice. Just put yourself out there. Flirt a little. It's okay to smile and speak sweetly and softly to someone else; there is just no cause to be mean or rude. I observe how the attitude of others changes when I smile and say something polite. And great looking shoes and lip gloss do make an impact. One of my students said on Friday that he read that the first thing people notice about you is your shoes. And in my experience they really do; buy a great pair of sexy heels, walk around like you know you look good, and count how many people will compliment your shoes. I have this patent leather black and white spectator pumps on which I get compliments all the time. Sitting in the lobby of the hotel in Chicago while waiting on friends to meet me for dinner, a woman came up the escalator eye-level with my shoes. I noticed the further the escalator brought her body higher, her head lowered to keep eye contact with my shoes. And then she spoke to me. We both laughed about loving shoes, and that was it.

The second thing they notice is your smile, because when you smile, you glow. And people get a glimpse of your heart -- the heart that God sees -- not your problems, not your shortcomings, just your heart. And then one morning you'll wake up, just like I do, and see yourself for the first time in the mirror, as the beautiful, special, wonderful woman you are. Maybe you've been hiding that wonderful woman you are under baggy sweats. Let yourself step out into the limelight. Don't be afraid to be who you are; learn to love yourself the way God does.

Side note to my readers who don't believe in God: Just because you don't believe doesn't mean you are not wonderful. You are beautiful as well. Don't get stuck on worrying about what religion I am or what religion you are. Right now, that is not nearly as important as you learning to love yourself.

Monday, November 22, 2010

One blessing that a divorce after the age of 40 gives to you is the wisdom which comes with age. I spent much time in serious reflection over my life. What I had done. What I hadn't done. What was it that I still wanted to do with my life? And I was given the opportunity to break out of the traditional family first mind-set and focus on my own dreams. I was serious, even as a child. I don't remember my parents ever telling me to do my homework; I wanted to have top grades, so I worked hard. Nothing ever came easy to me; at least, at first. In first grade, I still couldn't read. The school system was using phonemics; my mother helped me with phonics flashcards. But one day it happened; from that moment on I could read, and reading became my passion. And I got glasses. Talk about dealing with self-esteem issues; there was a day when glasses were not fashionable as they are now. At seven, I was the four-eyed girl. But I loved learning. Even to this day, I love to read, I love to learn, and I write poetry. So school was serious. And friendship was serious too. Due to the Army, we moved often, and so I don't have many childhood friends. So I learned to form friendships fast, and if I chose someone as a friend (or they chose me), they were my friend. And that was that. I had their back. My friend can have half my sandwich, my last dollar, or my favorite sweater. Nothing in this world is better than a true friend. The love of a true friend may indeed be your mate. And if you are blessed with a mate who is such, you are blessed beyond measure. Sometimes true love and friendship comes from other sources than a mate. I have been blessed with some really wonderful friends as an adult, and I take those friendships very seriously. I've been there for them in their rough times, and they've been there for me through births of babies, death of one of my children, death of my baby brother, and my divorces. But probably one of the best things I've learned from my friends is to not take myself so seriously. So with their encouragement, I picked myself (that sobbing heap of a woman on the floor who took herself and her marriage way too seriously) and stood up a better woman. A woman who remembered she knew how to laugh. That at 40 it really is okay to sneak in a little vodka to add to your soda at the movie theatre, so you and your girlfriends could watch Sex in the City with a cocktail. My friends thought I was too straight-laced until they reached into my Vera Bradley tote bag. But I am a woman who could play catch football with her kids and ride a bike. I am a woman who may not joke around all the time, but I do prefer to laugh than cry. I decided that it really was okay to admit that I like to be silly sometimes. In other words, I stopped looking at all of the things that were wrong with my life and worrying over them, and just decided to live in the moment. To have fun. To laugh. To play. Am I still a

22

serious person? Sure, when the situation requires me to be. And I'll tell you something else; sometimes I break out into song. Yep, like a musical, but just in my head. *"It's raining men, hallelujah, it's raining men…"*

I also decided that it was time I do things just for the experience of doing them. I didn't have to live my life the way my husband or boyfriend wanted me to. I didn't have to live my life the way my parents wanted me to. I don't have live my life the way anyone else wants me to. I can make decisions for myself. So I decided to go out West. After my divorce, I planned a road trip out West to Wyoming and the Dakotas. A friend of mine, a Paleontologist, invited me to go along on a dinosaur dig. Really, I'm serious. We found real dinosaurs, and I have pictures to prove it. For weeks, we roughed it out in the desert with shovels, buckets, and brushes. This trip required some serious planning and packing. I decided to collect satellite data to bring back to the geospatial analyst friends of mine to be able to recreate maps of the dig site. I bought a new digital camera with GPS capabilities and fantastic resolution, so my photography would be phenomenal. Some of the others were bringing their children, so I brought mine as well. Just because we are girls doesn't mean we can't go on an extreme adventure.

And this was an extreme adventure. What a way to celebrate a divorce than to have an adventure. Flying out of Atlanta was like any other trip I've taken, but then we switched flights in Denver. In the snow and freezing cold, in June, my daughters and I walked out onto the tarmac and boarded a prop plane with maybe 40 passengers. And that flight was the scariest of my life, but the views of the Rocky Mountains were worth it. The turbulence was so bad that the flight attendants never left their seats, and there were several times where we dropped several feet before stabilizing. But 45 minutes later, we landed safely in Rapid City, South Dakota. I drive a small little Mazda, but for this adventure I rented a giant tank of an SUV so I could drive off-road. I was literally going where I had never been before, but if I was going, I was going all the way. My sports car could have fit in the way back if you put the seat down. Men are not the only ones who are gear heads; I loved the power of driving that SUV off-road through the mud and over the bumps. I wish you could have seen me catch air. It was awesome. My daughters had a new respect; their Mommy can drive! You too can drive places you've never been. Are you scared? Is the thought of packing your car with essentials and an ice chest and just going somewhere different seem impossible to you? Maybe you think you can't do it. Well, you can. I did it. Sure, I was with friends, but I did it. Where would you go?

My friend met me at the airport, so I could follow him through the Black Hills to where we were staying in Wyoming. It was 38 degrees and raining for the first two days. For the first week, while we were digging at the site in Wyoming, we stayed in a motel, and our crew had total occupancy of the place. We were like a little army battalion with our trucks, our gear, and walkie-talkie radios. Most of the time cell phones did not work in the Badlands. And the trucks could only drive so close to the dig site, so we hiked through the muddiest mucky muck you can imagine. My hiking boots were so heavy from all the mud, and I was freezing cold. And then just like that, the rains stopped, the sun came out, and we had 90 degree weather. And some of the young people started getting heat stroke from not drinking enough water. We stayed in the field from early morning to late evening. The latrine was a hole dug in the ground several hundred yards away without even a tree to hide behind. There are no trees in the desert, only cactus.

I collected my data. I wrote field notes and drew diagrams of the bone locations. I took photos. I supervised the children. We had sandwiches and fruit in ice chests for lunch. I used my hunting utility knife to peel the oranges for the children. They loved how I'd cut spherically and make one long curly peel that looked like a snake. The children would sometimes help dig and sometimes they would go exploring. One day, I had just finished my work at the triceratops site and decided to hike over to the other dig site believed to be half a dozen bones of a Hadrosaur found in the hillside. Then my walkie-talkie crackled, "Allison, we need you to come back right away, your daughter needs you". Grace had fallen onto a cactus while catching a toad. And so I spent the next several minutes with her lying across my lap with a bare butt, while I plucked spines with little tweezers. Except for the cactus, this out West adventure was the best thing for my daughters to be in the company of all these real men who didn't sit in front of a computer or stagnate in an office. We hiked, we camped, we saw buffalo, and we roughed it. It was great!

I don't know if you've ever been camping, but this was roughing it in the day time. At least, at night we got to eat a hot meal, take a shower, and sleep in a bed. But I loved every minute of it. One of the other paleontologists said I made camo look fashionable. Just because I was going to be digging and sweating in the desert all day, did not mean I was going to forgo mascara and lip gloss and looking cute. Week two, we moved camp to North Dakota, and living conditions were even worse. Hunting cabins. No electricity. An outhouse. Field conditions were the same. The next day, my friend scouted out a farmhouse for the women and girls to move to. We had running water and could shower again. I was so glad to have a real bathroom, it didn't matter that there was no air conditioning. My daughter was embarrassed because I hung bras and panties out on the line to dry. To her, that was roughing it at the worst. We drove over an hour from town to the dig site. In North Dakota, we were digging fish for the Field Museum in Chicago, and somehow I ended up on road construction. The dig site was at the top of a butte, which is different than a mountain, because a butte is the piece of land that was not scraped away by a passing glacier, so the fossils are actually higher rather than lower. I enjoy learning about new things. And I learned many things about fossils and geology and survival and just how strong I really am. I spent three days – several hours a day – digging with a shovel to build a road up to the fossil location, so that the trailer could get close enough for the hitch to work. I've never done so much manual labor in my life. But after two weeks, I was on the plane back to Georgia, back to real life, back to my house for sale, back to the grass that needed mowing.

Wednesday, November 24, 2010

Tomorrow is Thanksgiving; a year ago today is when I came home from eating lunch with my mother and children and found divorce papers on the dining room table. And today I had a lunch date with the Doctor. One year had passed. I had totally forgotten what today was. And look how amazing this is, a year ago the day before Thanksgiving 2009 was one of the worst days of my life; and now, the day before Thanksgiving 2010 was really a wonderful day. Today I realized that I was willing to take the risk of getting hurt again. I realized that this man was worth it, and I didn't really want to date anyone else. I don't know what the future holds for us, but something changed in my heart for me. I knew, without any doubts, that the next man that asked for my number, for a coffee date, who emailed me, or whatever, the answer to any other potential date would be "It is very kind of you to invite me, but no." I had been on enough dates to have learned what I wanted and needed. I had two failed marriages, and I learned from the years of being married to those men what I wanted and needed. It was just lunch. Nothing fancy, but the connection was there. The click was there in a way it never has been before. I cancelled my on-line dating accounts. Don't panic if you are in doubt about narrowing down your dating pool to just one. You will know when it's time. No one has to tell you, and honestly, no one can. And I really had little reassurance that I was making the right decision. Only time will tell. And besides all of that romantic stuff, I was entering the holiday season. Last year, the holiday season was all a blur. My world was upside down, and I spent more time negotiating with my lawyer and financial planner than doing my usual holiday preparations. And this year, my plans for the holidays were essentially non-existent.

Dealing with Holidays after the Breakup can be tough, really tough. But it does have its benefits. For one, I'm not in the kitchen preparing a giant turkey and a bunch of side dishes, because there's no one here to eat it. Imagine a 20 pound turkey just for myself. Ha! The children are gone to celebrate Thanksgiving with their Father's family; my family was too depressed to have a Thanksgiving without the grandkids, so they went on vacation. So I'm home alone. Every year, I've prepared the huge Thanksgiving feast to share with family and friends. I even did it last year, because I already had everything planned out when my marriage imploded on itself. But you know, I'm really okay with being alone for Thanksgiving. I'm going to go have coffee and watch the parade at one friend's house in the morning. And then go to dinner with the neighbors in the afternoon. And then catch a movie tomorrow night. And no cooking. Now, I do love to cook, and part of me misses not planning and cooking a traditional Thanksgiving meal, but I am really thankful for my life, where I am today, and who I am. So really the trick I've learned about dealing with Holidays after the Breakup is to be flexible; let go of those things you just have to do. Instead just choose to have fun. Fun is what you want it to be; maybe reading a novel you haven't found time to read or going for a long walk, or visiting friends. Too bad the fitness center is closed tomorrow; I like working out. Don't dwell on what you don't have, but focus on what you do. Be thankful for making it through, being strong, learning who you are, for the people who do love you. Don't spend your day worrying about what you've lost. Stop worrying about your ex; after all, he's gone. Who cares? You don't need him to be happy. It doesn't matter who you spend your holidays with or how you spend them. It is possible to just enjoy being with yourself.

Friday, December 10, 2010

As a woman my age who is divorced with children, the probability of finding an eligible man who is not also divorced or widowed with children is highly unlikely. And if you do happen to find a man in his mid-forties or early-fifties who has never been married, he is probably not the marrying type and not worth your time. So all of that being said, I had to learn how to date around a visitation schedule. Not just my own, but his too. And so will you. My post-divorce dating philosophy is that children should not meet your date until you find the "one", so consequently, finding time to date can be difficult. I also cherish every moment I have with my children, and so I try to make my plans around their schedule. This basically means I can have 4-8 nights per month when my children are visiting with their father on which I can have a typical dinner and a movie type date. And while I've figured out how to fill up those available nights with dates, the best dates are really lunch dates. I love, love, love sneaking away from work for an extended lunch date. Okay, before you start thinking I'm ditching work and being dishonest, I give above and beyond to my employer and only take my allocated lunchtime. It just makes me feel sexier to pretend I'm sneaking away for a secret rendezvous.

Lunch dates are great, because there is no pressure to extend the date past the comfortable point -- both of you have to go back to work. Also, I don't always eat on a lunch date. Sometimes I pack a lunch and eat at my desk before or after the date. Then the date can be an activity which doesn't center on food. After all, watching someone eat is not always a romantic or exciting thing to do. And I can squeeze in twice as many lunch dates in a month as I can an evening date. And I don't feel guilty about being away from my children. Now, I'm lucky, my children are older, so they want to go stay over with a friend or go out with a friend, and so I don't have any need for babysitters. Like tonight, my children went out, and I stayed home, did laundry, and cleaned the bathroom. Now how's that for sexy? Yep, that's right, I'm home on a Friday night doing domestic chores. In fact, my vacuum cleaner is in pieces on the floor, because I'm trying to repair it. By the way, I have no idea how to repair a vacuum cleaner, but I thought, hey, it's already not working, how can it get any worse? If I can mow the grass, I can do anything. But I do not feel down at all about being home alone on a Friday night, and partly that's because I like hanging out with myself; partly, it's because I had an amazing lunch date today.

Sunday, December 12, 2010

To be honest, being the chief cheerleader, cook, and chauffeur was my way of life when I was married, and it's still my way of life now. Many of my friends jokingly say I've been a single parent much longer than a year *(much longer than my divorce),* because I've always been the one to pack the gear in the car, to fix the picnic lunch, snacks, and drinks in the ice chest, to drive the kids to the athletic events, dance lessons, and school activities, and to be the best cheerleader and photographer for moments of victory and the best comforter in moments of crisis of skinned knees or disappointing results. Like today for example, I began my day at 5 am to rouse the crew for a swim meet, out the door by 6 and in the pool by 7 after driving an hour in the rain and sleet. Thank God I live in the South, right? I've lived where it blizzards 8 months out of the year before, so you Northerners cut us Southerners some slack about whining about the snow flurries.

At the swim meet, in between handing out snacks, towels, and taking photos and videos of the swimmers, I planned the social activities for the rest of the holiday season, confirmed the dates of the summer camps everyone wants to go to, researched possible locations for a summer vacation in our now remaining available dates around my work vacation, camps, and their vacation times with their Dad, and did a little on-line shopping. How did I do all of this before I could google on my iPhone? Multi-tasking has taken on a whole new meaning with the use of 3G/4G internet connection 24/7. Okay, I'll admit, I did take 15 minutes pause to glance through a fashion magazine *(Thank you, Rachel's Mom)!* For those of you mothers out there, do you remember the day your name became "so and so's Mom"? "Hey, Grace's Mom, can you pass Grace the grapes?" That's something you'll have to deal with when your kids become older too, you will still be expected to do everything, be everything just in case, but when you actually get to the event and your little baby will sit with their friends and only talk to you when they need something. But don't go anywhere or be doing something else when they are in the spotlight or up on deck, because the moment they look into the stands where you and all the other parents are sitting and you're not watching, then you're in trouble. And I wouldn't trade these special moments of triumphs and trials for anything in the world. And 6 hours later, the car is repacked, and the chauffeur is behind the wheel again.

And now, we're home. The kids are watching a Christmas movie, I'm washing the towels used today and starting to prep for dinner. Oh yeah, and I'm working too. That is, if you can call writing work. When I finish this, I will complete the final edits on my dissertation for the copy editor, so the final copy can be sent to the printer for binding. And then, I'll really get going on dinner. Since we didn't have lunch until 2 pm (see why you have to pack an ice chest of snacks), no one is hungry just yet. Okay, I know you're curious, what's on the menu? The menu is sautéed chicken breast, red beans and rice, and a salad. I still haven't decided if we're having lemon bars or brownies for dessert. We may just have some pieces of Ghirardelli chocolate I brought back from San Francisco last month. Can you believe it? We still have uneaten chocolate purchased a month ago.

Monday, December 13, 2010

For nearly a year now, I've been telling myself you need to go have your photo taken. You know, with a real photographer, not one of those 500 prints for $9.95 with your kids in tow places, but a real photographer. And in the wee hours of the morning last night, I thought, I'm going to get my picture taken, for real. And so I hopped on Google and searched for photographers and looked at their web sites, and I sent an email requesting an appointment. And I said, I would come today if she could squeeze me in. And she did, and I had the most fun ever! More fun than I've had taking my photo in the longest time, because this was not pose for the Christmas card pictures. This was not a professional headshot for my portfolio or back of my book cover. This was more like yes, dangit! That's Southern for another phrase that's more apropos -- the acronym is YDFR. I'll let you figure it out. I'm a beautiful, sexy, fabulous woman who still looks awesome over the age of 40 in jeans, a sweater, and red heels, and I can work it in front of this camera. I cannot wait to see the proof sheet tomorrow! And I'm going to go again on another day for full body shots, but today I just wanted to get some gorgeous headshots to frame.

Beauty for a woman is an interesting phenomenon, because it's like a metamorphosis over time with stages of cute, gangly, dorky, pretty, worn-out, and just flat out hot! I must admit I had my cute childhood years, and then my pimply-nerdy early teen years, *(This is me with my brothers Ricky and Jason when I was 11.)* and then my wow, you're only 17, 18, 19 years, because you look 25 and then my frazzled young Mom years who didn't have any sleep and forgot what it was like to be a woman. It didn't help that during those years, my first husband told me every day I was ugly and stupid. And then my first post-divorce period when I did some runway modeling and discovered he was the stupid one because I was damn good-looking (and smart too), and then my second marriage years where I tried really hard to keep looking good where the best compliment I got was "you look nice", and then my second post-divorce period (after 40) where I look flat-out hot. Yeah, I probably am more attractive now at 41 than I've been in my entire life. It's crazy, because you would think in comparing 20 years to 40 years hands-down folks would vote that the 20-year-old, size 6, no wrinkles, no c-section scars, etc, would be much better than the 40-year-old, size 12, a few wrinkles, scars, etc. But she's not. Being 40 is so much better than being 20; I wouldn't go back there for anything. So in terms of beauty what makes the 40-year-old prettier than the 20-year-old? Okay, there's what you already know, good skin care, plenty of water, plenty of sleep, a healthy diet, and exercise. What you may not know is that beauty is more about a state of mind and the beauty in your heart than your actual physical appearance. That's right, being happy, having a positive attitude, loving yourself, loving your life, compassion, kindness, gratitude, etc, all add to your beauty more than any lip gloss will ever do.

Although, I really don't ever go without my lip gloss, not even to bed, really. I just reapplied my lip gloss while I'm sitting here in the bed typing on my laptop. The other good thing about photography today; it's digital! That means it's okay if you have a little cellulite, or a scar under your chin; the photographer can edit those little flaws. So don't worry about what you think are flaws in your physical appearance. Schedule an appointment with a really great photographer today and get your awesome self captured in a photo!

Tuesday, December 14, 2010

I am not a relationship expert even though I teach classes on interpersonal communication; I'm just a woman who has had more than her fair share of relationships which didn't turn out to be good. And I'm a woman who believes in fairy tales, and I am envious of those couples who married young and are still married, still in love, after 20, 30, 40 years. My professional background is communication, and I teach classes on building positive and healthy relationships by using effective and appropriate interpersonal communication. When I first got divorced, I was actually embarrassed, because I worried about what people will say. You know like the jokes people make about the marriage therapist who has been divorced five times. But over and over again I had friends who reassured me that I was a good person and that I was good at what I do. But not only that, friends and friends of friends kept asking me for relationship advice.

Even just today, a friend asked, "How do you know if the relationship you are in is the right one?" This question comes up over and over again; just with a different friend each time the question is asked. And being confident that your relationship is the right one is really difficult when you are having a disagreement or period of discontent. Honestly, I thought my marriage was a good one up until the last year of it. Why? Because I was just living my life the way I thought my life should be. I thought problems which occurred over the course of my marriage were normal and that all marriages had those same problems. I thought that if I kept putting forth effort, magically, my marriage would be good. But what I've discovered now, in retrospect, is that I had settled for just good enough. Even right from the beginning, because Stuart was better than what I had experienced before in relationships with any other man, he was good enough for me. And I should have been thinking is he good for me? And after I said "I do" and started living the married life, my marriage was good enough, because my second marriage was better than my first marriage. And I should have been thinking was my marriage good for me? Never be afraid to ask yourself if the relationship you are in is good for you. And then don't be afraid to listen to the answer to this tough question.

Of course, it's always easier to look back at your mistakes and shortcomings -- you can always see the things you didn't see when you were actually in it. That's just the way it is. But looking forward, I've learned not to settle for just good enough. Just good enough is not good enough for me anymore. I want it all. I'm not looking for perfection, because men are human beings too. I'm not perfect either, but I want to be good, not just good enough. And I do want my heart's desire, a best friend, a partner, a comforter, a man who supports my goals and ambitions, someone who listens to me for no matter how long I talk. I want a man who wants to know and values my opinion, whose sex drive matches my own, who likes me, whom I am deeply attracted to like oxygen molecules to hydrogen, a man who gives me as much of himself as I give of myself to the relationship, a match, a mate.

Side comment: This list is not in any particular order of importance. Some days some items are more important than other.

And that's something I've never had, because I settled for just good enough. And maybe that's what you did too. Deep down, maybe you knew even before you said "I do" that something was missing, even just a little something, and then over time that little something *(the enough)* became a

35

bigger something *(not enough),* and then before you knew it, you were divorced. Ironically, I spent a whole lot more money on my divorces than I ever spent on my weddings or any vacation which could have been an investment into an improved relationship. But that's a topic for another day. The bottom line is that I deserve to be in a good relationship, to be loved truly and deeply for the woman I am; you deserve to be in a good relationship, to be loved truly and deeply for the woman you are. My biggest mistake in love to date is not being patient enough to wait for what I deserve; for being so anxious for it to happen I imagined what I had was more than what it was. But here's the hard truth about knowing whether or not a man loves you. A man who beats you does not love you. A man who verbally bashes you or negates everything you say does not love you. A man who ignores and avoids you does not love you. A man who would cheat on you does not love you. A man who would steal money from you does not love you. A man who puts his interests and security before your own does not love you. Ladies, it is time we realize what love really is. Christian or not, read the Holy Bible - Ephesians Chapter 5 Verses 25-30 and 1 Corinthians Chapter 13 - the entire chapter. And then if you are not someone who prays, okay, fine, then, just reflect on what you read, and ask yourself if love is all of these things written here, have I ever been loved by a man like this, and have I ever loved a man like this? I don't know about you, but none of my past relationships could measure up to the standards written in the Bible. Those past relationships were good enough compared to other relationships, but no more. I'm holding out for good, honest, all or nothing, love. True love. And if you have the chance to find this kind of love, I'm hoping you'll hold out for it as well. And know that that second (or third, or fourth, or however many times you've had a failed relationship) chance couldn't have happened without the heartache you've experienced, and let all the pain go. Let

the pain go, and search for true love. You'll only find it if
you don't settle for a relationship that is merely good
enough.

Friday, December 17, 2010

Ho Ho Ho! Happy Holidays! Whatever your religious
preference, you probably are being invited to lots of
holiday activities. And now you have to squeeze dating into
your schedule. So here's the big question? Do you, or do
you not, take a date with you to your work holiday party,
your friend's party, or whatever? It depends. Definitely do
NOT take a blind date. If you don't know him that well,
then you are risking not being able to meet someone new at
the party, because the chances of a man approaching you
while you have arm candy is not very likely. Most men
struggle with how to approach a woman to start a
conversation, so you don't want to make the angst any
greater by causing them to think another 5 minutes about
how involved you are or are not with the man standing next
to you. MAYBE take someone with whom you've gone on
several dates and you really like.

Be sure you like him, because if you think your friends are
overly concerned about the latest celebrity breakup or
hookup, you haven't seen anything yet. Your friends, your
co-workers, they love you, just like my friends and co-
workers love me. And you, just like me, have gone through
relationship hell, and they've been right there with you,
praying for you, supporting you, sympathizing and
empathizing with you, and trying to cheer you up. Friends
want you to be happy. And it's not that I (or you) can't be
happy alone, because real happiness is not about having a
man. Happiness comes from within. If you are not happy,
in general, then you need to take action on that. Figure out

why you aren't happy. See a therapist. Reevaluate your career. Finally start that hobby you've always wanted to do.

I don't know about you, but I am a happy person, and I am an even happier person, when I have people in my life to love, and happiest when I am loved in return. But I'm getting sidetracked. I really want to talk about dating and the holidays. OK, two weeks ago, I went on the date with the Doctor to the Nutcracker ballet, a holiday tradition for me. And I had a fabulous time. I knew my friends would be curious; I even warned him that stepping out with me at the ballet where a lot of friends and business contacts from the community would be, that he may be noticed more than he would feel comfortable. And I learned that we haven't changed that much from middle school or high school. When he stepped away to take a phone call, "Who is that? He's really attractive. Wow, Allison, you've never brought someone with you to the ballet before. Is it serious?" I'm a really independent woman, and even as a married woman, I went lots of places by myself. My ex-husband didn't really like the ballet and cultural events, and I love them. I served on non-profit performing arts councils and boards of directors over the years. I have season tickets for many of the local arts organizations, and I love going to the art museum. But for the past 10 years or more, I've done all of things mostly by myself, or my mother, my daughter, or a girlfriend tagged along as my date. So for me to have a male escort to the ballet where I know personally about half of the audience and the cast is a really big deal and the gossip chain was flying.

For days after that, I received phone calls, emails, and lunch invitations to hear more about him or requests to gossip about me, because so and so wanted to know. I knew we would get noticed, but I didn't know just how much. And maybe it wouldn't be the same for you, because

38

if your job isn't a very public and community relations one, you may not know as many people in your local community as I do. And tonight, I'm about to go on another holiday date with the Doctor. And I'm very excited about this, because the holiday event is a Christmas program and concert at the local mega-church which is always fabulous. But that's not what is exciting to me about it. The invitation hits me in my core (my core values). I am a Christian, and the Christmas season is one of my most favorite times of the year. Not because of presents or Santa. But I love parties. I love how everyone does a little extra to make everything special. I love Christmas music and plays and concerts and church programs. And I truly appreciate the birth of Christ. And for the most part, my entire life, I've been in this alone. Sure, occasionally, if I begged, or if I took care of all of the details, my ex-husband would go, but not happily. Part of the reason why I wanted children was to have little companions, a little mini-me or two, who could go to all of these fun, holiday things with me. And for the first time ever, a man calls me up and says "at church on Sunday they were talking about this special program, so I went ahead and got tickets for Friday night on the chance you would want to go with me. Would you?" (*Would I? Are you kidding me?!! I have dreamed about that very sort of thing for twenty years!!! Of course, I didn't say all of that to him. I just said, I've love to go. Thank you for asking*). This is huge. This is a core value issue. This is not just a holiday work party. This is not just a holiday themed community event where you go to see and to be seen. This is celebrating the birth of Christ with a man I am deeply attracted to and care about. Now, this may not be as big of a deal for you. Maybe if someone asked you to do something else which was part of your core values, you would understand how excited I am. And I am very excited about this date tonight! Very, very excited!

Wednesday, December 22, 2010

I just found out, my ex is now engaged to be married to someone else. And if you haven't experienced this next phase of the divorce process, it's like getting divorced twice from the same person. Even though I'm okay with it, and there's no chance we would ever reconcile, it still is a bitter pill to swallow. And even though I'm moving on and am dating, it still doesn't make it easy. My children don't want to talk about it, but I'm sure they feel strange about it. After all, just over a year ago, they thought their parents would be together forever. And then in just one year, their parents are divorced and their father announces he's getting married again. It has to be weird for them. I guess that's normal. Even though my mother was married more than once, I've never known my biological father. My dad legally adopted me when they married. I've never had to do the visitation thing. I never had to deal with seeing my parents with someone else and feeling weird about it. The hardest part when your ex officially moves on and when you officially move on is actually accepting that the two of you were not meant to be together. For whatever reason, you made a mistake. You chose the wrong person and a relationship that was lacking in the necessary qualities to make it last a lifetime.

When you consider the divorce rate in our country, a lot of people are marrying people they probably shouldn't be marrying, or marrying people for the wrong reasons. In other words, they only kind of love the other person. And that's not enough. If I could have looked in a crystal ball and seen the future and known just how little he really loved me, I wouldn't have walked down the aisle. It would have been better to say no at the altar, than to deal with divorce. So if any of you haven't married yet, learn from the mistakes of all divorced people everywhere, if you're not 100% in love, loved, loving, totally sure, can't breathe without the other person, if that person is not your everything, then maybe you shouldn't get married. I'm sure one day, I'll officially move on too. Maybe I'll marry again. I don't know if I'll marry again. Even though I am enjoying the dating life, deep down, I'm a person who wants a partner, to build a nest together, to be totally committed and unconditionally loved. But right now the wounds haven't healed, and the thought of going through another marriage that fails stops time. I hope I've learned from my mistakes in relationships. I deserve real, honest, pure love. And my children deserve to live in a home where love lives also. To all who have had less than they deserve, may you officially move on to a real, no bull-shit relationship, where love truly exists. Personally, I'm excited about what the future holds.

Monday, December 27, 2010

So many people complain after the holidays about not getting exactly what they wanted for a gift. There's an old joke that a man should never give his woman a gift which plugs into the outlet to operate (you know, toasters, vacuum cleaners, etc). But you know the best gifts don't come in a box. And it really is the thought that counts. The thought behind the gift. The day before Christmas there was a commercial which said "Are you a procrastisanta?" This question directly hints at what I'm saying -- no thought -- just rush out and buy a gift so you have one, because you're obligated to give one. What I want, and I think what most real women want, is not an obligatory, because you'll be mad at me if I don't buy you a gift. What I want is a gift which comes from the heart, and it may be a tangible item symbolic of the giver's affection for me, or the gift may just be love itself. This Christmas I received the gift of time and a representation of the gift of time. Wrapped in a green blanket was a small box. Now, I will say all of my gushy romantic friends were really hoping I'd receive a ring from Christmas, because they too believe in fairy tales. But what I received was even better, a watch, a white ceramic watch surrounding my sparkling gemstones, his representation of thoughtfulness and care and a genuine desire for time to pass for us together, and the Doctor, my man, presented my gift in his family tradition of choosing one special person to receive his or her gift wrapped in a woolen dark green blanket rather than in paper. That day I became a member of the family, another precious gift. And these gifts were given in love which makes them more valuable to me than any past Christmas gifts I've ever received. So, for a week before Christmas Day I heard, you'll probably want to return it, but no, I'm keeping it. Forever and always. And I have an even better gift - contentment - I woke up with it this morning - something which has eluded me for many years. Deep down I've always kept hidden this feeling of discontent, especially around the holidays; even as a child, I felt this way. I've always been more comfortable with giving than receiving. I think it's because I fear being disappointed, by knowing that I don't have what I want the most (love), and the feeling that gifts received were not symbolic of true love. Of course my parents loved me when I was a child. I am not making any statements of criticism against my upbringing. This is about my fears and insecurities about not being good enough to be loved, not any statement of how much or how little others loved me. And as a woman, I have to give my exes credit for trying to love me. But a last minute run to Wal-Mart communicates a lot about the desire to express love through gift-giving. But this really was the best Christmas I've ever had to date, and I'm excited about a future of more time, of more love, and well, just more of the intangible things that don't come in a box and that make life worth living. So, I guess, I'm okay that I'm divorced and that relationship of not quite enough has passed away. In a weird sort of way, I guess, my ex gave me a gift by divorcing me, because we didn't have all of the love we should have had, and now I have the chance to receive the gift of love. Part of me feels grateful for being screwed over, because now I can move on to a better life. I know, that's a strange way to look at life. And maybe you're not ready to tell your ex "thank you for screwing me over, for leaving me, for not loving me, for hurting me", and that's okay. One day you will. And then you'll be content with your life, just as it is.

Wednesday, December 29, 2010

I woke up this morning with an overwhelming desire to make gumbo. So I ran to the store to buy a whole chicken, the veggies I was missing, andouille sausage, and file', a spice used to thicken the roux. Then I came home and started by boiling the chicken. I really do like to cook; it can be a lot of fun and it's kind of creative. You know out of a hodge podge of all these ingredients, one can make a fabulous entree. It's really kind of amazing. Every time I boil a chicken to get stock and the chicken, of course, for a dish, I remember a story a teacher friend told me about how her other teacher friends didn't know what she was talking about when she was describing a recipe for boiling a chicken. They had never boiled a chicken before. They always used canned chicken or just the prepared chicken breasts. I'm really surprised how many people today don't know how to cook anything that doesn't come in a box with all the ingredients inside. I never really thought cooking was this great secret super power skill until I heard other families talking about eating take out every night. My great grandmother was a dairy farmer's wife, and she cooked several meals a day for a huge family. My grandmother cooked every day too. And as a child, I just watched and learned what to do. Very few recipes are written down with complete instructions or ingredients lists. And measurements are always approximate (you know about a cup). From my mother, who was a professional woman, I learned timesaving tips like freezing casseroles ahead of time and using the microwave. I'm sure there are plenty of other women who are better cooks then I am.

But I do like to cook, and most nights, I'm going to put a home cooked meal on the table. Sure, sometimes we do have peanut butter or Spaghettios out of a can, or pizza. But I like to cook a meal from scratch when time allows. My youngest daughter has an interest in gardening; she's inspired me to use really fresh veggies. Each year her container garden gets bigger and bigger. You can cook a lot of dishes with tomatoes. Also whenever I boil a chicken to cook, I remember anatomy and physiology class where I had to boil a chicken completely removing all meat from the bones, bleaching the bones, and then reassembling the skeleton back together into a standing chicken. That was a really interesting project, and even though I really like science and animals, that project convinced me that veterinary school was not for me. I knew chickens were just the beginning of the animal skeletons, and building one skeleton was enough to last me a lifetime. So that's how I became an English major and started putting all of my energies into becoming a writer. And somewhere along the way, life shuffled me from writing to teaching, and now twenty years later, I'm doing both.

Sunday, January 2, 2011

I've always been a scheduled person, even as a child. I get up early, because I want to complete my chores early, so I have more time to play later in the day. On the weekends when I was in high school, unlike the typical teenager, I would get up super early to do my chores, because it was my goal to be completely finished, dressed, and out the door to go to the mall or a game or anything with my friends before lunchtime. I never really thought about it before, but I do the same thing as an adult with work. I picked a career where I could arrive really early - usually before everyone else - to get a lot of paperwork done. I teach early morning classes, and my goal is to be ready for lunch with co-workers or a date. And when my children were little, to have completed a day's work by 2:30, so I could pick them up from school and go do activities with them. My daily routine was something like this: wake up between 5-5:30, exercise, fix breakfast, wake the kids, hop in the shower, get dressed while they eat, help them get ready, get them off to school by 6:45, and then arrive at work by 7:15, work, leave at 2:30, come home, pack activity bags for dance, piano lessons, or athletic activities, and either prep dinner, so I could finish cooking within 20 minutes of returning, or pack an ice chest with dinner if the activities were going to be late, drive to activities between 3:30-4, either watch the kids do their activity, do volunteer work, grade papers, socialize with the other parents, or exercise, and then go back home to finish dinner, help the kids with their homework, etc, clean up, get everyone in the bed, clean some more, and eventually go to bed around 11 or so.

So that was my daily schedule before the kids started middle school and I got divorced. Interestingly enough, the biggest change to my schedule was the change in the kids' school start time. That pushed our entire morning back an hour. They also are more self-sufficient, although they do still like blueberry muffins or cinnamon rolls in the morning. They also get home from school later, so I stay at work until 4 now. But we still have all of the after school activities and chores to do. And even so, it seems like the to-do list never gets completely finished. I never have enough time to do everything I need to do, so again the importance of a plan. I keep an agenda for social activities and other important personal items, and then I keep an Outlook calendar which syncs with my iPhone for work-related items. I make a to-do list every night before I go to bed, and sometimes I even have an ongoing to-do list for the days later in the week, so I can write down XYZ needs to be done on Tuesday. Really being organized with a plan is what keeps the chaos under control and what helps me to be happy, because I know what to look forward to later that is fun. There's also a sense of satisfaction of crossing things off the to-do list. (One down - eleven to go). And I don't stress about unfinished things at the end of the day -- I just move them to the next day's to-do list. After all, work and chores will always be there waiting to be done. That's just a part of life. Planning is also important to changing your life; whatever resolution you made, if you're actually going to make it happen you must have a plan.

Sure, I can still be spontaneous. If a friend calls and says let's go see a movie, I'm going to move cleaning out the garage to another day and go to the movie. Or I'm going to work a lot faster to try to finish before the time of the movie. But that is also part of the plan, people are very important to me, and spending time with people who are very important to me ranks very high on my to-do list. After all, that's why I work so hard is to be able to spend time with the people I love when I can. Today's the last day of my vacation, and tomorrow I go back to work. I didn't finish half of the items on my to-do list of things I wanted to accomplish while on vacation, but that's okay. The messy closet will still be there next month. I better go make my to-do list of things that must be finished today to be ready for work and school.

Sometimes things just don't turn out the way you planned, and sometimes life is not spontaneous in the fun kind of way. And even though I'm a really happy person, I get depressed sometimes too. But I really try to focus on the positive. Although having a positive attitude can be difficult when people get mad at you for being happy. The other day my mother and I were discussing how much we miss the kids when they are visiting their father. For me, this is the most difficult part of divorce. I really brought my kids into the world with the intention of remaining an intact family. I wanted to be part of one of those families who made it, so that my kids could look back and say thanks for sticking together and keeping us one family. But life didn't happen that way. Also, I've crafted my career around the needs of my children. Even when I travel for work, I have flown my children and my mother out to be with me as often as I can. And so, when my children are away, I am miserable. I joke about how God is preparing me for dealing with the Empty Nest Syndrome. Anyway, she made some comment about hating that the kids were away, and I replied with something like, "I just want them to be happy, safe, and healthy wherever they are. If they are having a good time with their father, then I'm happy for them." To which, she replied sarcastically, "well, okay little miss sunshine and flowers." So maybe I am Pollyanna, but I already know my post-divorce life sucks, do I have to reinforce that it sucks by whining about it? Can we not just enjoy a nice lunch without kids instead of whining about how they aren't with us? Life is not fair.

I'm not going to have every little thing exactly the way I want it to be. This is not Utopia; this is the real world. And quite a large portion of the real world and real life will leave a bitter taste in your mouth. To be blunt and totally honest and have a moment of cynicism, if you're a good person, then you will probably get screwed over and deal with a lot of bull-shit at some point in your life. It has been my observation that the Bitches manage to keep their man twisted around their finger. Good Women get taken advantage of and mistreated and abandoned. Bitches don't have to be faithful; they just have to be demanding and manipulative. And men just seem to fall for the bull-shit and come back for more. However, I have a choice, and you have a choice; you can keep sucking on the lemons complaining about how sour they are, or you can take the lemon out of your mouth. I choose happiness. I choose to have faith that good things will happen even when everything is going wrong. This morning when I logged in, the quote of the day came up on my screen:

"Your success and happiness lies in you. Resolve to keep happy, and your joy and you will form an invincible host against difficulties" – Helen Keller

Now that is really profound. I have had a very difficult life, but really, in comparison to the struggles Helen Keller faced and overcame, really? I'm complaining? The difficulties you may be facing now are only temporary. Take a moment to reflect. Where are you right now? How bad is it? Write it down if you need to. Then store that piece of paper away for one year. In January 2012, dig it back out again, and compare to where you are then to now. If you don't give up; if you keep your faith; if you keep your joy, I can almost guarantee, you will be better one year from now than you are right now.

Wednesday, January 5, 2011

I have a love affair with words. I have an intense passion for words, and I must be honest and sincere with my words. Of course, I may make a mistake now and again and say something the wrong way, or may not be able to think of the right words to day, or whatever. But I'm really thinking about words on greeting cards. I really think about the words on greeting cards, and I must connect with the words. All of my friends, and even my children, know I like cards. I write cards; I mail cards *(yes, through snail mail);* and if I can't find a pre-written greeting card that expresses in words what I'm feeling, I have a huge stash of blank cards where I can fill in the blank with my own thoughts and feelings. I have a box of various stationary in my closet at home, and I have an entire desk drawer full of stationary at work. I am so emotionally connected to words. But you know how some people can just run into the Hallmark store and pick up any card appropriate to the occasion, sign their name, and then give the card. I can't do that. I cannot give just any card. The words written on the card must be a sincere reflection of my feelings. My last anniversary before my divorce I had a _____ (I don't even know what to call it, so I'll tell the story, and you can fill in the blank with what you would call it).

OK, so my 14th wedding anniversary was coming up, and we were having some problems in our marriage. The problems hadn't even been defined; for me, it was just this sixth sense that something was horribly wrong and that I was in my marriage alone. I had just a couple of months earlier even starting seeing a therapist to figure out what was wrong with me; why was I depressed and overcome with this feeling of dread, because an outsider looking in would have said I had a great marriage. And when I got divorced, many friends did say that, "I thought you had a great marriage". That's when I discovered that no one can judge the quality of someone else's relationship. If you're not in it, stay out of it.

So anyway, I went to the Hallmark store to buy an anniversary card. And one by one I started reading the cards to find the perfect card. As I read the words printed on each card, I was not having a love affair with them. Each card, instead of making me feel all warm and fuzzy and happy to be married to my husband, made me see one more way in which my marriage was lacking. All of those words were describing someone else's relationship. I became frantic -- seriously, there has to be at least one card which would be a reflection of my marriage and express how I feel. But they didn't. I ended up sitting on the floor in Hallmark, crying, unable to breathe, because if I can't find a card, what is wrong with my marriage? I hope you realize that if you're one of those people who can buy just any card that you don't have the same intense passion for words that I do. And that's okay. At least, you won't look like a crazy woman crying with a handful of romantic cards in her hand. I became paralyzed just standing there staring at the cards and asking myself over and over what is wrong with my marriage that I can't find a damn card. Even the humorous romantic cards weren't hitting the mark. We weren't even funny.

So I called my friend while I'm standing there sobbing and opening card after card after card to ask her what was wrong with me. And she simply said "you don't have to buy a card -- just go home." And I guess what's really crazy about this is that I'm not an overly emotional dramatic person. Most of my friends look to me for the calm, rational, approach to the relationship crises they are facing. So the only thing I can attribute to this is that I can't lie about my emotions, even with a greeting card, and that words are so powerful that my sense of honor and ethics won't allow me to use a greeting card to lie to someone. Did I love my husband, sure? But maybe you haven't bought a greeting card lately; they don't just say "Happy Anniversary - I love you". They talk about the depths of love, walks on the beach, holding hands, and all of that other romantic, gushy-gooey stuff. The stuff (the relationship, the marriage) I wanted to have. I was crying because I desperately wanted every word on every one of those greeting cards to be true, but some words on each of those greeting cards were just a tiny bit off. And it cut me to the core, and so I had a meltdown when the realization hit me that I didn't have the marriage I wanted to have. And not only that, I didn't know what to do about it. I didn't have to share this story with you, but I did for two reasons. One: because maybe you've experienced something similar, and now you know that you're normal because someone else has wigged out in the greeting card aisle too. Two: because I am having a much easier time buying greeting cards lately.

And I'm not buying just any greeting cards. After all, I'm not a greeting card junkie; I don't go into the Hallmark store and buy hundreds of random greeting cards to get a fix. But when I'm really happy, or feeling affectionate I love finding the right card with the right words. On another note, why hasn't the greeting card industry capitalized on mean, cruel, insensitive, breakup cards? Not that I want to buy one, and I definitely couldn't be the author of a mean card. But it just seems like some people would buy them. Maybe there should be a Happy Divorce Anniversary Card. Or thanks for having my baby; I'm sorry I didn't stick around to raise it card. I wouldn't buy it, because I wouldn't have the courage to mail it. So I guess someone who has the guts and mean-spiritedness to create them can make a million dollars off of that idea, because it won't be me. If you have the wherewithal to create a line of "I'm a mean Bitch" greeting cards, go for it! I give over my full rights to the idea to you. But anyway, there's just some sort of afterglow I feel when I have found the words to express my affection and romantic feelings. So it is a kind of love affair. And I guess if you're ever so fortunate as to receive a greeting card from me, you'll know it's a really big deal, because I don't say those words to just anyone.

Sunday, January 9, 2011

As I've gone through this difficult time of transition from married to single, I've learned that healing takes time. And really, I'm still in it; there is no timeline on this sort of thing. No one can say how long it will take for you to get over the pain of your failed relationship. Grieving the death of your marriage is just as tumultuous as grieving an actual death of someone you love. Have you ever buried a loved one, a grandparent, a friend, a child? I've buried my 12-year-old son, I know a little bit about the grieving process. Maybe now is not the time in the book to share the entire story of his life and death, but I'll start with how his life ended. September 12, 2002, in Montgomery, Alabama, at Father Walter's Memorial Children's Home, a long-term care facility for children with extreme medical conditions, with a Sponge Bob Square Pants cartoon on the TV across the hall, my son took his last breath.

That morning, early that morning, God woke me up and told me to go if I wanted to be there when it was time. And so, I called my mother, packed the diaper bag, and put my little girls in the car, and set out for Montgomery. I didn't know anything except if God said to go, I will go. I had been waiting for a miracle for over a decade, and I didn't what would really happen that day.

When I arrived and stopped at the nurses' station, I heard in the backroom, "Has someone called Matthew's mother? She needs to come now." And I said, "I'm already here." And the nurse came to the counter in surprise, "How did you...never mind?" And I went down the hall to his room. I knew when I walked in the room that today would be the end of 12 years of praying. There was a peace in the room I cannot describe. My husband Stuart who had always been like a real Dad to Matthew and my father arrived later and stayed for awhile, and then they took my daughters back home to Georgia. My mother and I sat with Matthew for several hours. I remember my mother making up the dialog for Patrick and Sponge Bob, because we couldn't hear their stupidity, only see the screen. Every time my children watch Sponge Bob, and it seems to be on TV all the time at my house now, I remember the day Matthew died. I cannot watch Sponge Bob, even though I know all the characters that live in Bikini Bottom.

The priest came to pray with us and to administer last rights. This was actually the second time Matthew had the last rights ceremony performed. The first time, he was just 19 days old, when the doctors said he wouldn't come out of the coma. But he did. And today, the priest performed the last rights ceremony again. I bowed my head to pray, and then I looked up and the room was filled with people. Every nurse, every staff person, the janitor, there was twenty people in that room to pray. And I realized we are never alone, and that my son was loved. He was not just another patient in a facility. Prayers ended, and everyone went back to their duties; and an hour or so later, he took his last breath. And I was there by his side. I was there when he took his first breath in the world, and I was there when he breathed his last. And what happened after that moment I don't remember very well. But I can tell you, I'm still not completely healed from burying my child. I'm still

53

haven't let go of the pain I felt picking out his tombstone all by myself. No one held my hand and stood by me with stoic confidence. By myself I picked the color of the granite, choose the design to be carved into it, and spelled out his name and the dates of birth and death.

Five years - ten years later, I'll still have a moment of despondency when a memory hits. I remember that moment every time I walk through the living room and Sponge Bob is on the TV. Do I laugh at Sponge Bob? Yes, death cannot steal your joy. You'll learn to live and love and laugh through all of it. If you're divorced, you'll have moments like this too. You may think you are over it; you're fine, and then you remember something *(a good or bad something)* and instantly, you're mourning again just when you thought you were over it. It's okay. For example, my friend said yesterday, "I'd really like to have everyone over to watch the game, but I'm probably going to lose my big screen TV in my divorce." And I replied "I lost my big screen TV too. It will be okay. Focus on the blessings you do have rather than the things you are losing and you will have more than you've ever had in your life."

A good friend is priceless when you are going through something. And I know you hear something like this and part of you wants to roll your eyes and say "you have no idea how I'm feeling" and then the other part of you says "thank God I have a friend who isn't afraid to tell me what I need to hear." Of course, you have to be discerning. Everyone you know is not your friend. Know who your good friends really are. I can almost guarantee you; you will be able to count them on one hand. A good friend isn't your friend for what you do for him/her. A good friend isn't afraid to tell you the truth. A good friend wants you to see you happy over anything else. A good friend will come over and take the trash out for you, so that you don't feel so alone. A good friend will call and say "I cooked a little something, and we have leftovers, I'm going to bring you a plate." They take care of your pets when you go out of town. They mow your grass as a surprise when they notice you've had many late nights at work that week. I have a few friends who are all of these things and more; they don't mind seeing my cry, and they will do something silly to help me find my laugh again. And real friendship is a reciprocal thing; to have good friends; you must be a good friend. And I don't do enough to thank my friends and to show my friends that I appreciate them. It's really difficult when your life is upside down and all of your energy is focused on putting it right again to be a good friend.

So today, I am thankful for my friends. They are just a few of the blessings that have enriched my life. They have made it better. And if I wouldn't have gotten a divorce, I probably wouldn't have discovered just how wonderful and good they are. There are blessings in the midst of storm; blessings you wouldn't have if you didn't have the storm. Here's a little something to think about, and it may sound silly. You may not appreciate having a large cooking pot, until a thunderstorm comes, and your roof leaks, and then you put the pot to catch the drips of water. You can curse the storm, or you can be thankful you had a pot. You have the tools to solve your problems. You can let your problems beat you. You can curse them. You can whine about them. Or you can just do what you need to do; take it one moment, one day at a time, lean on your friends for support, keep a positive attitude, and you'll make it through. The storm won't last forever. In the beginning of my separation, I didn't feel like it would be okay. I was in the midst of the storm. But one day, I woke up, and I knew, it will be okay. And it is.

Monday, January 10, 2011

Oh my goodness! I haven't seen this much snow since I lived in Europe! My father was stationed outside of Nuremburg, Germany. My brother and I went snow skiing with friends all the time. Sometimes, on a Saturday, my family and I would go walking. I would pull my youngest brother on his sled up the hills, and then he would sled down the other side. We have a lot of fun playing in the snow. But I never thought much about snow when I was child. Snow was all around me. I wasn't in Georgia when I woke up this morning, because I have lived here for 15 years, and I've never seen this much snow around here, and it's still snowing. When I went to feed the cats and make some coffee, I opened the kitchen door onto the back deck and had an actual snow door. There was 8 inches piled up in the door frame. The patio bar stools had snow up to the foot rest bar and the steps to the deck were invisible. So then I went to the front window and looked out at the driveway. What driveway? And I thought, well, I do own a snow shovel, although I have always repurposed it for other yard work besides shoveling snow, but I could shovel some snow.

I am just amazed; all has been washed white with snow. That's a purifying metaphor - to be washed white as snow. Do you have snow where you are? Is the untouched, unplayed in, undriven on, pure snow, how white is it? I bet it's whiter than you ever thought white could be. I've been thinking a lot about love lately, and I want a love that is pure, like snow, that covers over all of the past hurts, pain, the scars, the lies, the mistrust, etc, and makes all of the past disappear as if the past never existed. I want to be able to love someone like snow falling, quietly, effortlessly, definitely. Snow, like love, when it comes; you can't stop it. You can't say to snow, I'm not ready for you. I don't want you to fall on me. Snow, go somewhere else, fall on someone else, because I don't know if I can trust again. When snow comes, you have to accept it. Love, is kind of like snow, you may think you're not ready. You may think you've closed off your heart to love. You may think you can't trust again. I felt that way just a short while ago, like I wasn't ready, my heart was closed off to love, I just wanted to play, I thought every man would hurt me anyway, so why be open to love, but then I was given the opportunity for real, pure, love. It fell into my life like snow is falling on my house and yard now.

And just like I haven't seen snow like this snow in Georgia today, I hadn't seen love like this before. Now, a cynic would say, the snow will melt; the love won't last. It's just a matter of time when the snow will stop falling, and the sun will shine, and the snow will be no more. But love is a miracle. Love will become the sunbeam which warms your face. In each season, you will see love again, ever present in your life. If you've ever thought you were experiencing love, and then that love disappeared (and okay, you and I are both divorced, so we know that's happened), maybe you weren't experiencing love at all, but just thought you were. Maybe you don't believe that love can be real. But if you can believe in the snow and the sun, you can believe that love exists also. Maybe you only believe in snow when you see the snow. And maybe you only believe in sun when you see the sun. And maybe you will only believe in love when you see it too. Be open to seeing love; just accept love into your life when it comes. If you're a cynic, don't worry about what will happen when the snow melts; just accept the love as it is today, let tomorrow be tomorrow, watch love transform into greater, deeper, miraculous love with the seasons.

Tuesday, January 11, 2011

Everyone has thoughts -- personal, deep, intimate --
thoughts. Some thoughts you share openly; some thoughts
you keep to yourself, and some thoughts you have, but you
haven't even admitted to yourself that you have those
thoughts. When I first realized there was a problem in my
almost 15 year marriage, I went to see a psychiatrist. I
didn't even tell Stuart that I was going to go, that I felt like I
needed to go, or what was even bothering me that would
make me even consider going to see a therapist, counselor,
or psychiatrist. I was feeling a change in the climate, like
something was wrong, really wrong, like all of the peace
had gotten sucked out of the air, and I couldn't breathe. And
I started thinking something must really be wrong if it feels
wrong, and so I decided I needed to talk to someone about
it. And that person was not him. So basically, I had
thoughts that I was ready to admit to myself, but not ready
to share with my spouse.

Okay, this is something I wished I would have had known
at the time. If you don't feel like you can share all of your
thoughts and feelings with your spouse, you have a
problem. I had a problem. While I loved him, I had all of
these thoughts that I was keeping to myself like a secret
part of my heart and soul that was mine alone, and he didn't
have a right to know them. I was afraid to share my
thoughts and feelings -- afraid to be open and vulnerable --
afraid to trust him with my most intimate thoughts. And I
wasn't sharing these thoughts with anyone. And a
psychiatrist was duty-bound to keep whatever I said in the
room 100% confidential, so it was almost like talking to
myself, but a little more than that. My thoughts are a great
treasure, and many of these thoughts wove their way into
my poetry or surfaced on the pages of my journal. I didn't
keep a journal before I started seeing the psychiatrist. That

was her suggestion to start writing down all of my thoughts. Actually her instructions were to get a very pretty journal which would make me happy when I looked at it, find a pen I enjoyed holding and watching the ink glide onto the page, and hide it from anyone else. She even gave me ideas on hiding it -- put it in a bag in the freezer, put it in the bottom of a drawer, and so on.

Do you want to know where I hid my journal? In plain sight. It sat on my nightstand at night when I was sleeping. And still does. Sometimes I wake up in the night and just have to write something down. And my journal went to work with me in my briefcase every day. My ex seemed so disconnected from what I was doing in my daily life; I don't think he even noticed I was spending time in my bed writing in a journal. Now the journal I was keeping when I was married, I shredded page by page. You see, when he left me, I became afraid that he really did know it existed, and if I didn't want him reading my intimate thoughts when we were married, I sure didn't want him to read them when we were getting a divorce.

I started keeping a new journal today, but this journal is a record of my thoughts and feelings. One day, I hope to be in a relationship where I'll want my man to read it. My journal, my heart, my secret thoughts and feelings will be my gift to him. But anyway, keeping a journal is really important to knowing how you feel and why you feel as you feel. You don't have to write eloquently; you just have to write it. And you get to choose with whom you share your thoughts in your journal. When I was married, I must have felt unloved, unsafe, and too vulnerable to be completely open. It's not like my most intimate thoughts are scandalous -- I'm not a mass murderer or evil person. Honestly, some of my journal entries are nothing more than the details of my day -- my thoughts about snow and love --

or in the springtime -- my thoughts about grass growing -- or why I wanted to paint the bathroom gray -- or why it makes me happy to see the cans of vegetables in the pantry lined up with the labels displayed to the front in order -- or the significance of how mowing the grass for the first time empowers me when I feel weak and insufficient to be on my own. It's a good thing I like to write, because I am spending a significant portion of my day (well, most days) writing. I keep my journal, I write letters to friends, I write for work, I write my blog, and sometimes when I feel inspired, I write a poem, or just lines of poetry which become a poem later. And maybe you don't like to write as much as I do, but I do encourage you to start keeping a journal. Make it a pretty one that you feel good when you see it. Hide it if you need to do so to feel safe to write down anything you are thinking and feeling. But write in it. Putting your thoughts on the page will help you to admit that's how you feel and help you learn how to deal with your feelings and help you get one step closer to finding the happiness which is eluding you now. Putting your thoughts on the page will help you to heal. It's time for you to start letting go of the past.

Wednesday, January 12, 2011

I'll admit it, and then all of you sleepyheads can groan and throw your pillows at me, I'm a morning person. I wake up early. My mother said I woke up at 5:30 when I was a toddler ready to play. My mother is not a morning person. And I always took the earliest possible classes in college, because I was up anyway. And I like getting up early now. Some things never change. But I get up early in the morning for two reasons -- first, because I just can't sleep any longer, and second, because I find joy in the morning. I had a business mentor who challenged everyone to join what she called the 5 o'clock club. Successful people start their day early. But although I like to have purchasing power, and my creditors would like me to pay my bills, I've never really been motivated to live life for the pursuit of making money. I'd rather care about people, and so I'd rather get up early to cook breakfast or to write thank you cards or to do something nice for someone else.

On my coffee table, I have this beautiful glass mosaic candle holder. And in the evenings, you can burn a candle, and it looks really pretty to see the flicker of the flame through the little multi-colored panes of glass. But in the morning, magic happens, and I discovered the magic by accident. I discovered the magic on a morning when I was feeling a little sad about my situation as a single parent which I never wanted to be, my failed marriage which I never thought would happen, and so on. I wasn't really praying, but I was thinking "God, are you going to take care of me?" as I walked down the stairs into the living room. And the sun had just come up enough in the sky to shine brightly, directly, intently through the transom over the door. And magic, little pieces of prismatic confetti were dancing all over the coffee table, the floor, the furniture, and the walls. Little spots of light. I sat down on the sofa, just like I'm sitting now, and the little colored squares of light shone on me as well. Beautiful. Wonderful. Amazing. A little morning sun, a simple candle holder transformed into a light show in my own living room, and I knew in that moment that everything would be okay. Finding joy that morning unexpectedly reminded me that there was more for my life than what my current situation was. The dancing squares of light only last about ten minutes -- just as long as it takes the sun to move a little higher in the sky and not shine so directly through the transom over the door.

Every morning, the sun rises again. Every morning, the sun shines through the transom again. Every morning, whether I am there or not, the sun and the glass candleholder play together and create magic in my living room. Every morning when I am still home to see the sunrise, I look for my own personal light show, and each time I am equally dazzled and amazed as the first time. Until this morning. This morning, something different happened. I didn't sleep well last night. My father was taken to the hospital late at night by ambulance. This is the third day in a row we've taken my Dad to the hospital. Yes, during this snowstorm, I have driven back and forth to the hospital. Each time the doctors have sent him home and told him to go back to bed. And so I've been up every two hours getting word about his condition. I have a horrible, splitting headache, and I know, I could still be sleeping. But thank God, I'm not sleeping, because something happened in my living room this morning. The sun rose as it always does. The light show happened as it always does.

But today, I discovered something else. There was a rainbow on my ceiling. When the sun moved just a little bit higher, I looked up for the first time at the ceiling, and there was a rainbow. The large, round, mouth of the candle holder and the sun were painting a rainbow on the ceiling. Beautiful. Wonderful. Amazing. A rainbow is a promise after the storm that the storm will never destroy you. A rainbow is a reminder that all will be well. And this morning, I found a rainbow. And I feel joy in my heart. I crawled out of bed this morning worried about what would happen today, and now I have a promise, a reminder, and joy. When you focus on what is going wrong in your life, your problems are magnified. But when you focus on the beauty and joy around you, your spirit is renewed and your problems seem almost nonexistent.

Do your problems sometimes feel like they are going take you over the edge? Do you ever lose your confidence? I do. And when I do, I usually just pretend like I'm the same confident woman as always with most of the people of the world and keep on going. But today, I'm just not feeling like it. I'm tired. I'm feeling weak and vulnerable. And then I see the lightshow in my living room again – that little reminder that I will make it through. So, when I have moments like this when my faith in good things to happen now or good things to come in the future is shaky, I have to remember a time when I made it through. Twenty-one years ago, there was a time when my life was really upside down; what I'm feeling today is nothing in comparison. On December 1, 1989, my son was born, just a couple of days before my twentieth birthday. It hadn't been my plan to be a mother so young in my life; I really wanted to focus on my education and my career, but sometimes babies just happen. I had a difficult delivery; don't worry, this is not a baby delivery story. We had fun taking care of a newborn baby, and he was like all other newborn babies.

Then we had a horrible ice storm when he was 19 days old, and we lived in Louisiana, so just like the snowstorm that has swept the South this week, it was unusual weather. That ice storm was a lot like the one we have Georgia this week. And driving to the hospital to check on my Dad over the icy roads caused me to remember driving my son to the hospital in December of 1989. I couldn't get him to nurse, and he was lethargic. We braved the ice, snow, and cold, and took him to the ER where I was mocked for being a new mother who just didn't know how to take care of a newborn and told to go home and try again. Two days later, he stopped breathing. And I did CPR on my baby as my first husband drove us back to the ER. The doctors took my baby from my arms, hooked up the machines, and did all of the doctor things they do to save a child's life. The doctor said I could stay in the room if I'd be quiet and stay out of the way, and because I can't stand not knowing what's happening, as hard as it was to watch the doctors and nurses insert IVs and a breathing tube, I was glad I was right there. The doctor said Matthew wouldn't live through the night, so we had the priest come and do a last rights ceremony. They put him in PICU, and had these rules about when he could or could not have visitors, and so I pulled a chair out of the waiting room and sat in the hallway outside the door to the PICU when I wasn't allowed to be in the room, and then I was in the room when I was allowed to be in the room.

For days I sat there. Most of the time, I sat there alone, just waiting. Some nights my grandfather would come in the middle of the night, and he'd just stand in the hallway. My friend, a Baptist minister came a few times. My first husband was there often the first day or two, but as each day passed he came less and less. I didn't want to leave. I couldn't leave, and so I sat in the chair quietly waiting for the next visitation hour. And each day, the doctor would say, that he won't live through the night. But he lived. The nurses started having me express breast milk, so that when he woke up, they could give him my milk, and so I did. There was a big breast pump machine – huge, like factory issue size – in a small room at the hospital. I felt like a cow on a dairy farm hooked up to this industrial machinery expressing my breast milk. And on the seventh day, he woke up, and he ate. And each day, he got a little stronger, and about this same time 21 years ago in January, I brought him home from the hospital again. And there began a 12 year journey of being the mother who never heard an encouraging word from a doctor ever again. Every day someone said, he won't live through this day, this month, this year. Every day someone said, it's hopeless, stop expecting something good to happen for him. His brain will slowly die away; his body will get weaker and weaker. Needless to say, I was discouraged and feeling weak and vulnerable and scared. And some days it was really, really hard to believe that he would get better.

But I believe in miracles. I believe that anything is possible. I believe in things I don't see, and consequently, I see things that other people miss, like rainbows on the ceiling, and divine intervention in my life. There's a scripture that says just have the faith of a mustard seed. A mustard seed is really tiny -- almost microscopic. And with just a microscopic amount of faith you can move mountains. Mountains are not literal mountains, but the insurmountable odds and struggles and difficulties in your life. I was always asking for prayer, at church, from the evangelist passing through, from everyone. I even worked for the local Christian television station. One time, a preacher who was there to record his show, said that if I just had more faith, then my son would be healed. I had enough faith. But God had a plan for my life, and getting my son out of his wheelchair was not part of the plan.

A few weeks after my son died, someone asked me if I still believed in miracles. And I do. And they asked me how could I possibly believe in God after watching my son suffer all these years, praying, hoping, waiting for a miracle, and never getting one? I did receive a miracle. The miracle was with me; God gave me the strength, the hope, and the joy, to make it through. I still have laughter, I still have joy, and I still have a song in my heart. I could be a bitter, shriveled up, mean-spirited woman who hates life and everything in it. Because I can tell you this, reader, if you've never buried a child, I pray that you never will. It is the worst pain a mother can ever experience. Worse pain than a failed relationship, even though losing your marriage is very painful. And so when I worry about today, and when I feel down, I remember what I have made it through, and then I realize I can make it through this too. I still believe in miracles. I still believe in love. I still believe that you and I can find happiness, peace, and contentment if we will just hold on and believe just a little bit that good things will happen today and good things will happen tomorrow and good things will happen in the future.

But I'll admit it is difficult to believe that good things will come out of the bad things that happen in life. It is difficult to believe in miracles. It is difficult to believe that you can love again after a failed relationship or a divorce. My heart used to hide in a little frozen prison box; frozen in fear that I would be hurt again. I guarded my heart, and so I would allow myself to love cautiously, just the pieces that could see through the bars would have the opportunity to love. Unfortunately, I entered my second marriage with my heart locked away. I wanted to love. I did love in a way. In a guarded, cautious, maybe things really will be okay, maybe if I do this or that the right way, then I can let me heart out a little bit more and my heart won't be trampled. I thought I had made a safe choice, and so I gave all of myself that I could, but still part of my heart held back. Why? Partly, because when I married, I left part of my heart behind with my son who was in a long-term children's health care facility, because as a new bride I thought if I followed my new husband to another state and supported his education and career, I would receive in the love department all I ever wanted.

The first year of my marriage, I was in Georgia, and I was really depressed about losing my son, about feeling alone, and was really scared. And I kept this mostly to myself. Even though my ex didn't notice this about me, some of the ladies at church did. On Mother's Day, they surprised me with roses. You see, all of the children surprised their mothers with a rose during the service as a way to say "I love you, Mom." And each of my friends brought me a rose and before I knew it, I held a handful of red roses. I cried, because a few women I had known only a few months had seen my heart in its hiding place. My ex didn't understand; I guess, he couldn't see into my heart. Maybe he did understand, but just didn't know what to do. I don't really know about that; all I know is these other women empathized with my loneliness. Years passed, and I continued to give of my body, my time, my energy, and my talents, but yet, my heart was reserved, frozen, just waiting to melt from too much love. I lived in fear, waiting for something to go wrong. And it did.

Did I pray for all to be well in my marriage? Yes. Did I read books, attend women's retreats on being a better wife, and did I keep giving even if I wasn't receiving? Yes. Did I try to be the perfect wife and fulfill every request my ex had? Yes. I was a good wife. But I was not good enough for him. Or, in his defense, I wasn't right for him. He didn't love me the way I needed to be loved. And I couldn't let my heart out of the box completely without love. My heart responds to love; when I receive love, the ice imprisoning my heart melts. When I don't receive love, my heart retreats to a safer place within, and I've learned that I have to guard against that. Maybe you are like that. Maybe you can't even connect with what I'm describing. And that's okay. Here's what I really want to say. In this year or so of healing after my separation and divorce, I have opened the door to my heart's prison. I want to give all of my love, my whole heart, even the secret pieces of fear and pain. If I, or you, want to ever be in a relationship that lasts, that's the courage we've got to find. To let the ice melt. To take the guards off of our heart. To love again. Love is not something you can do halfway. Love is a constant. Actions may not always reflect our true feelings. Words may not always come out the way you want them to. That's because, we're human. I'm human. I'm not perfect. I can try as hard as I want, but I'll still mess up sometimes. And if I'm loved, I'll be accepted for being me with all of my imperfections. When I was married before, I tried to make a relationship work. Now, I'm just going to accept a relationship just as it comes, and a relationship with real, honest, open, trusting, love will melt me and free me to love. I am waiting now, not for something to go wrong, but for the day when my heart will be out of the box completely. Don't believe me? Just wait. One day, I don't know exactly when, but I'll write about the moment when I'm loved completely, openly, and honestly, without reservation and with total acceptance. Now that's a miracle I will wait my entire life to receive. And I believe in miracles.

Sunday, January 16, 2011

It's a privilege to be able to choose what to do with your time; not everyone has that luxury. And I'm thankful, I do. And this weekend, I spent quite a bit of time just thinking and reflecting about what's important to me, what I want out of life and what I need to be fulfilled. On Saturday night my friend and I were discussing how someone makes it to their dreams and becomes the successful person they are supposed to be. The people in your life – your parents – the person you marry – your friends, they all have some influence on you. My friend made this comment that he didn't think I could have reached my full potential with my ex. And so, when I reflect about reaching my potential, or another way to put it, I guess, would be when I think about being the best me I can be, when dreams *(career, family, relationships, and all other aspects of life)* really do come to fruition, your partner, spouse, or significant other, really does impact your potential. For example, when I completed all of my coursework for my doctorate, passed my comprehensive exams, and started researching and writing my dissertation is when Stuart told me he wanted a divorce.

Stuart and I met in graduate school in January 1993. We were both working on our Master's degrees in Speech Communication and Theatre. We both had graduate assistantships with the university theatre department. Now, I had known him for several years as a casual acquaintance, because we had acted in different theatre productions over the years, but we'd never had a single conversation with each other. So we really didn't know each other, and the first conversation we had shouldn't have sparked a relationship, but over time we became friends. I started mid-year, and all of the other graduate assistants had started in August, and so they all had staked out their space in our tiny 8 x 10 office with three desks and chairs intended to house 7 graduate students. Four other students were sitting around talking when I arrived, and I asked where should I put my books, because every square inch of the desktop and bookcases seemed crammed full of someone else's things. One guy said just move that stuff over, and he pointed at the pile belonging to the man who would become my second husband. Another guy grabbed a box and with a sweep of his arm slid the pile into the box. Let's tell him that he lost his assistantship when he comes in. And just like that, they all decided to pull a prank on him. I didn't know him, and I thought, surely, his friends wouldn't do this if he wasn't the kind of person who would think it was funny. I was the new kid, so I just went along with the prank, because they seemed so sure. After awhile, just I and another guy were sitting in the office, and he arrived. And he noticed immediately his stuff in the box and started asking questions. And then I did something I shouldn't have done. Succumbing to the peer pressure, I pulled the prank, and told him he was fired, and I was his replacement. He thought I was a bitch, and rightly so. He was angry at first, and then, he started to get happy. He didn't want this job anyway, and then my sense of fairness pricked my conscience; I couldn't let him leave thinking he didn't have a job when he did. So I confessed. And then he really thought I was a bitch. But over time, we became friends, and then we started dating. We had compatible career goals; we both desired to become college professors. The other guys I dated were exciting and fun to be around, but they didn't want out of life what I wanted. And I wanted to be married to a friend, a man who was kind to me, and I envisioned eating brown bag lunches sitting on the bench in the Quad at some university somewhere twenty years from now discussing philosophy or literature. Approximately three years later, we married, the week after I graduated with my Master's degree. He had already started his doctorate, and I thought I would begin immediately on my doctorate. A decade would pass before I enrolled in my doctoral program. I followed him to Georgia, when he changed his mind about what doctoral program he wanted to complete. I got a job, so we'd have insurance benefits. I had babies. I started teaching part-time at the local community college. I sold cosmetics to make extra money. I did some copy-editing to make extra money. During those ten years, he changed his career goals, and when he did, everything changed. My dreams of working beside my husband as we both taught college evaporated. I decided it was time to go back to graduate school. I had delayed my dreams for a decade in an attempt to be the perfect wife. Little did I know that in another five years, he would be sitting in the chair across the room from where I was sitting on the bed telling me that I was a good wife and that he didn't want to be married to me? Our marriage wasn't perfect, and this wasn't the first time we had discussed divorce, but this time I knew deep down in my gut it was really going to happen.

And I thought two things: one, I cannot believe that I supported him with all he needed to complete his degrees, and when it was finally my turn to focus on my goals, he wouldn't be there to support me; and two, I'm going to finish this no matter what, I'm not going to stop. That's determination and perseverance in the midst of a crisis. My dreams, my goals, my purpose, my potential matters. What I do, how far I go, impacts what my daughters believe they can accomplish in their lives. What I do, how far I go, impacts everyone else in my circle of influence. So reaching my potential will help others reach their potential. Isn't that amazing to think about -- how the life of one woman makes a difference? Do you stop and think about how your life makes a difference, not only for yourself, but for everyone else you know? First, I have to visualize where I am going, and then I have to believe I can get there, and then I have to have the courage to start the journey, and then I have to do the work to make it happen. At this moment, I'm talking about personal career goals, but it's the same for relationship goals too.

First, I visualize what type of relationship do I want to have, then I believe that it's possible to have it, have the courage to put my heart out there and commit to finding it, and then do my part to make it happen. Of course, I don't control the other person in the relationship. But doesn't that kind of go back to what I said earlier, that the right person for you will support you so you can reach your full potential? And you know the other thing I've been thinking about, what a miracle it would be if each person in the relationship was the right person for the other person and each person supported the other person in reaching his/her full potential, how much more could the two of them as a couple accomplish together than apart? How much greater would the positive impact be on the people around them -

their families, their children, their friends, their co-workers, or just total strangers?

I really do like being outside no matter what the weather or what time it is. Last night, my man and I took the four-wheeler for a ride through the woods about midnight. We found where the deer were nesting in a cove of trees. I never knew that it was possible, to see at night more clearly than you could see in day. And I never before heard the music of little pieces of ice bouncing down the snowy, icy slope, after the wheels disturbed their rest. We parked the four-wheeler and just walked hand in hand mesmerized by this magical Georgia winter night. The almost full moon was so bright, that with the crisp, white, snow decorated with a layer of glistening ice, you could see the shadows of the tree branches. I never knew that it was possible, for moonlight to cast a shadow. So much is possible. Stuff you never ever imagined could really is possible. Visualize the impossible. Believe the impossible. Embrace the reality that the impossible can be possible. Take action on making the impossible possible. Just because it *(whatever it is)* hasn't happened before; just because you've failed in your past relationships before; just because you haven't accomplished your goals yet, doesn't mean those things are impossible. The impossible happens every day; you just haven't seen moon cast shadows on snow before.

Tuesday, January 18, 2011

Part of my dreams I envisioned back in graduate school did come true. I am a college professor. Divorced and sharing brown bag lunches with friends. Sometimes your life will not be the way you think it will be. And sometimes you get what you really want by going through something else. I am back at work. It's freezing in my office. Of course, I knew it would be. It's always freezing in my office in the winter. I'm at the end of the hall right next to the most used exterior door, so every time someone opens the door, there's an arctic blast. I have been in this office for I think five years, and I'm cold every winter. And every winter, I talk about getting a space heater, I think about buying a space heater, but I just don't do it. You know, it's pretty bad when I get so cold that I can't stand it any longer, and I go sit in my car to blast the heat and warm my bum with the electric seat heater.

So here's the question you're probably thinking, why don't I solve the problem? Why have I spent 5 winters freezing at work when I could simply just get some heat? And if you could see me, you'd probably ask why don't you have on a coat, hat, scarf, and gloves? Well, the simple answer to the last question is I can't type or do my work when I'm bundled up like I'm ready to hit the ski slopes. The answer to the real question about why I haven't done anything about it is more complicated. Some people might say I have a personality flaw, because it is my natural inclination to put others first and to put myself last. I wouldn't let a friend go without heat, but yet, I will. And so I need someone to remind me that I'm deserving and worthy and am not being selfish when I look to my own needs. My failed marriage is kind of like my office is too cold problem. I knew there were things missing from my relationship with my ex just as I know that there is heat missing from my office. But I ignored the tell-tale signs of lack of emotional intimacy, lack of companionship, lack of sex, etc, just like I'm ignoring the signs of freezing hands and blurry vision because of the cold. For years, I got up each day saying "My marriage is good" and I went to work each wintery day saying "My cold office won't be that cold" and for both, I can make it through one more day. I can't possibly be the only person who does that.

Have you done that? Did you know deep down that there were warning signs that your failed marriage was not meeting all of your needs? Now in the defense of all of us and a gentle reminder, there is a difference between needs and wants. You can't possible have all you want, because seriously, if I could have all I wanted, I'd be on some secluded tropical beach making love all night and all day with the love of my life with no financial worries, no responsibilities, and no failed marriages issues which drive me crazy. Like a permanent and perfect vacation. But that's not reality. So real life is somewhere between permanent vacation of my dreams and what I have now. Now I have a chance to start over with someone who desires to meet my needs and wants to hold close to me in the middle of all of the financial worries, the responsibilities, and the failed marriage issues which drive me crazy. And a real office is somewhere between top floor suite with all of the luxuries and what I have now. And I'd be happy with my tiny corner office just as it is if it could have heat in the winter and no ants in the summer. So maybe I should get a space heater and warm up this office. Maybe it's time.

And like always I talked about buying a space heater, and I didn't do anything about it. Two days have passed, and a miracle happened. An answered prayer. I have heat in my office! Can you believe it? I have heat. After 5+ years of a cold and drafty office, I now have heat! I can now add to my list of my favorite things: a tiny ceramic space heater. For all these years I have complained about being cold, and no one has ever worried about me being cold until now. And I am so grateful, so extremely grateful, for the warmth surrounding my body, and even more grateful for the warmth steaming my heart. This gift of heat was given to me in love, in genuine care and concern for my well-being. While I was getting ready for work this morning, my man called and asked me if I had time to swing by his office on my way to work, because he had something to give me. And he put into my hands a tiny black ceramic space heater. Finally a miracle, a man did something to meet my needs as a human being. I didn't know it could happen. But it did, and it was very nice, very nice indeed. This feeling is better than, well, you know.

I read an article the other day on the internet that said that gratitude brings about happiness. And I am very happy today. I am happy in spite of all of the disappointments of daily life, the death of my loved ones, the destruction of my marriage, and the drama of dealing with divorce issues. If you were to pile up all of the bad dealings of my life on one side of the scale against all of the good on the other, it would appear that the bad outweighs the good. It would look as if there was more bad than good. Because no matter how sad and depressing my life appears, I am happy I have had the life I have had. I am happy that my story can help you find strength and courage and hope to make it through your struggles. I am happy that I have discovered what love really is. The warmth I am feeling today would not be as warm if I had not lived without warmth. Are you deprived of the warmth of real affection? Have you lived without sacrificial, unconditional, selfless love in your past relationships? Before you whine and moan about what you have not had, pause for a moment, and reflect on what you have. Be grateful for your circumstances just as they are. Life is never going to be perfect. My bank balance is low, I have no savings, and I still owe money to the lawyer for my divorce. My house still is on the market and is in desperate need of repairs. My kids have outgrown their clothes, and I can't afford to take them on vacation. My brother has just been diagnosed with terminal cancer. And the list goes on and on.

But I am grateful for what I do have. Good friends. Good health. A positive attitude. My children. Love. Warmth. My parents. And that list goes on and on as well. But if you're still waiting to receive your heart's desire, then be patient. Persevere through the pain, believe that good things are to come, and be thankful that your prayers will soon be answered. Thank God for listening and answering my prayers! Thank those around you who care about you and love you for the person you are. Thanks to my friend's stepmother who gave my phone number to the blind date who has now given me this tiny ceramic space heater for my office, and my dear friend who encouraged me to accept the phone call and to open my heart, because without their belief in good things to come, then it would still be cold in my office, and I'd still be waiting for my prayers to be answered. Thanks to my man for kindly caring about me, for being my friend first, for loving me just as I am, imperfect as I am, and for giving me the gift of his heart.

Wednesday, January 19, 2011

I really like to walk. And I walk for a variety of reasons. Sometimes I walk around the neighborhood just to get a little exercise with fresh air instead of a stuffy workout room on a treadmill. Sometimes I walk to get where I need to be, like walking across campus to go to a meeting or to talk with a friend. Sometimes I walk because I'm bored; like when I was in San Francisco for work, my friend Thomas from New York and I criss-crossed 6 square blocks for the two hours between our meetings just for something to do besides sitting and drinking another cup of coffee. Sometimes I walk because I am overwhelmed, and I walk to try to walk off my anxiety, like this past summer day I got the phone call my grandmother was dying, I just starting walking and crying and thirty minutes later I found

76

myself 2 miles away at my friends' house. I did feel better by the time I got there, and a little better by the time I talked with Nicole for awhile. And so walking back, I actually felt the sunshine and heard the birds chirping and enjoyed myself a little.

Sometimes I walk to appreciate the natural environment around me. Have the tulips sprouted yet? Oh, that's where the rain water coming out the downspout gullied pine bark mulch into little piles and dams carving valleys of Georgia red clay and rich brown topsoil. The carpet of snow has melted a little more over there exposing the brown oak and maple leaves. Sometimes I walk to enjoy a quiet moment with someone special. There's comfort in knowing that he feels the same cool wind across his cheek as I feel, and peace in knowing that he sees the hand of God sprinkling the outstretched tree branches with soft powdery snow, and contentment in knowing that we are walking together instead of alone. Have you ever felt this way? Did you feel this way with your spouse, partner, or friend before the relationship failed? Did you ever even take a walk with him/her? And if you did, did you walk together? Or if you've never felt this way, do you wish you could? Do you dream about walking hand-in-hand through a quiet wintry wood or on a sandy beach with the salty sea spray sprinkling over you? I really like to walk, and going on a walk with someone is a good test of compatibility. I bet you've never thought about that before. I didn't either, until recently. In the past, I've gone on walks, and sure, I found it annoying when my walking partner and I didn't have the same pace. One of us would walk faster or slower than the other. Or one of us would walk more purposeful and determined and the other more reflective and observant. And I guess, it is okay if the other realizes the difference in pace and adjusts to meet the needs of the other and then you continue on from that moment of realization walking together. But it's not okay if the other keeps on going and abandons his/her partner without regard.

So, maybe a walking stick will be your measuring stick, and the walk will measure the merit of your relationship. I really like to walk, and I'm extremely happy to have taken several walks lately, and I'm full of hope for future walks which bring contentment and care, peace and passion, warmth and wonder. And I pray you will enjoy the next walk you take whether your reason is exercise, for stress relief, with your dog, or to discover if you have the same pace as someone else. And sometimes you may have to decide to walk a different direction. Sometimes you may have to walk alone. Today, I walked into the jewelry store to have my watch battery changed, and I decided it was time.

Choking back the tears, I scolded myself for being so sentimental and such a baby. I sold my wedding band. The saleslady asked me if I was sure I wanted to sell it, and I said, "I'm divorced. It's been awhile. And it's time. I need to let it go." And while I waited for her to do whatever transaction paperwork she needed to do, it felt like I could feel grains of sand soaked in molasses dripping through an hourglass, and I just kept telling myself, "don't cry, don't cry, don't cry." And so I sold that white gold wedding band and all it represented - the unbroken circle which was broken, the forever covenant which was no more, the promise to love, honor, and cherish which was not kept. And as I walked out of the jewelry store into the sunshine, a tear slid down my cheek. I got in my car and texted my best friend and called my man to tell them what I had done. I didn't feel good about it, but I thought, I can use this money to buy something for my children. I can sell the diamonds next and put that money towards a new piano my daughter really wants, which she'll play every day. The thought of selling my wedding ring has been gnawing a hole in my stomach, but I just kept pushing the bile back ignoring how I was feeling. Have you been worried about something and just kept pushing the feelings further and further down into your stomach just hoping they will go away? After your divorce or failed relationship, what did you do with your symbols of love, honor, and devotion? Did you sell your jewelry? Did you throw it into the river? Do you have a collection of mementos lined up in a box marking each and every one of your failed relationships?

So on Wednesday I sold my wedding ring. And today, on Friday, I have my wedding ring back. Standing in front of him with the ring in the palm of my hand; he said "Allison, you can't erase your past; your past is a part of you, and this wedding band is a part of your past and so a part of you. You should keep it, at least a little while longer; until you really know for sure that you want to let it go. And maybe you really want to keep it forever." How can there be a person who can hear my heart speaking when I say no words? Why does he care about my heart? Why would he care about my wedding ring given to me by another man? My man had bought my wedding ring from the jewelry store and gave it back to me.

And so I've cried all afternoon, because he's right, my failed relationships have made me the woman I am now. My failed relationships are a part of me, and while I'm ready to move onto something more, something better, and something new, I can't erase the past. I take my failed relationships with me into my new relationship. No matter what happens in the future, your past is a part of your future. You have to have peace about your past before you can have peace about your future. I'm a better woman for having the life that I've had, and maybe my wedding ring still means something, just not what the same as on my wedding day. And so, today, January 21, 2011, I received a most precious regifting of gold and love, a wedding ring I received for the first time on May 27, 1995. And I'm going to keep my wedding ring, because it was given to me in love the first time and with unconditional love the second time. My heart spoke in silence to another heart, and I feel cherished for the first time in my life. I talked myself into selling it because I thought I wasn't loved. My ex had written in our divorce papers that we had a loveless marriage from the very beginning. And so, I questioned the symbolism of my wedding band, because I didn't feel loved. But today, I feel loved beyond measure.

Saturday, January 22, 2011

I love waking up on a Saturday morning; there's just something calming about knowing I can lay in the bed propped up on pillows, drink a fresh cup of coffee in my favorite mug, not rush to get a shower and dress for work, and just reflect about yesterday, last week, making it through 2009 and 2010 when my marriage fell apart and I survived an entire year on my own, my life as a whole, and what I'm going to do today. Do you ever take the time, whether it's when you first wake up in the morning or a few minutes in the afternoon sitting at your desk at work or just before you go to bed, to stop the gerbil wheel and just think? What do you think about? Sometimes I think I've wasted so much time, put so much energy into a relationship which was doomed to fail. Do you feel like you did so much to make your relationship work, and then you feel more like a failure, because you just couldn't do it?

Sometimes I think I should have been smarter when I was a young woman -- waited longer before I had sex, focused more on my education than having fun with friends, been strong enough to stand up for myself rather than allowing others to take advantage of me, to not have married my first husband just because I was pregnant. Of course I thought I loved Roger, as much as a 19-year-old understands love, and I did intend to stay faithful to my marital vows forever, but I decided that divorce was better than death. I should have refused to move from Louisiana to Georgia after marrying Stuart, my second husband, because leaving my child behind in the long-term children's care facility was the last thing on earth I wanted to do which I agreed to do because I believed that a wife should follow her husband and put his needs before her own, and more. I am still trying to figure out why I do that. Why do I put the needs of the man before my own? Why don't I expect more for myself?

Basically, I regret some of the decisions I made. Do you have regrets? Do you wish you had made different choices? Do you think about what your life would be like now if you had? Sometimes I do think about what my life would be like if I had done things differently. Let's take the major milestones and see what would be different. First, I wouldn't have had a child when I was still a child really. But then, being the mother to a special needs child with tons of medical problems saved my life. Second, I wouldn't have married the first time to an abusive man, because I would have remained focused on my writing career. But then, my writing wouldn't be as meaningful to you, because I would have written for travel magazines and newspapers rather than surviving hardships and feelings and all of this "having a positive attitude after failed relationship stuff." Third, I wouldn't have married the second time, because I wouldn't have been looking for a man who was so extremely different from my first husband. And if I wouldn't have married him, then I wouldn't have my beautiful daughters who bless my life so much. Fourth, I wouldn't have put off getting my doctorate, because I would have gone to LSU and finished back in the 90's. And changing that would have meant that all of these years I've loved teaching at the community college here in Georgia would not have happened. And I can go on and on.

But the bottom line is this, I have received so many blessings and good things in my life which wouldn't have happened the way they did if I wouldn't have made the decisions I made and lived the life I had. And now, I feel even more blessed, because I've been given the opportunity to bless others in ways I never imagined. I can listen to my students and friends more empathetically, more compassionately, more lovingly, because I have experienced something like their present troubles, and a person with a broken heart understands a broken heart, and a person with a broken heart that has healed, or is in the process of healing, understands that a broken heart desires to be healed, to be loved, to be nurtured.

And now, I have what I would consider the best opportunity and the greatest blessing which just blows the bad out of the water. As a divorced woman with children, I have the opportunity for a new beginning, and my new beginning will blend two divorced and broken families. I don't know exactly when it will happen, only time will tell, but the opportunity is there. This is an answered prayer, because I always wanted to have more children. Some years, I was afraid to have another child, afraid that he/she would be sick and die like my first child. Some years, I was tired of feeling like a single parent carrying a baby in a carrier and holding the hand of a toddler while also being a pack mule determined to make it into the church for services, because I went a lot of places alone, just me and my kids. Some years, I was worried my marriage wasn't good enough to bring more children into it. For the last few years of my marriage, after Jason, my youngest brother died, I really wanted to have another child. My extended family felt so small, no nieces, no nephews, no cousins for my children to play with, and I saw my family dying away with the generations.

I had never worried about getting too old to have more children until Jason died. He was eight years younger than me and was in his twenties, and I just knew he would eventually get married and have children and do his part to give my parents more grandchildren. I was his big sister, and we were very close. He joined the army after high school, and he lived with us in between his tours of duty. He dreamed of going to West Point, and when he came from Germany, he was accepted. One day, during morning drills, he had a seizure. They sent him to Walter Reed Hospital in D.C., and he was diagnosed with adult-onset epilepsy. Eight months later, his honorable medical discharge was processed and he came back to Georgia to live with us until he figured out what he wanted to do. The girls loved having their Uncle Jason around all the time. He was both a big help and a burden. One time the three of them were sitting in the living room eating cereal. And as he walked into the kitchen, he had a seizure right there on the kitchen floor. I asked him later why did he get up from the couch if he knew he was about to have a seizure. And he just said that his last thought was he didn't want to drop the cereal bowl on the carpet.

Another time he decided he would help with some yard work while we were at work. And he decided to burn the leaves and branches he had piled up. And then he called me, he used the fuel from a Coleman camping lantern and flash burned himself accidentally. I raced home and took him to the hospital where I spent the next six hours pouring saline water on his burns. This was just one of the many accidents he had over the years. He struggled with trying to find the purpose for his life after the army. The weekend he died, he finished making picnic tables for the elementary school. My brother Jason never had any children. And in my grief, I longed for another child. Stuart and I had decided after the birth of our youngest child that we were done. That we had enough children, but I was just afraid of having more children. I really wanted more. And now, with my brother's death, I wanted to try again.

We considered adoption: I did all the research on adoption, I spent hours on the computer looking up children who were available, to adopt US or adopt abroad, I called friends who adopted children and listened to their stories, and I made an appointment to go to the adopting parents class offered by the county. We went to the appointment, and then my ex said he couldn't do it. He couldn't adopt. So no child. Then we did the things we needed to do medically to have a baby, but we didn't do the things we needed to do relationally. Do you have children? Did you birth them? Did you adopt them? Do you want to have a child, but it just hasn't happened?

And so as each year passed 2006, 2007, 2008, 2009 without a child, my heart hurt a little more. Even my children were sad, because they wanted more siblings. And I have prayed and prayed about this over the years, and then I hardened my heart against wanting more children in my life. And even when I first started dating in 2010 after my divorce, I told people when the topic of children came up, "I'm 40. I have children. I just want to focus on my career. And I'm okay with that." But I wasn't okay with it, but I just pushed those feelings further and further down into my gut. And now, I realize that while divorce among families is devastating for the children, and I believe that children shouldn't be forced to suffer from the bad marriages and even worse divorces, something positive can happen after divorce for the children. A new family can form; a family that is more unified, stronger, and has more love in it than the two families which split apart. Of course, this wasn't my plan for my life. I planned to be married forever, and I wanted my children to grow up in a loving household with their biological parents forever. But things didn't go according to plans. But maybe this is God's plan for my life. Maybe I've been through what I've been through, so that I would be ready and able to love and mother more children, so that I can help their little broken hearts which have suffered so much because of the weaknesses and selfishness of their parents. I wouldn't have come to this realization that maybe I'm meant to be the mother of more children if I wouldn't have had the life I've had. For what has your life, your failed relationship prepared you? Have you thought about what good will rise out of the ashes? If you haven't taken the time to think about these things, maybe it's time to take the time. Maybe it's too soon after your failed relationship. Maybe you're not ready to find your purpose. That's okay. Just keep moving forward. Take things one day at a time and see where you end up tomorrow. Keep hoping. Keep praying. And keep trying. Rebuilding your life is a process. You will get there. One Saturday morning, you're going to wake up, stretch your arms, yawn, look at your life, and say "yes, life is good."

Monday, January 24, 2011

My grandmother and my mother made my clothes when I was a little girl. I never even wore anything besides a dress until I was in third grade, when the teacher asked my mother to have me wear shorts under my dress for when I played on the monkey bars. So it's not surprising that I like to wear dresses now as a woman, and I'll be thankful when the

85

weather isn't so cold, so I can wear dresses more often. Now that I have heat in my office, it's not so bad wearing a skirt in the winter. Some women don't like to wear dresses. But I like being a woman, and I like looking like a woman.

My grandmother used to tell me stories about how she and her sisters would barter between each other to get enough feed sacks with the same design on them; my great grandfather was a dairy farmer, and when the huge delivery of grain would come in, the girls got new dresses. Yes, people actually did make dresses from feed sacks in the 1930's and 1940's, and some folks today complain  when they can't afford another $300 Coach handbag. I almost always had handmade clothes; at least until middle school, and even then special occasion dresses were handmade. My homecoming dance dresses, my junior prom dress, my wedding dresses, all handmade. My senior year, I begged my mother to please let me buy my senior prom dress from the store, and she did. I finally had a special occasion store bought dress. And then we recycled that dress into my first wedding dress. *(This is my first wedding dress made by adding some lace to a recycled prom dress).* And now, my daughters and I watch this reality TV show "Say yes to the dress" where the bride will cry about not having an extra $1000 in her budget to get the $6000 dress she really wants. My entire budget for my first wedding was $0. And my budget for my second wedding was less than $1000. So I'm not really a demanding bride, and I'm willing to put time and energy into something I want to be special rather than just writing a check or swiping the plastic card.

But sewing is not something I just love to do; it's just something I can do. I can sew because my grandmother thought that every woman should know how to sew. So for Christmas when I was 12, I received my first Singer sewing machine; I asked for a horse, and I got a sewing machine. So like most things in my life, I wanted one thing, but I got something else. And somehow later I discovered that things were as they should be. Over the years, I learned to sew. My mother still helps me, and sometimes will just sew things for me when I'm too busy to sew it myself. Together we made my wedding dress for my second wedding, because I couldn't afford to buy the dress I really wanted, so we did our best to recreate the design ourselves. *(This is my second wedding dress in ivory brocade and satin).* You know, it feels kind of weird counting my wedding dresses, but that's just the way my life is. A woman is only supposed to have one wedding dress, but unfortunately, I have two. And after my second wedding; since I didn't think my future daughters  would ever appreciate my style, I recycled that dress. I covered our wedding photo album with pieces of the dress; I made Easter dresses out of the skirt for my daughters later. I thought it was very creative of me at the time. Looking back, it seems like a weird thing to have done. And I still have pieces of it saved in a box in the closet if my daughters want to take a piece and add it to their own dresses, even if it's just a little piece sewn underneath where only they know it's there. Then their "something old" will actually be a little something from when their Mom and Dad got married. And even though we are divorced, I still think it is a romantic idea for my daughters.

Where is your wedding dress? Did you cut it up, sell it, or give it away? Were you like me, and you did something with it before your marriage failed? Or did you have some sort of post-divorce destroy the wedding dress ritual? Are you saving it for your daughters? My favorite picture of my oldest daughter when she was a small child is the one where she played dress up with my wedding veil, because she wanted to get married to Daddy like Mommy did when she grew up.

Over the years, I have made clothes for Barbie dolls, costumes for recitals, curtains for the kitchen, decorative pillows, Christmas stockings, and quilts. The last big sewing project I was working on before my divorce was a t-shirt quilt for my husband. Over the years, I had saved all of his special shirts, the ones he and his friends designed in college, the activities in which he had participated, mascot shirts, and just whatever. It took years, but I had two boxes of shirts saved, and this quilt was to be his Christmas present in 2009. But we separated, so it didn't happen. There are lots of special things I made over the years, and it's really emotionally difficult to look at them now. Decorating for Christmas was really hard, because I made the stockings, and one remained in the box this year when all of the others were hung from the mantle. Were there things you made for your ex, or with your ex, left in the box? What did you do with those ornaments, crafts, and other handmade things from your failed relationship?

I try not to think about the things that I made and all of the hours I spent making them, because it seems like such a waste of time and energy. And it makes me sad. Sometimes you lose a button. And being able to sew the button back on is the positive. I can dwell on what I've lost, and be sad, or I can put my talents to use to make others feel special. Today at school, one of my daughters lost two buttons off her new jacket, and I sewed them back on for her. And I even sewed a button back on one of my own jackets. And I'm going to sew the elastics onto the tiny tap shoes which belong to a little sweetheart of a girl. After all, I have lots of practice sewing pointe shoe ribbons and ballet slipper elastics. When my girls were in their dance classes in all of their growing up years, I sat in the hall night after night sewing this, that, or the other. I sewed several costumes for ballet productions and church activities. My grandmother was right; knowing how to sew has brought a lot of joy to my life. Because when my daughter said "thanks, Mom", and smiled, and when my little dancer's eyes sparkled as she grinned "you mean, you can fix my shoes? Really?" The joy in my heart from seeing their joy replaces all of the sadness of what could have been, but wasn't. I'm so thankful my grandmother gave me a sewing machine. I'm so thankful my mother taught me how to sew. I'm so thankful to have my children and to have other children to love in life. And I'm so thankful that sometimes you lose a button.

Tuesday, January 25, 2011

I used to never have text messaging on my cell phone. I've had a cell phone ever since they were invented in the 80's. Yes, I had one of those bag phones. I bought the bag phone for security reasons. For the same reason, I owned a handgun. I was just a little bit paranoid about being stalked by my first husband. To him, visitation with his child was an excuse to find me, and he would follow me as I went to the grocery store and curse at me as I walked from my car into the store. Ironically, I taught at an inner city school, and I was never worried about driving through the bad parts of town. There, I felt safe. I always felt like if I had a flat tire, I could knock on any door in the projects, and the person would say "Its tha' purty lil English teacher. She gotta prob'im wi' her car." And they'd help me. I never worried about getting hurt, even though my car was vandalized more than once, and after a football game in Shreveport, our school buses were riddled with bullets. I crawled along the floor of the bus checking each student for injuries. Luckily no one was seriously hurt or shot. Even then, I felt safe.

I taught high school literature and history. I had 156 students, and only 6 of those students were not black. No matter what integration laws are created, people still cluster in racial groups. The white folks figured out how to move to the other side of the river and start another town with their own school system. I just graduated and divorced; I was barely older than my students and I was a single parent. It was difficult to pay my bills on a teacher's salary, especially the extra medical bills for my son, and I never really received any child support to speak of. My annual salary was $17,000; after taxes, I netted less than $1000 per month. I couldn't afford the premiums for health insurance, so I didn't have any. And I lived in government subsidized housing, a white clapboard house down the street from the First Baptist Church. Ironically, my students had the preconception that because I was white and pretty, that I was also wealthy. Little did they know I didn't own furniture or a stove, and that my car was borrowed from family? It took a few weeks to gain their trust. On Saturdays I would go over to the school and pick up kids to take them to the park to play football and eat peanut butter sandwiches. The first time they asked to go with me after I mentioned my son and I were going on a picnic, I thought they are just trying to sweeten up the teacher for brownie points. But then I realized that all children want is to be loved, and that children who have grown up feeling unloved, want love more than anything else.

I've always had the cheapest cell phone you could buy; usually it was the one which came free with your plan. I am really not a technology kind of person. I still prefer to write with pen to paper. And I prefer to talk face to face with someone than to call them on the phone. I would rather drive 30 minutes to have a 5 minute conversation, than to be in a separate location talking on the phone. I've always enjoyed spending time with people I care about – whether it's my students, my family, my friends, my significant other and his children – just getting together is most important. What about you? Are you really into technology? Do you prefer email or letters? Do you prefer talking to someone or talking on the phone to someone or just texting someone? Until the year before my divorce, I didn't even have a Smartphone. I actually got my first Smartphone with texting and all of those features, because when I asked my friend for advice to improve my marriage. She told me to find something my ex and I could share; he was into technological devices, and so I asked him to help me get a Smartphone and show me how to use it. In so many ways it was a waste of money at the time, because I didn't know how to use half of the features on it, I didn't understand texting, and I didn't want to pay the extra money to have my email come to my phone, and it didn't improve our communication with each other.

After my divorce, I had to change my cell phone number and so I bought an iPhone. And I love using my iPhone. And I know the Apple Corporation is happy, because now I own an iPad too. I didn't hardly have any text messages on my plan, and then in the first week of my teenager getting a cell phone, I was over my limit, because she texted me non-stop. I called the cell phone company and added more texts to my plan. And now, I probably need to go to unlimited texting, because I have figured out the joys of texting. My co-workers and I text each other during meetings about what we think about what is being said by the speaker; my kids text me about all sorts of details throughout their day. And this is something I've learned about their generation - I prefer face to face; they prefer texting, and they feel like we've had extended, special, deep and meaningful conversations if we've exchanged several texts especially if there's a smiley face at the end. I can text a friend just to let him/her know that I'm thinking about them or praying for them or to ask a question. What I like best, I guess, is that the moment I think of someone, I can take action on that thought or feeling rather than waiting. And it's really great when that someone texts back. So how often do you text? Do you even have text messaging as part of your cell phone plan? Maybe you should consider trying it out if you don't have it. Today, I received a text "you are so hot." That right there should make you want to have text messaging on your phone; come on, don't you want to receive texts about how great you are?

But if you don't want to text, it's okay. You can always call someone. How many times a day do you think of a friend or family member, but you don't stop what you're doing and pick up the phone to say "hi, how are you?" Why don't you? Are you worried they won't be receptive to your call? One of the things I learned post-divorce is there is a dating rule. You shouldn't answer your phone every time it rings. I didn't realize it in the beginning of my new single life, because I'd basically been married or in a relationship with someone since cell phones were invented. Whether or not you answer your phone when someone calls you is an indicator of how important the person calling is. For example, when the phone rings at home, my children always yell out "the phone is ringing, the phone is *ringing*,

THE PHONE IS RINGING" and then I usually check the caller ID and say "it's a telemarketer, just ignore it." And when you first meet someone, or maybe you've just had the first date, and even though you may be really excited because it's a new relationship and you really want to know what's going to happen next, you shouldn't stop everything you are doing that moment to answer the phone.

This is what you need to realize, it is a privilege and an honor for that person to have your time and attention. You are giving him/her a gift of you when you answer the phone. I bet you thought answering the phone was an obligation. You are not Pavlov's dog who responds automatically to a bell. Just because the phone rings, you don't have to answer it. You choose to answer the phone. And trust me, the person who is calling knows you chose to answer the phone or not. Answer the phone because you want to answer the phone. Call someone because you want to talk to them. Send a text message because you want them to know they are in your thoughts at that moment. And over time, as your casual dating relationship turns into an exclusive relationship, then the amount and frequency of your communication should increase. And when you decide to answer the phone when your significant other calls you, you are letting him know that he is a priority in your life. So, really the dating advice is don't make a man your top priority by answering the phone each time it rings unless that man is your top priority.

And really this phone advice applies to other relationships as well. My list is really short: my significant other, my children, my parents, my close friends. You probably will choose to answer the phone whenever your children call you. You will probably to choose to answer the phone whenever your elderly parents call you. You will probably have one or two very close friends who will receive the gift of you answering the phone when they call. But everyone else on the planet gets voicemail unless I'm bored and have nothing else to do. And even when I am bored and have nothing else to do, the telemarketer is still getting the voicemail. When you choose to call someone, or to text someone, or to drive across town to talk to someone, you are sending a relationship message. When someone chooses to answer the phone when you call, when someone texts you back, or when someone sits down to talk to you, he/she is giving you a relationship message. I had to learn how to text, and I had to learn what was appropriate phone communication for the context when I started dating again after my divorce, because the only rule I knew was "you should always answer the phone when your spouse calls." I didn't know the rules about phones and dating. I had to learn the dating rules, and you'll have to learn the dating rules too. And you'll probably make a few mistakes. You'll probably call a few too many times before you realize that person is not interested. I did that. You'll probably answer the phone too often. That's just all a part of the dating world. But in time, you'll meet someone who is worthy to be called your significant other and to be your top priority to call and to answer the call. And then you can choose to give him the gift of you. You are special. And the time and attention you choose to give someone is a gift.

And your true love and your real friends will actually appreciate you for all of the ways in which you communicate. And if reading this blog makes you think of a friend or someone special in your life you haven't called or texted today, pick up your phone right now and dial their number, and when they answer, say "Thank you for answering the phone, and thank you for being my friend, my sister, my child, my partner, (you know, just whomever they happen to be to you), my life is better for having you in it." You'll feel better, and they'll feel better. I feel better just thinking about all of you smiling while holding your phones. But there is something better than a phone call. And that is, putting pen to paper.

There is just something about putting pen to paper -- the way the ink flows from the tip of the pen delicately drawing lines and loops -- the way what should be random lines and loops form letters and words which express what I'm thinking or feeling. There is just something about putting pen to paper that is not at all like typing on a computer keyboard. What do you like better? Pen to paper? Or computer? Even though I'm typing right now, I don't have the same emotional connection that I do as when I'm writing with a pen. I really have to imagine that I am talking to you, that I can see you, and I have to form an entire sentence in my head and then let my fingers fly tap-tap-tapping the characters out until the thought is visible on the computer screen. Sure, it's neater when I make a mistake, because I can backspace, erase, and start over. My handwritten notes will sometimes have letters that don't turn out just right, or sometimes I will have scratched through words or scribbled over the misspelling trying to fix it.

Pen to paper is messy and imperfect and heartfelt. Life is messy and imperfect and heartfelt. I can't write words onto a page without feelings, and I can't roll through my life without feelings. When I'm writing, I'm reflective and full of thought, and if I'm writing a letter to someone, then I spend a long time just reflecting and thinking about that person before I write the letter. And I think about how I'm feeling. And sometimes I even pray about what I should say which will help that person feel better about their situation. You know, we all have days or moments where we just don't feel good, and it's difficult to keep going with positive thoughts when we feel down or depressed. I have

95

those times. Really, I do. And one of the coping mechanisms I have learned over the years is to take my focus off of myself and pay attention to someone else. I've never been in the financial income bracket where I could donate thousands of dollars to charity or pay someone else's bills. So buying extravagant gifts is not something I can do. But I can write a letter. And so I keep lots of pretty stationary on hand and when I stop running around doing a bunch of errands or seeing after the kids or working frantically on a project, I will write a letter to someone about whom I care very much. When my kids go on vacation away from me, I always tuck a handwritten letter into their suitcase. I want them to know how special they are, that I love them, and that I want them to have fun and enjoy life when they are away.

When one of them was at summer camp last year, I mailed a letter the week before to be sure it arrived. That letter was the only piece of mail received by any camper that week. Now, this is how great kids are. The other kids didn't whine about how come my parent didn't write me. No, they celebrated the letter. They had a letter parade through the camp. And then at bedtime, all of the campers in that cabin gathered in a circle, and they read the letter out loud like it had magic properties, and each of them imagined the "I love you" was meant for their little heart. I will always, no matter how crazy life gets, remember that one letter mailed to my little camper, and take the time to write a letter again. Do you write letters? When your friend tells you about their horrible day, do you stop and write your friend a letter of encouragement? I'll be honest; I don't do it as often as I should. But I try my best to write when I can. Most of the mail a person receives is depressing: a bill or overdue notice, a political flyer about what's wrong in our society, some legal paperwork related to their divorce, a request for money from a charity which is really depressing when

96

you're praying your home doesn't get foreclosed, and you can't afford to buy your child a new pair of shoes, and junk mail. Nothing personal and loving. Nothing kind and considerate. Nothing to remind you that someone cares about you. Okay, maybe you haven't received a personal, loving, kind, considerate letter lately, and reading this is depressing you now. So what do you do about it?

Write a letter to someone. If you write them, they'll write you back. Maybe not the first time. You may have to love on them with pen to paper and words of encouragement for awhile, but they will write you back. And you'll feel better after you write the letter. Putting pen to paper has always been a source of joy for me. I went to the gift shop during my lunch break today and bought some new note cards to add to my collection. I have several friends who have been on my mind lately, and I was in the mood for something different on which to put pen to paper. Just looking at the pretty paper makes me feel better. Oh, and the pen matters too. You have just got to find a pen that makes you feel good when you see it, fits just write in your hand and flows freely as your heart feels. And just something as simple as a pen with ink in your favorite color will make you smile, and in the moment when you focus on the pen to paper, you'll forget all about your problems. I found the perfect purple pen, and I ordered four boxes. I shared two boxes, and I'm down to my last half dozen. It's about time to order some more pens. It may be silly or sentimental. I may sound crazy, but if a special pen makes you happy, you just got to keep writing with it.

Friday, January 28, 2011

Sometimes life happens, and you think I have dealt with so much, but this, THIS, is more than I can bear. Yesterday evening was such a time as that, more than I could handle, completely overwhelming, and yet, I just held tightly to a sliver of hope, the tiniest, microscopic, almost nonexistent sliver. And I made it through the night. I slept some. I cried some. I prayed some. I talked some. I slept some more. I cried some more. I prayed some more. And I made it through. Do you ever have nights like that where it feels like your whole world is caving in around you, and so much is happening, that you can't even comprehend just what is happening? Please say you do; I can't possibly be the only person who feels that way sometimes.

Last night was like that for me. It was a parenting issue. Being a parent after a divorce is more difficult than anyone who is not a divorced parent can imagine. And the problems of post-divorce parenting are compounded when your children are teenagers and search for ways to push your buttons. I'm not going to tell the specifics of this story, because if you are the parent of a teenager, you can fill in the blank with your own "my teen and I are in conflict over this major issue" story.
If you don't have anything to write about now, give your teen some time, and something will happen. Even the best of kids have their moments; it's all a part of the growing up process. And it's a part of the coming to terms with the divorce of your family and the moving forward into your new life.

I made it through the night. And when morning came, I woke up, with swollen and puffy eyelids, with a groggy, cottony mind, but the sliver of hope I had last night grew just a little bit bigger. As the sun painted the morning sky with streaks of orange, pale pink, and lavender, I began to look forward to today with a giant piece of chocolate cake slice of hope. This morning was better than last night. The problems of yesterday didn't disappear as from a magician's cabinet; the problems of yesterday still exist and still need to be solved. Taking one small step forward in faith that God would solve the problems, I drove out of my driveway expectant that today would be better than yesterday.

And trust me, it wasn't easy to believe; I had no confidence, the follow up events to last night were discouraging, but I was determined to see the day through, to hold on, to keep going, to not give up. When was the last time you felt like just giving up? What was happening? Was it the day you gave up on your marriage? Was it when you realized there was no way you could pay your mortgage note, and you packed up your car, and left your home behind? There are many people in my neighborhood who have. Was it when you had to give tough love to your teenager and you didn't have the strength and fortitude to be tough, but you had to be? Were you sick, really sick and you thought, so what if I live 2 years or 5 years, the cancer is going to get me anyway? I could probably list a hundred situations and still not mention yours, so you'll have to remember the time you felt like giving up. Maybe you did give up on that one situation, but you didn't give up on all things.

You're still here. I'm still here. And there is hope. Do you still have your hope? Is it a sliver, a slice, or complete? If each day will be better than the day before, it's only a matter of time before our lives meet our expectations and our hopes and our dreams. Yesterday I felt like giving up. I had so little hope, I couldn't even think of one thing to encourage you. I only had enough hope and faith to see myself through until morning. But I didn't give up. And I'm not going to give up. I made a decision that I'm holding on and I'm holding out for all of the blessings and good things, and love, and commitment, I deserve. I made a decision that I'm risking it all for the chance to have it all. Whatever happens will not overwhelm me or destroy my belief that good things will happen. I refuse to give up. And I don't want you to give up either. Failed relationships mess things up for most of us. After a failed relationship, you learn that the love story of fairy tales is not real life. After a failed relationship, you learn that some people will hurt you. After a failed relationship, you learn that some people can't be trusted. And if you give up, if you lose faith, if hope fades away, you will never learn that your own life story, your own love story, is better than any fairy tale. I learned that today. Today is better than yesterday. I am so grateful for the little moments of happiness I experienced today which made today better than yesterday. And I am going to keep praying that tomorrow is better than today. And that the next tomorrow is better than the next today. And so on. That's my prayer for me. That's my prayer for you.

Sunday, January 30, 2011

I don't want to be one of those people who knock people over the head with the Bible. And I still don't want you to be worried about religion; if you're not a Christian, I'm not trying to convert you. I'm just trying to share little bits and pieces of my life with you in this book, and my religious beliefs are a part of who I am, and so occasionally, scriptures will weave their way into my life story. Just enjoy the happy thoughts and reflect on what you want for your life. So, today is a day of anointing, and I am beginning this blog with Psalm 23.

1The LORD is my shepherd; I shall not want.
2He maketh me to lie down in green pastures: he leadeth me beside the still waters.
3He restoreth my soul: he leadeth me in the paths of righteousness for his name's sake.
4Yea, though I walk through the valley of the shadow of

death, I will fear no evil: for thou art with me; thy rod and thy staff they comfort me.

⁵Thou preparest a table before me in the presence of mine enemies: thou anointest my head with oil; my cup runneth over.

⁶Surely goodness and mercy shall follow me all the days of my life: and I will dwell in the house of the LORD forever.

It is only fitting that this beautiful day began with an anointing, because my cup of blessings is running over. This morning, I was invited to church by my significant other to be anointed for a new beginning and for miracles and blessings in 2011. The invitation by itself is a blessing. And then, the support and encouragement from him, my family, and my friends is another blessing. Sure, life is still not fair. And some of the problems I had earlier in the week still exist. And figuring out all of the details of life after a failed relationship is like muddy and murky water where you can't see the bottom, you don't know what will happen next, and you're not sure of all of the obstacles hiding in the fog in front of your boat. But you just keep rowing, because you believe that good things are ahead. I believe that good things will happen.

And today, was just another glimpse at just how good those good things will be. The afternoon sun warmed my heart and soul today as we picnicked on fried chicken and potato salad at the barn. I haven't felt sun that warm in so long, I just wanted to lean back in the lawn chair and soak in the sun like a kitty cat. Have you ever felt that way? Do you ever just stop, like freeze the chaos, and just stop whatever it is, and sit in the sun, close your eyes, and take it all in? Sometimes the blessings are already there, you are just too focused on the chaos and the drama and the problems to realize that good things are already happening to you. Today, we went horseback riding through the woods together, and it was so wonderful to not wear a coat and gloves and just feel the warmth of the sun on my face and the warmth of the horse beneath me and the warmth of a hug. In moments like this, it's like life can't possibly get any better than that. Moments like this are a blessing. Moments like this are kind of like the promise in Psalm 23. Moments like this restore my soul and calm my internal struggles and worries over what will go wrong next. What are you doing when you experience a moment which brings calm? Playing with your dog? Singing to your children? Going for a walk? Snoozing in the sun? Days like today remind me that surely goodness will be with me all the days of my life. Like the first ray of sunlight which breaks through the clouds of night, I can see a glimpse of the goodness which is to come.

And I am so excited to have more blessings than burdens in 2011. Today is a day of anointing. Today is the beginning of a new beginning. And I'm walking under the warmth of the afternoon sun, feeling the glory of God in my life, love in my heart, and peace in my soul. And if you need to read one more thing to make today just a tiny bit better: Friday I didn't buy these cool boots at the store because I was worried about spending the money, etc, etc, and last night I ordered those same boots online where they were on clearance for half as much in the store with free shipping. I've never bought a pair of boots and spent such a small amount of money to get them. And so in a few days, I'll be able to go for another walk in my new boots. Now doesn't that thought just make you smile? It makes smile. Yeah, good things are going to happen. Better things than a new pair of boots. Blessings and miracles are to come. Every day will be better and better than the day before. Go back and read Psalm 23. Think about each line of it in reference to the feelings and experiences you've had in dealing with your failed relationship. You probably had times where you were lacking what you needed. You couldn't rest. You needed restoration. You felt like dealing with your divorce or the drama of a failed relationship was like walking through a valley, probably the lowest emotional valley you've ever walked, worse than grieving a death almost, but then something happened, and you didn't feel alone. Maybe you felt the presence of God. Or maybe you just realized that you had friends who wouldn't abandon you and you wouldn't go through rebuilding your life alone. There is a plan of restoration for your life. Accept your anointing, as my man and I accepted ours this morning, and allow blessings and goodness and grace to come.

Monday, January 31, 2011

This evening while I was waiting for my child at practice I realized that waiting is something I know how to do. And something I've been doing for years and years and years. As I sat in the car with the music softly playing and the heater gently blowing watching dusk become dark and raindrops softly falling against the windshield, I thought about all of the hours I've spent waiting on all of the various days for all of the various reasons. And then I thought, waiting isn't sitting around with nothing to do, waiting is an action. Where were you the last time you had to wait? On what or for whom were you waiting? Why were you waiting? Were you bored? Were you anxious? For some people, I guess, waiting tries their patience and is nearly impossible. But for me, waiting is a part of my life. Waiting is something I do for people I care about. When I first began driving a car, one of my family responsibilities became driving my baby brother to his after school activities. I waited at Taekwondo and little league baseball practice. I still can see his little cute self with his curly hair and the little white outfit as I watched through the window as he bowed to his classmate. I waited on customers to decide what they wanted to order when I worked in restaurants to pay my way through college. When my son was really little and would need to go for a check-up, our appointment at the clinic may have been for 9:30 in the morning, but I would wait until mid-afternoon before he would be seen by the neurologist. And I waited many, many, times by his hospital bedside for him to recover from pneumonia or surgery or whatever other medical issue he had that week. I waited quietly beside his bed for the last six hours of his life on earth.

I have waited in the hallways of hospitals, dance studios, swimming pools, and gymnasiums for my children. One time a friend of mine teased me and said that I spent more time in a day waiting on my children to finish their activities than I spent at work earlier that day. And yes, in some respects that was true, because at that time I worked from 8 am - 2 pm (6 hours not counting lunch), and then waited for them from 3 pm - 9 pm or later in the evening at least three nights a week at some activity or another. Consequently, I've become a master packer. There's a tote bag for every activity. I almost always have an ice chest packed with snacks and drinks in the car. I wait for teeth to be cleaned, for the school bus to come, for the rain to stop, for the flowers to bloom, for the kids to request a snack, for the show to start, for the stars to come out at night. And I love it! I wouldn't miss a minute of the waiting, because sometimes the best moments happen when I'm waiting. If I don't have enough waiting to do with my own family, I've been known to volunteer to go pick up a friend's child from school or to go to their little league game just to wait on them. Now doesn't that sound silly to you? Its okay, you can say it, because it sounds silly to me. Why would I spend all of that time waiting? What am I waiting for really? I'm waiting for the good part, and I want it to see it live. Because I waited for so long, I really appreciate the good part when it happens. Think about it -- if I waited at the swimming pool for 2 hours a day 3 days a week for 3 years, I've witnessed a lot of belly flops, but the first fantastic dive off the block that was perfect, I saw it. And I waited just as many hours and years, if not more, for the dance classes to be over for the evening, and I felt the frustration when the girls couldn't remember the right step or fell down, but then I was there when one of them leaped high in the air across the floor. And tonight, while I was waiting for one of my children at yet another practice, I realized, waiting is not only something I know how to do, but something I enjoy doing.

Waiting is a gift I give to those I love. And in return, I receive the gift of being there for the good part and knowing that moment was the exceptional moment because I was there for all of the not-so-good moments. And here's what is really neat about this entire concept of waiting. What have you and I both been waiting for really? We are waiting for real love and a relationship which can stand the test of time, right? So in a way, it doesn't really matter what happened in our failed relationships, or how many years we've been waiting for something better, something more, something great to happen, if you wait for the good part willingly, patiently, happily, it will happen. It will. One day, you'll look back and realize you haven't been waiting for it to happen, you've actually been living it, and you'll appreciate the real love you have in a real relationship that lasts forever. And you won't be discouraged by all the time you wasted by waiting, you'll just be happy. I'm happy that I was there for all of the in-one-second-of-time moments which make the other 359 seconds worth the wait. I'm happy there is more to come.

Thursday, February 3, 2011

When I would sit in was a little girl, I really valued the time
I spent with my grandfather, the ordinary, everyday,
nothing special, just me and him kind of time. I would sit
on the bathroom counter with my legs dangling while he
shaved his face. And then wherever he went, I was his little
shadow. If he went outside to feed the animals, I went
outside to feed the animals. If he went into the kitchen to
get a drink, I went into the kitchen to get a drink. If he
hauled off trash to the dump in his pickup truck, I rode
shotgun, and then we'd stop by the 7-eleven, and he'd buy
me a cherry and coke frozen ICEE. If he walked up the hill
to the mailbox, I would walk with him. Whatever he
needed to do, I just quietly and quickly tried to keep his
pace. Most of the time, my grandfather said very little to
me. He didn't explain to me what he was doing; I would
just watch and learn. I really valued the togetherness. I just
felt connected and special. And then I grew up. I forgot the
value of just being together, and I became accustomed to
doing everything by myself. And the more independent I
became the less content and cherished I felt.

What was your childhood like? Was there a significant
person from your childhood who made you feel valued,
respected, and cherished? Have you ever thought that part
of what you are searching in your relationships today is that
same feeling of togetherness you felt as a child? Maybe you
grew up and forgot what you really valued as well. What
you value is what you really need. So I grew up, and then I
became a mother.

Because my first child had so many medical issues, taking
care of him and being with him was more of a duty, but it
was nice to have a constant companion. But he spent his
entire life in a wheelchair, and there were many days where

106

it was difficult to take him everywhere with me. One time I
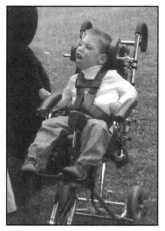 needed to go to my college to
meet with an instructor, and I
brought him with me. And then
when we were there in front of
that old brick building with the
twenty some odd stairs leading to
the entrance doors, I cringed.
And then in my quiet determined
manner, I unbuckled him out of
his wheelchair and set him on the
bottom step. I folded the
wheelchair and carried it to the
top, and then I went back down,
picked him up, carried him to the top, buckled him back in
his wheelchair, and went into the building. I wasn't strong
enough to carry the combined weight of him and his chair
up a flight of stairs. This is just one story of many about the
difficulties of caring for a child with severe handicaps and
medical problems. You would think that as difficult as it
was, I would have been happy to be relieved of the burdens
of his care when he needed to live in a long-term children's
care facility to insulate his immune system from the
exposure to everyone's germs. But I wasn't. I missed him.
When he was five, I moved to Georgia while he stayed in
the center.

A few years later, I had other children, and I took a year's
maternity leave with each one, and then decided to change
my career to be able to spend as much time with them as I
could. I rediscovered the value of togetherness. When my
youngest daughter Grace was in pre-K, I would pick her up
at noon, bring her back to my office, and while I worked,
she would sit in her child chair at her child table next to my
Mommy chair and Mommy desk. She would eat her lunch,
she would color, she would talk to me when I wasn't on the

phone, when I had to walk to another building or to check my mailbox, and she would walk with me. I can close my eyes and see her in her little uniform and pigtails with ribbons, her blue eyes sparkling as she excitedly created another crayon scribbled masterpiece. And then wherever I needed to go for whatever I needed to do, she would quietly and quickly keep pace with me. Sometimes we would feed the rest of her bread from her sandwich to the geese by the pond.

As the years passed, my children got older and became more occupied with their own activities. I never stopped to think about that I'm the kind of person who needs companionship and togetherness. I always thought I was really independent, because I went and did lots of things by myself. If I wanted to go on vacation, and my spouse didn't want to go or couldn't get off work to go, I would just go by myself or it would be just me and the kids. I really have no problem with driving for hours and hours by myself. It wasn't really that I wanted to be by myself, it's just the way it was. What type of person are you? Do you crave connection or do you need autonomy to be happy? Are you independent, because you truly want to be, or because you don't have a partner who wants to stay connected with you? After my divorce, I spent a lot of time thinking about what type of person I am and how much I really value togetherness. And I really need to be totally immersed in the lives of the people I love. I don't want to go on a long hiking and camping trip by myself for the solitude of being in nature.

As much as I love to walk in the woods, I don't want to walk alone. And for me, a romantic moment is something as simple as folding towels together and enjoying the calm of togetherness, a spontaneous embrace, and quiet conversation cuddled under the covers late at night. And for me, joy is seeing the smile on a small child's face when I place a fuzzy bunny in her hands when we are at the barn, and then hearing the little footsteps behind me and the incessant chattering as I do all of the barn chores. And contentment is leaning back on the shoulder of my man while I softly read a bedtime story to all of the children piled onto the bed. It's even more wonderful when the teenagers sneak into the room to listen to the story too. They won't admit it, because that wouldn't be cool, but I think they value togetherness too. And this is priceless; you couldn't pay me any amount of money; there is nothing I value more than this kind of intimacy. Yep, togetherness - that's what makes me happy. But I like being my own companion too.

As I was leaning back against my man, he petted my hair, or least that's what I call it; a more accurate description would be to imagine having your hair brushed without a brush. Never before knowing him has anyone ever petted my hair, and I had no idea just how wonderful it feels to have such a comforting, soothing, and gentle touch like that. My past was just not like that. I never knew that I even would like such an intimate and sometimes playful gesture. If someone would have asked me, do you like to have your hair petted, pulled, stroked, I would have probably said "What kind of question is that? What do you mean?" I discovered something about myself and what I enjoy only because he is caring and confident enough to just touch me. When we first started dating, he asked me if I was an affectionate person, and I replied "I don't know." I really didn't know, because I've never been a really touchy kind of person, mostly because I didn't trust that other people would be kind to me.

As I got to know him, I grew to really trust him; I had to learn to put the past in the past and enjoy the moment. Each

relationship is different, and you will be different in a new
relationship. Usually when someone has been abused, they
shy away from physical touch. But I crave, need, and want
to be touched in gentle and loving ways. And so, I choose
to put the past in the past. I let the bad touch of the past go.
And sometimes it's a conscious decision I have to make,
because worrying about what could go wrong seems to just
pop up unexpectedly. Have you ever reached out to pet a
puppy, and it pulled back like it was afraid? That's a self-
preservation instinct. The touch of the past was bad or
painful, and so instinct says avoid the touch in the future.
And so the puppy doesn't allow himself to be petted. And
what is really sad about that is not the abuse or bad touch or
pain that the puppy has suffered in the past. What is really
sad is that the puppy won't relax and trust and allow good
to come into his life completely. It doesn't matter if we're
talking about the type of touch or demeaning words; it is
instinctual to avoid putting yourself into the position of
being hurt again. So what happened in your past
relationship that makes you afraid to trust that today will be
better? What did the last person do, or not do, that causes
you to avoid reaching out or accepting something better
from the person in front of you? But this is the hardest part
about experiencing a failed relationship. The conditions,
like the way you were treated, hinder your ability to
connect intimately with a new person.
However, you have choice. The puppy has a choice. You
can be willing to trust the new person and experiment with
touch and affection like you haven't ever experienced
before. You can, you really can, put the past behind you,
and let it all go. Dream about what you really want in a
relationship, and then go for it. Be open to
new experiences, different types of touch, discover what
you really want and need with a partner. If you're a little bit
like me, you may not know what you like until you've
experienced it. I didn't know that I liked my hair to be

petted until he did it. Each moment we are together, I'm intrigued to discover what else. What else will I be open to trying that I will discover I enjoy? What else will be one more thing I want to put on my list of I always wanted a relationship like this where this sort of thing happens? Do you want to have enjoyment and happiness? Do you? Really? Perhaps some of you haven't even been willing to go on a date yet. I've been in that I just don't want to even put myself out there phase. Some of you have started in a relationship, but you're holding back, waiting for the catch. I've done that where I tried having a relationship with someone new and realized fairly quickly that I just couldn't do it. I wasn't ready. Are you just waiting for something to go wrong? I struggle with picking the flaws in a man like you pick tiny pieces of lint off your sweater. I need to learn to just let go of the past and enjoy the present and hope for the future.

Monday, February 7, 2011

I'm so excited, because the new boots I ordered came by FedEx Saturday evening, and I wore them for the first time yesterday. They are a mocha-colored, weathered leather, lace up and side zip, rugged Diba boot that just mold to my foot and ankle. Not only do they look awesome and are very comfortable, I also got them for a great price. And I had a coupon code for free shipping from DSW. So, nearly $100 boots for only $39. And because I've been doing so much walking and horseback riding in this crazy Georgia winter, I finally bought a really good, outdoor, insulated, inclement-weather coat, a bright red Tommy with a fur trimmed hood, at Macy's, on sale for $59. That was almost $175 off the MSRP. It was amazing good luck. Do you like to shop? And are you the kind of shopper who doesn't even look at the price tag, but just buys it or charges it, no matter the impact to your budget? Or are you

111

the kind of shopper who cuts coupons and only shops a sale? Or you the kind of person who puts off buying stuff for yourself, because you don't want to spend money on yourself? Even though I love shoes, and I love fashion, I am actually frugal compared to many women. And I'm sure compared to other women, I'm not so frugal.

My family never had lots of money, and when I was a teenager, my Mom would give my brother and I each $100 to go buy my school clothes for that season. And I only shopped the sales racks and looked for the really great deals. Brands didn't matter so much if I liked the fit, color, and style. But I'd usually come home with a huge pile of stuff. My brother would come home with a shirt, a pair of jeans, and maybe a belt. I'm really somewhere between the sale shopper and the kids first/Mommy last shopper. That's why I haven't bought a good outdoor coat since before I graduated from high school, and thankfully, I've lived in the South all that time, and I could suffer a few weeks of cold and rush into the building or car before I got too cold.

I encourage you to buy things for yourself, to spoil yourself, and that's because I've always been the kind of person who is more likely to do something for someone else before myself too. And like the instructions on the airplane, but the oxygen mask on yourself before you help someone else, it's important to meet your own needs first before your children. And this is really, really hard to believe that you are worthy enough to come first. But this is the really unbelievable part, your children won't really be happy, or figure out how to resolve problems that come in life, or learn how to love and know what being loved is really supposed to be like, or manage money appropriately if you don't show them. You can't tell them. You have to show them. Sometimes my children struggle with post-divorce issues too. It's hard on them to witness all of the emotional ups and downs their parents go through; it's hard for them to believe that love lasts when their parents fail at keeping the family together; it's hard for them to live at a different material possessions level. If you are a parent, what are the post-divorce issues you've observed your children struggling with? If you're the child of divorced parents, what did you go through? Your children need to see you pull yourself up by the bootstraps *(I'm so glad I have a new pair of boots)*, dust yourself off, and get back in the saddle. Just let it go that you failed in the past; learn from your mistakes and move on. Get going.

As you move into your new life, your family is going to change. And your children will watch you to know what is expected in this new family. And here's the crazy part you probably haven't thought about before – you only have to get accustomed to one new family structure; your children went from one family into two families post-divorce. You have one set of rules, one set of expectations, and your ex has another. You do things one way, and your ex does things another way. That's normal for divorced families; unfortunately. But as you move into your new life, and you will probably make some mistakes or not handle things wonderfully all the time, and that's okay. I've had to learn the right and wrong way to handle things too, by experience, and sometimes you have to make a mistake to know what not to do the next time. Stay positive. Stay focused on building your relationships with your new partner if you ever have one, with your children, with your extended family, and your children will fall into the happiness at their own pace over time.

Do you know these sayings? Love with your whole heart. Dance like no one is watching. Live. Love. Laugh. Sometimes there's a lot of wisdom in cliché phrases. It's taken some time, but I'm finally doing the things I need to do to take care of myself, to be happy, to love through my actions, to laugh and play and dance with a carefree attitude a small child has, and I can see my dream life unfolding before me. I am living my dream life, and each day, more and more of my dream comes true. Embrace your new life with a positive attitude, and don't be your own obstacle to happiness. If a new pair of boots makes you smile, buy them. If you meet a man who makes you happy, love him. It's okay to move on from your failed relationship into a new beginning. I'll be praying for you to let your past go and for you to find happiness.

Wednesday, February 9, 2011

Expectations - we all have them. Sometimes we expect too much. Sometimes we don't expect enough. And sometimes others expect us to do or be somebody we are not. In marriage and in relationships, we have expectations about what the other person should or should not do. And many times, we are disappointed, because we haven't clearly communicated what we really want specifically, and so the other person doesn't get it quite right. But I guess, if they try to get it, that's something. Think about the last time you were disappointed. Were you expecting something to happen? Was it something good or something bad? Were you expecting someone to say something just a certain way? Did someone try to do meet your expectation, but just not get it exactly? Did someone do something that was way beyond your expectations?

And oh, think about a particular romantic date on the calendar coming up in a few days. A lot of people have expectations about Valentine's Day. I've never really had expectations for Valentine's Day, because after I got out of the grade school years of cutting and gluing paper hearts to a cardboard box and giving cards to everyone, Valentine's

Day just became one of those things that other couples did. Even though I'm a hopeless romantic, I just never had a romantic partner before. I don't know if it's because I'm so independent, or because if I'm in the mood for a vase of fresh flowers, I just buy flowers for myself, so I didn't give him enough time to do the thoughtful gesture. Or maybe it's just I chose men in the past who didn't do the mushy, romantic stuff, and

I just came to accept that was normal. So I just didn't worry about it. I made an effort to do little things for my children and to help them make Valentine's cards for their classmates. I put up Valentine decorations around the house. But I never really expected gifts. And I still don't expect to receive a gift now.

I have learned the best gifts are unexpected. This morning on my way to work, I decided to do something nice for my significant other and the ladies who work in his office, because they work so hard and go non-stop throughout the day, I dropped off some Cinnabon rolls to them. They weren't expecting me, and they weren't expecting a treat. So that's what made it really great! I just loved seeing happy faces consuming deliciousness *(even though we did all joke about how much we needed to work out now)*. For me, that was one of the best gifts. Being able to do a little something unexpected for someone else that makes them smile is all the gift I need. But when I arrived at his office, I received an unexpected gift - an early Valentine's Day gift - a gorgeous pair of white Coach Sunglasses. Tres' Chic! It was so exciting and so thoughtful. And I am so grateful for this unexpected gift. I would never indulge by buying something like that for myself. Really it's just too much. And I just don't expect to receive such nice gifts. Thank you. But this was not the only unexpected gift I received today. A co-worker brought me a cup of coffee in the middle of the afternoon, because I had been working for hours on paperwork. Thank you. A sweet child read me a story afterschool. Thank you. I was invited to supper. Thank you. I received the gift of time, care, and safety. Thank you. I didn't expect any of these gifts today. That's what makes them so wonderful. The best gifts are unexpected. What did you expect to happen today? Did you receive some unexpected gifts that you haven't stopped long enough to realize you received a gift?

You see, this is what I expected for my day -- finish up the laundry, feed the pets, take the kids to school, rush to work, work at work, talk a little to people at work, work late, rush home, do household chores, check email, write, get the kids ready for bed, brush my teeth, go to bed. That has been my typical day for as long as I can remember. That's all I expect out of life. But this is how blessed I was today -- finished up the laundry, feed the pets, take the kids to school, buy cinnamon rolls, order a Valentine's surprise to be delivered Monday, received smiles and laughter, hugs, kisses, some fantastic sunglasses which look fabulous on me, rushed to work, worked at work, talked a little to people at work, received a cup of coffee, worked until my normal time, did a little unexpected shopping, listened to a story, shared a supper, realized how much my man cares about my safety and well-being, received a little extra time, bought gas on the way home in case the snow was worse than expected during the night, did the chores, checked the email, got the kids ready for bed, brushed my teeth, and in a little bit, I'll go to bed. I received so much today, way beyond my expectations, and I am so thankful. You probably received many unexpected gifts today, stop and count them up. Thank you for reading my book today. I hope a few of my words on these pages are on your list of unexpected gifts you received today.

I'm really not the kind of person who measures value by how expensive a gift is. I have received gifts before that I didn't like, and I always feel guilty about that, because I really appreciate that someone would do something nice for me. But sometimes, you just don't like something. And that's okay. As I tell my children, thank the person for giving you the gift. The person is of value, not the item. If you follow celebrities, then you may think that if it's worthwhile or worth having, then it must be ostentatious, flashy, and expensive. You probably think if you don't live in a mansion, then you're living a deprived life. We normal people dream about winning the lottery or hitting it rich with stock investments or getting the high-paying job of our dreams. Do you? What do you value? Most of the time, or at least some people, acquaint the good life with how much money they have, but really, it's the little things that count. The good life doesn't have anything to do with money, or what kind of car you drive, or what kind of house you live in. The good life is when you find happiness despite your circumstances.

Now I live in a really nice house in a good subdivision with a picket fence. Kind of like the American dream, but not quite like what I expected. But I haven't always lived in a nice house. What was your first home as an adult like? Was it an apartment? Or was it a tiny house in desperate need of remodeling? After my divorce from my first husband, I lived in a white clapboard house that had been split into a duplex. The interior walls were pressed wood, and my entire living space was smaller than one room in my house now. I only had a dorm-size refrigerator and I didn't have a stove; I cooked on a hot plate and in a microwave. And some of the plumbing didn't work. I did have electricity and a phone. I didn't own a bed, so my son and I slept on the fold-out sofa in the living room that was borrowed from a family member. My rent was $75. Yes, $75 in 1992. And I could barely afford that after paying the medical bills, the car payment, the insurance, and the electric bill. I didn't have cable. I didn't have artwork hanging on the walls. But there was a rose bush that grew beside the front step which I got from the First Baptist Church down the road. When the church was redoing their landscaping, they just threw away the old rose bushes. I picked one up and threw it next to the front steps. I intended to dig a hole and plant it, but I never did. Rose bushes are supposed to be picky and difficult to take care of, but that little rose bush did fantastic. I never watered it. I never fertilized it. But it had the most beautiful tiny pink roses. I had a little patch of grass in the front. And when I say little, I mean like less than 4 square feet, and I never mowed it. I just whacked at it with a weed eater and a pair of scissors. So even though I've lived in a house with a grassy yard, that's why I said, I learned to mow the grass this past year. You too can mow the grass.

One day my Grandmother came to visit, and as was her habit wherever there were flowers and grass and blue sky, she would walk around looking for four-leaf clovers. And wouldn't you know it, she found one. And I still have that four-leaf clover in a frame, because it's the little things that count. That four-leaf clover is priceless, especially now that my Grandmother has passed away. This past summer, a few weeks after she passed away, my children and I were at the orthodontist. One child was finished, and one child was having lots of brackets put in, so it was taking awhile. In front of the orthodontist office, there were flowers and grass and blue sky. My daughter asked if we could walk around in the grass while we were waiting. And so we did. And I told her, you know, if Gigi were here, she would be looking for a four-leaf clover. And so she said, "Can we look for one?" And so we did. And we found one. It's the little things that count. You see, we searched for nearly an hour, happy in our pursuit of a little thing. It was like Gigi was with us stooped over inspecting every blade of grass and every leaf among the clover.

Some people search for wealth, but even if they find wealth, they will never be as happy as we were when we found that four-leaf clover. What do you search for? What do you put your faith in? If you put your faith in the things that don't really matter, then you won't find happiness. If you live only in pursuit of money, then you will miss all of the joy offered to you in this world. I am grateful for the financial blessings I've had in the past - oh, my goodness - nearly twenty years. But my goal in life is not to be wealthy financially. And that's why I didn't sue my ex-husband for tons of money. That's why I settled during mediation instead of dragging the divorce process out for months and months. I want to be happy. And no amount of money could ever make restitution for not having a loving and happy marriage. I want to be loved and to love. I want to share what I have with those I care about. I want to find more four-leaf clovers and to always be happy walking in green grass under a blue sky no matter how much money I have in my bank account. I want to always appreciate the little things. You too can learn to appreciate the little things.

Saturday, February 12, 2011

When I was a little girl, I always dreamed of owning my own pony. And you also know that dream has been realized because my parents are gracious enough to share their horses with me and my children. We all have a childhood wish. Some little something we wish we could have, like a pony, or a sports car, or to catch a baseball at a Braves game, or ____. Why don't you fill in the blank? What is the one thing you've always wished you could have? My grandfather from North Louisiana always would talk about wanting two things -- a pet koala -- and if he had the money to buy any kind of car he wanted -- a Jaguar. In his lifetime, he never got either one, but he was always hoping. I remember the years he tried growing eucalyptus trees on his property. After all, one can't keep a koala if you don't have any eucalyptus leaves. If you do wish for something, you should be putting forth some effort to get it. Or at least, learn more about it. Read a book. Or talk to someone who has what you want.

What about love? Is being loved in a special way something you've always wanted? Are you putting forth some effort to receive your wish for real love? Real love isn't as easy to recognize as a koala, so how do you know when you have it? Well for starters, when someone really loves you, they surprise you by their kindness and thoughtfulness with a gesture or gift that makes you feel loved. And the really amazing thing about expressing your love for someone, or that person expressing their love for you, is that you don't have to spend a lot of money. For a couple of weeks, I've been planning a Valentine's surprise for my man, but I'll tell you about that a little later. First, I want to share with you a loving gesture I received. Last night, one of my children was not feeling well. This is Dad's weekend, so he called to talk about taking her to Quick Care. While I was listening to her symptoms, my man scribbled a note to me on the back of an envelope that he would take a look at her if we wanted him to do so. Alright, I guess, I'm going to have to finally tell you, because that offer of providing medical care doesn't mean as much unless you know that my man is the doctor from the blind date I had a few months ago just shortly after I began writing this book.

You see, God does answer prayers. And God provides what we need when we really need it. And so, I received an expression of his love, an immediate, whatever you need, whatever your daughter needs, I am here to take care of your needs, gift. Real love satisfies your needs happily. Probably within the first week of dating him I learned that the one thing for which he has been wishing is an alpaca. He told me. I heard others tease him about wanting an alpaca. Even his ex-wife made a sarcastic comment about shoveling alpaca "poo" with Allison. And I thought to myself, everyone should get what they want in life; everyone should have one thing that makes him/her happy. And if he wants an alpaca, he should have one, or two, or three. Why not an alpaca? I know it may sound silly that someone dreams of owning an alpaca, but you wish for something to, and your wish may sound silly to someone else. And so, I did a little research. I read about alpacas. I found a nearby alpaca farm in North Georgia, and I talked with the farmer, and made an appointment to drive out that way and see the alpacas. So this afternoon we had a few hours of fun fulfilling a wish. We drove out to Windy Hills Alpaca Farm in Jasper, Georgia, and Elwin happily showed us the alpacas, explained all about alpacas, let us feed them, and pet them, and play with them. We had so much fun, and except for a few gallons of gas, we didn't spend a dime. After all, how can you ever buy an alpaca if you've never even been close enough to one to pet it before? Real love supports your dreams. I support his dreams; he supports my dreams. Every day he encourages me to write more or to do something to promote my book project by giving me words of positive affirmation. He's not a writer, but he supports my dream of being a writer. And so, I am all for alpacas. Keep dreaming and wishing and hoping. Do something every day to get you one step closer to realizing your dream. Every day, I write down another story. Today, he petted an alpaca. My grandfather planted eucalyptus trees. What are you going to do today?

Sunday, February 13, 2011

"With this faith we will be able to hew out of the mountain of despair a stone of hope" - Martin Luther King, Jr. In 1963, civil rights leader, Martin Luther King, Jr. gave what is considered to be one of the best speeches in American history where he talks about his dream for a better life with peace, equality, and justice. This speech is about enduring struggles, trials, and inflictions, about dreaming, hoping, and praying for a better tomorrow, and about inspiring others to make the choices which will lead to a better life. Many of us, especially those of us, who have experienced a failed relationship and have dealt with post-divorce issues, have at least a few times felt like they had a mountain of despair. I know I have, and more than once I've cried over my mountain of despair. Have you ever felt that way? Have you felt so depressed, so despondent, so full of despair, that believing you could be happy one day was as nearly impossible as climbing Mt. Everest? If so, then you know what I mean. In Matthew 17:20 Jesus said *"if you have faith as small as a mustard seed, you can say to this mountain, 'Move from here to there' and it will move. Nothing will be impossible for you."*

So think about your mountain of despair; if you have faith, your mountain will disappear. The entire mountain, all of your post-divorce issues, all of the pain, hurt, and betrayal, all of the unfulfilled dreams, just all of it, can become like a little stone or just go away. Can you even imagine how awesome that is? Do you even get it? The other day at work, a co-worker told this story about visiting a cathedral where the priest rolled out a huge timpani drum, and on top of this drum was a large round bowl full of stones. Some

122

stones were broken with jagged edges. Some stones were smooth. Each stone was slightly different than the other stones. He asked everyone to take a stone. And then he talked about how these stones were once much bigger or parts of a boulder or rock face of a mountain, and over time, these stones were broken. We, too, are broken like these stones. Each and every one of us will face some challenge in our life which breaks us. The sharp, jagged, stones were recently broken; and for some us, these stones represent a recent dissolution of a relationship, or a hardship. The smooth stones were broken a long time ago; the smooth stones have received pressure over time or rolled through mighty waters which has smoothed out the jagged parts; the smooth stones represent those of us who were broken in despair a long time ago.

And in my head I was thinking, my divorce was finalized almost a year ago. When my marriage first ended, I had a mountain of despair. The emotional pain was devastating. A year passed, and my mountain became a stone of hope. It didn't happen all at once, but day by day, a little more was chipped away, and over time, the pain grew smaller, the difficulties became easier, and the needs became fewer. Seriously, hope was all I had, and my faith was shaky, but I held on. And since then, my stone has become smoother and polished; a stone that actually feels good to hold in your hand. Have you ever picked up a smooth stone, maybe out of a creek bed, and just held it in your hand? One of my children has a hobby of rock tumbling, and so we have bowls and bowls of rocks which were once rough and jagged, but are now smooth after being tumbled. I've been tumbled. You've been tumbled. And our stones are a little smoother than yesterday. And tomorrow, our stones will be smoother still.

So then, my co-worker continued with his story, the priest had everyone drop their stone back into the bowl on top of the timpani and just listen to the "booomp" echo through the cathedral. Close your eyes and imagine dropping your stone into the bowl. Do you hear the sound of your stone echoing through the cathedral? Do you hear the first "boomp"? Do you hear the echo "boomp" faintly in the distance? I hear it just as well as I hear my own heartbeat. When I drop my stone -- which remember was a mountain of despair at first -- the sound of it echoes. Maybe if you close your eyes and listen, you can hear it the sound of my despair echoing in your own heart. And I hope it causes you to have a little more faith than you had before.

So do you believe? Do you have faith that your mountain will become a stone? If you do, later, others will be blessed by hearing your story. This morning, the minister talked about 12 stones. The 12 stones which represented each of the tribes of Israel built as a memorial when the Israelites crossed over into the Promised Lands after 40 years in the wilderness. You see, those that suffered through the wilderness had faith. I have suffered, and so I have faith, because I have seen God's hand in my life. But others are just starting out; maybe they are in a relationship for the first time or newlyweds, or new parents, and so they don't know what will happen. And sure, we can pray and hope and dream that they will never suffer abuse, or death of a child, or divorce as I have. That would be my greatest desire for everyone, but unfortunately, life is hard. Sometimes we lose our way, or we make bad choices, or we lose our faith, or we forget what's really important in life. The stones representing the faith of others who have come before us are a marker for the path that leads to freedom. He talked about how when we are lost, we can look at those stones, and find our way. And he talked about how we who have made our stones into a memorial of

124

God's faithfulness and promises need to show our stone to others.

So we sat there in church listening to his sermon about not throwing out the stones which represent the foundation of our faith, I thought of our children, all seven of them when you put them together, and I thought all that I have gone through, the entire 40+ years of my life, the hewing out of my mountain of despair, the smoothing of my stone, will all be worthwhile if only our children will be able to stand on a solid foundation of faith and have wonderful lives and real love. I know, you are thinking seven children; it seems impossible to try to blend together seven children from different families into one family. But I guess nothing is impossible with God.

When I was a child, I dreamed of owning a pony. And as I went through school, I dreamed of becoming a writer, and I'm in the midst of realizing my dreams of being a writer. When I grew up and became a woman, I dreamed of having real love, and today, my dream of the future has expanded. My dream is to one day sit in church with the arm of my man lovingly wrapped around my shoulders and to look down the row and see all of our children and their spouses and their children right there with us. Because when that day happens, a whole bunch of hearts, broken by the pain of divorce, will have been healed. And when that happens, I'm going to give each one of them a gift of a smooth stone engraved with the word HOPE. I don't know exactly what my future family will be like, but I have hope that no matter what happens, I will always hope for the best. May you never lose hope?

Monday, February 14, 2011

Happy Valentine's Day! Okay, so you know the date on the calendar, and you knew I had to go there. And I'm sure if you're still struggling with your emotions from your failed relationship, or you aren't in a romantic relationship at the moment, you're probably thinking, "Why, oh why, does this holiday exist which reminds me of what I don't have?" Are you a little bummed out, or depressed, about today? If you are, it's okay. When I was looking at cards the other day, there actually are cards for people who like just met somebody yesterday and want to give them a card; there was "I know we just met, but I want to give you a card" card. I really cracked up at that one. Did you buy anyone a Valentine's Day card? Did you receive a Valentine's Day card? I received three pieces of mail today. One - a card from my parents, and I must say what was really neat about it was that my mother wrote my name beginning with Dr. instead of Miss *(because we all know it's not Mrs. anymore).* And that was a great reminder that during the year after my divorce, I finished my dissertation and completed by doctorate. Two - a card from my friend with a pig in a diaper with a bow - that said "Have you seen Cupig?" That card really cracked me up as well. Three - a letter from the Homeowner's Association demanding I paint the exterior of my house within the next 15 days, or I'll receive an abatement. I don't even know what an abatement is, but unless Cupig also has a house painting business on the side and can work some magic for me, that's not happening.

My house has been for sale for a year as a condition of my divorce, the mortgage payments are a struggle, and let's see, oh, yeah, my lawyer is still waiting for me to pay the rest of my fees, so even though I already knew my house needed painting, it's not going to happen anytime soon.

Also, someone reminded me yesterday it's about time to file taxes. So, I'm not feeling the love from the HOA. But I do have parents and friends who love me, so that's good. And when, and if, I ever purchase a home in the future, I want to be out in the country and as far away from an HOA as I can get. I like walking in the woods anyway, so that would be better for me. But this is just how life is. Nearly everyone who gets a divorce struggles with financial issues. It's worse for some than others, but it's not good for anyone.

Something I've discovered lots of women learn to do after their divorce is mow the grass. A couple of weeks ago, a woman sent me an email which said she read my blog, and she learned to mow the grass too, and she's gotten so good at it, she makes a diamond pattern like at the ballpark. Well, she's better than me, because I'm doing well if the grass is just not too high. But I think that's really awesome. If she ever invites me to her house, I'll probably take a picture of the diamonds cut in the grass. There are just so many things to do when you're a single parent – yard work, housework, childcare, work work - and there's just never enough time to do it all. Look around your home. What do you still need to do? I need to clean out the fish tank and take a pile of stuff to Goodwill and throw out the Christmas wreath still on the front door and paint my house. I bet there's more to do than one person can do. And then, to make it worse, you look at yourself, and you feel guilty that stuff is undone, that you can't do it all. Well, guess what? You cannot do it all. I cannot do it all. No one can do it all by his/herself. So just do what you can, and let the rest of it go. The kids will survive unvacuumed carpet one more day. The HOA will still exist if I don't paint my house. I'll just get another letter next month. The grass won't be that much longer the next day. All you can do is the best you can do, and you can't do anything more than your best.

So are you thinking, where is she going with this, because I thought we were talking about Valentine's Day, and now we're talking about chores and childcare? Part of doing the best you can do is to keep your priorities in order. It's more important today to sit down with your children and look at their Valentine's cards they got from their friends at school than to vacuum the floor. It's more important today to call a friend who doesn't have a romantic date tonight; wish them Happy Valentine's Day. It's more important today to do something to treat yourself. Bake cookies. Paint your toe nails. Kick back, relax, and watch a movie tonight. Go visit a friend or family members for a few minutes just to say hi. Today is special to me, not because it's Valentine's Day, but because today is the birthday of someone very special to me. So tonight, I'm not going on a romantic date; I had lots of romance this weekend already, I'm going to go wish her Happy Birthday, and maybe eat a cookie. This is what love is to me. Happy Valentine's Day!

Tuesday, February 15, 2011

What's for supper? Tonight at our house, we are having lasagna and fish sticks and chocolate chip cookies. I know what you're thinking; that's a strange combination. The real entree is lasagna, salad, and garlic bread. However, one of my children has been sick for the last few days, and she wants fish sticks. Normally, I do not believe in cooking multiple meals, because my kitchen is not a restaurant. But when it's a special day like a birthday, he/she should get to have for supper whatever he/she wants. Or when a child is sick, if he/she wants to eat anything, I'll gladly fix it up. After all, how much harder is it to throw a few fish sticks on the baking sheet next to the garlic bread? So what are you fixing for supper? Don't be ashamed if you say I'm just picking up a pizza, because I did that the other night. And last night, we had Spaghettios and Vienna sausage and cheese. I love to cook, but I just don't always have the time. And then of course, after supper, we have to have fresh-baked cookies. That's almost a given at my house. All of my children's friends ask to come over just to have a cookie. The girls complain about having to answer the "what kind of cookie did your Mom make yesterday" question at school.

Now, before you start thinking I'm super Mom who can work all day and still find time to bake cookies. I'll let you in on a secret. The little dough boy already did a great job mixing the cookies, cutting the cookies into pre-measured pieces, and all I have to do is pull them out of the little yellow package and throw them in the oven. Sure, I can bake cookies from scratch, but if you don't have time, you don't have time. After work, I have so many things to do. So while I am writing, the lasagna is in the oven, the towels are in the dryer, a load of clothes are in the washer, and my children are taking their piano lesson. We've already been out to the barn and fed the horses and the bunnies. I still need to clean the fish tank and the litter box, but I did throw out that Christmas wreath last night. I felt guilty about still having a Christmas wreath on the door in February. If you're a single parent, then you're a multi-tasker just because you have to be. It's just the way it is. If you're a two-parent family, you may still need to be a multi-tasker, you just have a partner who is doing some of the tasks as well. If you're lucky enough to have a partner who shares in the fun and does the chores with you, then you really have a partner. That hasn't been my experience, so single parenthood hasn't been that much different for me physically, only emotionally. I believe a family is a team. The team plays together, and the team works together, and the team pulls together in a crisis.

Unfortunately, divorced kids don't have a great example of the pulling together in a crisis, but two out of three isn't that bad. The kids have always helped out with the chores; at least, the things they are able to do. One day I had a business friend stop over at our house when she had an unexpected layover in Atlanta. My children were just toddlers then. And I remember my two-year-old taking off her shoes in the living room. And I said, "Okay, now you've taken them off, go and put your shoes away." So she got up, picked up her shoes, and disappeared down the hall. My friend asked, "Where is she going?" She couldn't believe it; I showed her to my daughter's room where she was putting her little shoes in the closet with the others. Yes, toddlers can put their things away. I do many, many things for my children, and I have been accused of being Super Mom, but I want my children to be able to do things for themselves, and so I have encouraged them to be self-sufficient and to pull their own weight. I will admit it was easier to train toddlers than to track teenagers. But I expect my kids to help. And I don't give an allowance. My grandparents and their siblings worked on the family farm. My parents helped their parents. My parents expected my brothers and me to help them. I started doing laundry at age 10, so I'm very efficient at completing household tasks, because I have 30 years experience.

But here's a problem I had when my divorce first happened, I started doing everything for my children. When they were gone visiting their father, I spent the entire 3 days cleaning, cooking and putting up, the washing, just everything, because I was afraid that my children would resent doing chores with me. I was afraid that I wouldn't be fun; that I'd be the "all work and no play" parent, because my house had chores, rules, homework, etc. Do you worry about that too? Do you try too hard to be fun that you don't teach your children the important principle of teamwork? Teamwork is a skill we first learn at home; teamwork is a skill we need to be successful on our jobs. Children like to pitch in. Completing tasks together as a team builds self-esteem and family unity. And post-divorce families need to feel as much like a family as they can. Tonight is Tuesday night, and the one TV show everyone really likes to watch is Glee, and so we'll have supper, finish the laundry together, and then sit down with some fresh-baked chocolate chip cookies and watch Glee together. So one of the things that will happen to you during the post-divorce period is that you will get a little off-track, but after awhile, after your emotions stabilize, after you stop competing with your ex about being the most fun parent, after you start believing that you're a decent person again, after you have some conflict with your children and re-establish that you're the parent, eventually, you'll get back on track. The days will settle down, and things won't seem so hectic. You'll start to feel like you're getting things done. You'll notice someone taking out the trash without being asked. Homework will be finished and ready to be signed before you remember that it's getting late. It really will all be okay. You can manage your family by yourself. And one day, you'll meet someone who wants to partner with you, shares the same values as you, and who will help you merge two teams together into one. It just takes time. And consistency in parenting and living your values. And faith that dreams will come true.

Friday, February 18, 2011

The last two weeks have been super busy. I have been too busy to take lunch, and that is really unusual for me. One of the things I like best about my job is that I am able to take long lunches. And so I really look forward to having a lunch date, or lunch with a friend, or a chance to run errands on my lunch break. Today, finally, since I've worked like crazy to finish up tons of paperwork and

131

writing every day this week, I got to go to lunch with my friend. She and I have a lot of things in common. We were both really young mothers. We have both been married before; thankfully, she's still happily married to her second husband. We are both professional women who look gorgeous for our age. We have both buried a son. We have the same values in life such as faith and family first. I really appreciate the advice she has given me the past couple of years; she's always honest with me and willing to point out my mistakes, but she always supports me and encourages me through whatever I'm going through. Do you have a friend like that? A friend who has had similar struggles as you? A friend who has made it through rough times and come out better for it? A friend who always encourages you and never makes you feel bad about what you need to do just to make it through whatever you're going through at the moment? She is probably my most empathetic friend.

There's just something especially comforting about having a friend who shares an experience you do. Like, I understand why she doesn't come in to work and stays in bed all day on her son's birthday, because I really struggle on my son's birthday. Since he died in 2002, I have celebrated his birthday in silent memories by myself. Well, every year until this last birthday, because on his birthday a couple of months ago, my man had lunch with me and looked at his baby book with me and listened to the stories of his life. After my brother died in 2007, my mother understood for the first time the pain I felt. Please don't misunderstand, my mother always supported me. She made sure I ate, bathed, and dressed for weeks after my son died. One day last autumn, my mother joined my friend and me for lunch; I reminded each of them beforehand that we were all mothers who had buried sons. And that was comforting to know. Like, this woman across the table from me will understand when a tear rolls down my cheek and won't ask any questions kind of comfort. She'll just know that my heart aches at the same time my heart feels joy. Being happy does not mean that you have no pain. Being happy means that you choose to be happy even when you are in pain.

So, when we have the occasional opportunity to go to lunch, like today, I never really know which one of us will need to talk and which one will need to listen. But it doesn't really matter. I am just as happy to be the empathetic ear. That's what friends do for each other. And friends are also there to help us celebrate in the little things and the big things. I turned 40 the week after I was served with divorce papers in 2009, and my friends helped me to celebrate. It was actually the first birthday party I had since I was 16 years old, and we had it over lunch. And then my 41st birthday was even more special. The birthday before my divorce was okay. The birthday in the middle of my divorce was good, really good. And the birthday after my divorce was great! How do you celebrate your birthday? Do you celebrate your birthday? You're not too old for a party, you know. So, if you haven't had everything that you've wanted in the way of celebration, just be patient. Give it time. Keep moving forward with hope, and each year will be better than the year before. Or plan your own party and invite your friends. Women need to be able to share the celebrations as well as the sorrows with their friends. So I'm equally thankful when my friend cheers for my good news as when she listens to my problems. And I'm excited to be included in her good news too. Bad stuff and good things. Good times and bad news. So I really don't like it when life gets so busy that I don't have the time to find out what is happening with my friends, or when my friends are so busy, they don't have time to return phone calls, or when they do, the message is "I don't have time to talk; I'll talk to you later." So I'm really glad my friend and

I took the time to go to lunch today; I wish it could have been a longer lunch, because we probably only talked about 1/10th of the stuff we wanted to, but there's always next week.

And next week, I'm really excited about having lunch with my friend who is flying in from California. Laura is a publisher friend with whom I've worked on several development projects, and I'm hoping she'll give me some advice on this book, and maybe discuss writing another book. And I'm really, really excited about friends coming over for pizza tonight. It's Friday night. And yes, if you have gone through a lot of painful struggles in your life, you'll be like me sometimes, where I'll be laughing one minute and fighting back tears the next. And that's okay. It really is okay to cry when you feel like, to whine occasionally (just not too much), and to be angry or disappointed. Just remember that your strength will come in the joy, so the only way to make it through the tough moments is to find the source of your joy. My joy is found in my children and in my friends. My joy is found in quiet moments leaning against my man's strong shoulder or laughing at a funny story. Life goes on. Every day, I choose to let the pain go. Every day, I choose to find the positive in my surroundings. Every day, I choose to smile and be happy despite the disappointments in my present circumstances. You can't change the past, but you can find the joy in the moment. And when you find your joy, when you experience a happy moment, you change your future for the better.

Sunday, February 20, 2011

This morning before church, I read a short excerpt in a little book called Married for Life talking about making love last through all the years of marriage. This little book includes stories of couples who have been married for more than fifty years. The truly amazing thing is that the advice they give on love is really quite simple. It's not complicated at all, but love involves choices. Some choices are little things like always making your spouse a cup of coffee. Other choices are big things like not having an affair when someone comes along.

This morning, at the beginning of the service a young man talked about how he was faced with the choice of losing his wife and family or changing his career. You see, his career caused him to be away from his family at night; this made it difficult for him and his wife to communicate on a daily basis, and didn't allow him to spend time with his children as he wished. And he realized that his actions were causing his wife to lose faith in him and to feel unloved. But he made the difficult choice to change his career rather than get a divorce. This was a selfless decision. He chose to put his family first. Think back to the last few months before your relationship or marriage officially ended. You had some choices, didn't you? And this is tough. Would you have quit your job if it would have saved your marriage? Would you have agreed to move if it would have saved your marriage? Would you have changed the way you spoke to your spouse? Would you have changed anything about yourself or the way you do things? How far would you go?

Granted, it probably shouldn't be that hard. Your mate shouldn't be making it difficult for you to love him/her. Both of you should be choosing to put the other first, but if it took self-sacrifice, could you, would you have done it? Or maybe you did everything you knew to do. Maybe you sacrificed all that you humanly, possibly could, but it wasn't enough. I moved to another state for my spouse. I put off my education and my professional career for my spouse. I'm not a saint. I'm sure there was probably more I could have done which would have made my spouse happier. I'm sure my ex could make a list of things he wished I would have done, but I don't know what would be on the list. I tried really hard to make my marriage work, and I thought I was a doing a good job. If you tried your best, then even if your relationship still failed, you did your part. You did your part to show love to your ex. And this is also really tough. You will still be called upon to show love to your ex as an ex, because if you have children together, he/she will always be in your life. I Corinthians 13:4-13 talks about what love is. Many people only think about love between romantic couples, but there is love between a couple, love between friends, love between parent and child, and yes, even love for a stranger, or love between divorced parents. *Love is patient, love is kind. It does not envy, it does not boast, it is not proud. It is not rude it is not self-seeking, it is not easily angered, it keeps no record of wrongs. Love does not delight in evil but rejoices with the truth. It always protects, always trusts, always hopes, always perseveres. Love never fails.*

So let's think about this. Love is patient and kind. That means that you are willing to wait for someone without being huffy and put out because you had to wait. That means that you speak in a kind tone of voice to your ex on the phone, especially when your children are in hearing range. That means that you do little things for your friend, your child, or your next partner just because it will make them happy, and you do it with humility and tenderness and affection. Love is not envious. As the saying goes, "beware of the green-eyed monster." It is really difficult when you are going through your separation and healing phase to be jealous of friends who are in loving relationships. Be happy for others who have real love. Oh, and this is another jealousy issue that divorced parents who date other divorced parents experience, when the choice to love the other is to put the needs of the children first. That means driving home late at night when you're really, really sleepy instead of sleeping over to honor that morality agreement. That means being willing to eat hot dogs and macaroni and cheese with the kids instead of a romantic dinner for two. And if you are not being jealous and you are being patient and kind, then you are happy to make the choice and you enjoy being with the children as much as the times when you get to be alone on a date.

Love doesn't keep records of wrongdoings. Remember how I keep telling you to let it go. Guess what? This is the same thing. If you don't keep records of wrongdoings then you are letting it go. You can forgive your ex for what he/she did to you, and just let it go, and move forward into a new relationship of co-parenting post-divorce. To be honest, I'm not totally ready for this one yet. It's really, really, really difficult for me to forget all that happened in my failed relationship and move on, but I'm trying. And I know, that once I can, then I will be happier than I am now. And my children will be happier than they are now. And you will move on to a new life after your failed relationship. And when you do move into a new life, remember all that you learned about love being a choice and choose to love others and not yourself. Love is honest. Always be honest. I have a past. I have failed relationships. To have real love and a real chance for happiness in a new relationship, I must be willing to share every detail with honest communication. Love always protects, love always trusts, love always hopes, love always perseveres, love never fails. I choose to love again.

I feel blessed to have the opportunity to love again, to have a new relationship with a wonderful man, to have more children in my life to love. I will always make the choice which protects all of their hearts, their safety and well-being. Even when I get scared, because when you have been hurt in the past, sometimes you get scared that the past will repeat itself, but I will choose to give my man the benefit of the doubt, to trust that he has loves me and will always consider what is in my best interest, that he will protect my heart as well. It is my prayer to have a marriage and to experience love that would qualify us to have a story to go in that Married for Life book. Of course, I'm getting a late start, and I'll be close to hundred years old when I could actually meet the being in a committed and loving relationship for 50 years mark. But whether I am only blessed with real love for a year or fifty years, I choose to love patiently, with kindness, honestly, truthfully, with trust, with respect and unselfishness, with a smile and gentle touch and soft words, every day, for my man and for our children. I hope you will have the same opportunity to choose to really love, forgetting and forgiving the past, and to move forward to your new life post-divorce. And for those of you who have not yet been married, I pray that you'll just get love right the first time.

Monday, February 21, 2011

When my son, only a few weeks old, was first hospitalized back in 1989, I did not know what the future would hold. I did not know how devastating his illness would be, how many years I would despair as a mother praying daily for my child to be healed, to be without pain, and to have a chance to be a mother of a healthy child. He never learned to speak, so I never heard him say "I love you, Mommy" or "Thanks, Mom" or any of those other sweet things children say with pure love and gratitude found only in their little hearts. But in 1989, I asked God, why me? Why did he choose me to be the mother of a child who would spend the 12 years of his life in a wheelchair or in bed? I considered my son to be a special gift from God, and I'm sure I made mistakes as a young mother, but I loved my son the best

138

that I could. One woman sent me a newspaper clipping which said that parents of disabled children are given a greater capacity to love than others. I looked back on my life and saw how God prepared me for the task. In high school, I babysat for a family with three children, one of which was wheelchair-bound. Also, my mother designed daycare centers for the local hospitals, and on the weekends, she would sometimes have handicapped children spend the night with us to give the parents one night of rest. I always enjoyed the time spent with these children just as I enjoyed spending time with healthy children.

And so, while my heart wasn't really prepared to grasp the magnitude of the difficult life my son would have. Thank goodness we are only asked to live life one day at a time, because if we really knew ahead of time how bumpy the road would be, we may not have the faith to keep going. I did feel somewhat prepared for the task at hand. And so I didn't give up on him or lose faith in God. My first five years of motherhood were nearly impossible to bear, but I made it through one day, one night at a time. The next three years of motherhood were extremely lonely, but I made it through one day, one night at a time. Are there times when you feel extremely lonely? What about the first night you slept alone after your relationship ended? Maybe you had many nights in bed without a mate before the relationship ended, and so your children helped feel the void. If so, did you discover after your divorce the loneliness of being away from your child? For you, maybe the first night your child ever slept away from you came after your divorce. Being away from my children has always been one of the hardest struggles for me. My son was in a children's long term care facility back in Louisiana and later in Alabama, and so I had several lonely years of being away from one of my children. I really wanted to have other children. I did find out I was expecting shortly after my divorce from my first husband, but that child was never born. The doctors said I'd never be able to have a healthy child, and so I thought this is all I will ever have. I will be the mother of one child who is too sick to be in the same room with me. Without hope of ever giving birth to a healthy child, I lost another during gestation. This was the darkest day of my life. I was without hope of ever having a better life. I was alone in a hotel room in Dallas, Texas. I became a walking, breathing shell of a human being. I was in such despair that very few people even knew what happened. I didn't tell anyone except my friend who nursed me back to health and my other friend who cared for my son when I was at the medical center. Writing this now, I find myself shaking at the memories. I may never be able to share all of the details. But I could not give up on life. My son needed me. I found the strength and the courage to continue. I faced all of the criticism with a fierce determination to make it anyway. I fought to find hope again. In time, I learned to smile again. I married again.

Eight years later, I gave birth to a healthy daughter, and then two years later, to another. I felt so blessed. Luke 6:38, the scripture reads, *"If you give, you will receive. Your gift will return to you in full and overflowing measure, pressed down, shaken together to make room for more, and running over"*. And because I was so blessed with two beautiful, healthy children, I shared my blessing with my family. As they grew, I allowed them to be free to love others. I didn't hold tight to them as some parents do afraid to even get a babysitter for a dinner out with their spouse. Did you date your spouse before your relationship failed? Or was every meal out at a McDonald's playground? I allowed the grandparents to have as much time with them as they wanted. And even though my mother's heart was full and overflowing, I was shaken to make room for more.

In 2002, my son died, leaving an empty place in my heart. I tried so hard to be brave, and to be grateful for what I did have, and to love my family just as it was. But I was miserable. I still felt unloved. But I just kept going. I just kept hoping. A few more years, my youngest brother Jason died of a terminal seizure in his sleep. Followed by the death of my second marriage in 2009/2010, I didn't know what I was supposed to do. No more children – none of my own, no nieces, no nephews. I had an empty place in my heart. I had more love to give, but no one to give my love to. I felt like my gift of love was rejected by my ex. I loved the children born from my womb with more love than they needed to feel loved. So, I felt really blessed to meet a man who had five children. Don't misunderstand me; I was not out looking for an available man with children. In fact, I was a little scared to date a man with children, because I didn't know if I could do it; I didn't know if I'd be able to love someone else's child. See I have faith in God, but I lack faith in myself. But I loved the man before I ever met the children or knew much about them. In fact, I love all of my friends and their children; so many of them I consider to be the nieces and nephews I never had. But to have more children to call my own – that exploded hope in my life.

Once I truly realized just how many children I was being given the opportunity to love, and I felt reassurance after praying that I had more than enough love for each and every one of them, I was overjoyed. And I determined at once that I would pour all of the love I had into their lives, and that is what I've done. 1 Timothy 1:5 says *"Love springs from a pure heart."* I wish I was so worthy and good of a person to call my heart a pure heart, but I'm not referring to my own heart here. My heart is not pure; I just love the best I can with the imperfect heart I have. I try to show others I love them as well as I can. I am a romantic in the classic sense. I will keep a scrap of paper containing loving words. I don't delete any of the voicemails where my significant other has said something kind and loving in the message. I wear a letter K, my man's initial, on my Tiffany necklace daily. He's a romantic too, because he asked for a letter A to wear, so I gave him one last week, and he wears a letter A with the cross his parents gave him. Last night, the youngest of our children called me just before bedtime, and gave me the gift of pure love. She told me that she saw the A for Allison on her Daddy, and that she knew he wore it because he loved me. And that she loved me too. And that she wanted me to be with her always, every day, because she missed me so much when we are apart, that she wanted an A for Allison to wear too, so that I would be with her everywhere she goes. Her love from her little pure heart is a precious gift.

And in one miraculous moment, the empty place in my heart was full beyond measure and running over. This is the amazing thing about love. The more love you give away, the more love you receive in return. I am overwhelmed with love. And so, tomorrow I have two dates: a lunch date and a dinner date. My lunch date will be in the elementary school cafeteria with my precious new goddaughter, who gave me the gift of her pure love, where she will receive a letter A, so that she will know that I love her back and that I want to be with her always too. My dinner date will be with my man who gave me the gift of his heart first, and because of our love for each other, and the love we both have for our children (all seven of them) the youngest returned my gift of love with the pure love from her pure heart. I am truly blessed. And now my prayer is that one day all seven of them will feel deeply loved and will love deeply in return. I don't think love will come that easily as

142

each one is unique and special, and each one has a heart needing to heal from the pain of divorce.

Wednesday, February 23, 2011

Today, I actually got angry about my divorce situation and raised my voice. It was just a few minutes, but it was a major event for me. I'm still shaking on the inside. I tend to just hold stuff in and keep it to myself, put on the polite face, and keep on going. I try to practice dual perspective; that simply means I try to see the situation from the other person's perspective before I act or say something. I try to think of how my actions or my words will create a positive outcome for any situation. And I really do want the best for everybody in every situation. I really do want the best for my children. And I want the best for myself. And today, I just got tired of putting everyone else before myself. I've never really ever gotten angry at anyone for the way I was treated. I may have thought of a lot of horrible words to say to someone, but I kept my thoughts to myself. I didn't talk back to my parents as a kid. One time in high school, a girl was mad at me and threatened to hit me, and I told her to go ahead and do it. Another friend had to rescue me, because I wouldn't fight back. I have seen some women get angry about their situation, call their ex on the phone, and scream all sorts of profane words about whatever, even in front of the children. I've never done that.

Have you ever yelled at someone because you were really angry? I have friends who, when they found their marriage was ending, threw things and broke things and punched holes in the wall. Did you do that? If you did, it's really okay. Everyone deals with the breakup of their relationship differently. I sorted through the household items to divvy things up fairly when I found out my marriage was ending. I worried over whether he'd have enough towels or plates or what would he do in that apartment by himself. Was I hurt? Yes. Was I angry? No. I was in shock. Eventually when reality set it in, I cried. Were you angry when your marriage ended? What did you do to express your anger? Or are you more like me and have difficulty expressing anger? When most people get angry, they take a stand. They draw a line in the sand, and say, this is it; I'm not going any further. Well, today, I drew a line in the sand. And so I'm finally ready to be honest about it, I'm angry that the previous forty years of my life was not a fairy tale, and that I didn't get married and live happily ever after. I'm angry that I made vows to love, honor, and cherish for the rest of my life, and for what? I'm a divorced woman.

And because I am a divorced woman, I am free to make my own choices. And I only have to answer to my conscience and to God. And no matter how much my ex husband wishes he could tell me what to do and how to do it and what I can say and what I can't say, he's not my husband any more, and his opinion about my choices no longer matters. And it is my choice how to live my life. It is my choice how to describe my life. This is my story of my life. Is it biased? Is your story of your failed relationship biased? Of course it is. Your story is your perspective about your life. My story is my perspective about my life. And that's just the way it is. That's what I got angry about – writing this book. Often when a couple with children gets divorced they go to family counseling because the courts demand they do. Sometimes the parents end up at the counselor's office because their child struggles with dealing with the breakup of the family. We were at the counseling appointment to discuss how to co-parent and to have similar rules of behavior, so family life would less confusing for one of our children and so she couldn't do the "but the other parent said I could" manipulation thing. And instead of focusing on our child, when the counselor asked each of us to say what is one thing that you would like to see the other parent do to make things go better, he mentioned my blog, and how he didn't like what I wrote. He even brought printouts of pages and highlighted offending excerpts, because it could be possible that our children could surf the web and read my blog. My blog is how I started working on my book, and I have wanted to write this book long before we ever got divorced. This book doesn't have anything at all to do with him, or any other man I've dated previously or am involved with currently. This book is my story. This is how I'm learning to be happy and positive after a life that both sucks and is wonderful at the same time. Some women may take up a hobby after their divorce. Other women may start living vicariously through their children or volunteer at a local community organization. Whatever you want to do that helps you to heal and to have hope is okay. No one has the right to tell you what to do any more. You are free to make your own choices.

I'm a writer. I have notebooks of poetry. I have notebooks of short stories and play scripts and the beginnings of novels. I have journals or notebooks. Sometimes I don't like what I've written, and I tear it up and throw it away. Most of what I write I keep hidden, and when I'm alone, I dig out that notebook, and I reread the words I've written. Maybe you're not a writer, but it is really cathartic to write down your thoughts. Do you keep a journal? I really encourage you to start one. One journal I keep is a love journal where I record the special feelings I have about my man. Keeping this journal really helps me on busy, hectic days to remember that being loved and showing love is my top priority. I keep another journal where I write down my hopes and dreams for the future, so that I will remember to make choices which will move me in the direction of making those hopes and dreams for the future a reality.

145

And I keep another journal for when I'm feeling poetic, and unfortunately, poems usually come to my brain in the middle of the night, and so if I've written several new poems, then I haven't been sleeping much. I came up with a motto to entertain a friend who was feeling down about her recent breakup. It's not poetry, but I think you'll appreciate it more than poetry.

I don't love him any less,
but I don't have to be a f***ing mess.

Being happy and positive doesn't always come easy, and sometimes that means I have to dig through the muck to find the lost treasure or piece of wisdom which points me in the direction of being happy and positive. That lovely motto a few lines up – well, my friend and I laughed for thirty minutes on the phone repeating that in many different tones of voices. Maybe you just need to say that out loud a few times and see if you don't feel better. I don't have all the answers. But I read my Bible to search for answers. I am not perfect, and I don't always make the best choices. But I do the best that I can. And hopefully you will, just like me, try to do the best that you can to.

Friday, February 25, 2011

When I took out the garbage earlier I noticed the tiny sprouts from my tulip bulbs in the flower bed along the sidewalk. Yes, you too can take out the garbage. I'm so excited, because that means we had enough cold days (remember all those days of snow) and enough warm days recently for the tulip bulbs to do their thing. So this means that spring is really on the way. I had been really worried about my tulips, because I was so distracted early in the fall that I forgot to dig them up before the ground got too hard. I also didn't have the time to trim back my rose bushes.

Usually we don't have cold enough winters in Georgia for the tulip bulbs to hibernate enough. The best thing to do is dig them up, store them in the freezer in a bag, and then replant them in early spring about this time. So there's your gardening tip for the day. And then here's another one I've learned recently, if your yard is perfectly kept all the time, then you have too much time on your hands. Go have some fun.

But even though I wasn't the most conscientious gardener, the tulips are sprouting. I'm being rewarded with their beauty even though I didn't do everything I should have done. And in a few more weeks there will be gorgeous blossoms of red, yellow, orange, and pink. Isn't it ironic how the bad wintry weather is necessary for beautiful flowers to blossom? Another metaphor for life, I think we have here with the tulips sprouting. Maybe we need the bad stuff that comes in our lives to grow and blossom. Maybe we need to be thankful for the problems we've had. But that's so hard, isn't it? Are you grateful you've had problems in your life? Are you thankful for the pain you've suffered? As I listen to friends talk about their relationship issues, they sound anything but grateful. So I really doubt that you are thankful. No one is happy to have had problems. And it's nearly impossible to be thankful for a failed relationship. Maybe I needed to experience all of the difficult things in my past to become the woman I am now - - a woman sprouting into a new beginning. Just as the tulips have broken through the surface of the ground, I have broken through the pain of my divorce. Just as the tulips will bloom brightly, I hope to do the same.

When I see the tulip blossoms standing proudly on top of the bright green stalks, I smile. I hope that when others see the beauty my life has become, they will smile. I heard a song on the radio today, "smile, even though your heart is breaking..." were the lyrics. And every lyric was somewhat similar. The advice was to smile no matter what you are going through, because there will be a tomorrow. And tomorrow will be better. And you'll appreciate the better tomorrow for having the bad yesterday. So no matter how impossible it seems to be thankful for your problems, be thankful anyway. No matter how difficult it is to smile when you're having a rough day, smile anyway. Let the worries, the pain, the anger, and the anxiety, melt away from the warmth of the spring sunshine. Let it all go, smile, and be free. Because you are free. Free to grow. Free to love. Free to be yourself. Free to find someone who loves you for you. And that's a wonderful thing. I can't wait to see the tulips bloom in a few weeks. I can't wait to see how much better my life is by the time the tulips are blooming. The worst of winter is over. The sweetness of spring is here. That relationship which wasn't good for you is over. A relationship which will nourish, sustain, and fulfill you is coming. Wait for it.

Saturday, February 26, 2011

There's a song from the Broadway musical RENT titled Seasons of Love. I actually learned of this song last year when one of my daughters sang Seasons of Love for her school chorale concert. Now, we have it on CD, and every time I hear this song, I understand a little more about the love between a woman and a man. Here's just a bit of the lyrics...

Five hundred twenty five thousand
six hundred minutes
How do you measure, measure a year

In daylight, in sunsets, in midnights,
in cups of coffee, In inches, in miles

in laughter, in strife,

Five hundred twenty five thousand
six hundred minutes
How do you measure a year in the life
between a woman and a man
How about love? How about love?

So a year can be measured in the number of minutes that passes. Or a year can be measured by the moments of love we share. Or a year can be measured by the days we make it through when we don't believe we will make it through. No matter how you measure a year, if you are divorced, or in the midst of the separation or divorce process, I can almost guarantee you that the last year of your life has not been easy. So what has happened in your life in the past year? What has happened in the past two years?

For me, 2009, was the rocky year where there were moments of love and *(I don't even know what you can call them, so let's just make up a word to describe it. Think about how you felt, and then you'll know what I mean)* moments of *unlove*. That's our new word for today. So I guess you could say, a year for a divorced person is measured by moments of *unlove*. That rocky year marked the best year of my marriage and the worst year of my marriage, because just before my marriage ended, I experienced what I thought at the time was the best moments a couple could share together. The type of moments songs are written about. The type of moments when you think, yeah, we've made it through the crises and the year markers where couples usually fall apart, and we're still together. And then in November 2009, we separated. And I started measuring off another year -- a year of being alone and discovering who I really was as a divorced woman. I was no longer an "us", but a "me".

149

So what follows next is not what you'll find written in the lyrics of a song; this is how a divorced person measures a year. The moment you found out your spouse wanted out of the marriage. The moment you came home to an empty house and realized he/she was not coming back. The moment you sent your children to spend the night with the other parent. The moment you stopped referring to him/her as your spouse. The moment you stopped wearing your wedding ring. The moment you were served with the divorce paperwork. The moment you consulted with a divorce attorney and realized financial ruin comes with divorce. The moment you learned your spouse had met someone else. The moment you learned news about your marriage you really should have known long before. The moment your divorce was finalized and you held the pieces of paper in your hand. The moment you realized that you couldn't really survive your divorce alone, and so you reached out to a friend, a family member, or to God. Does this sound familiar to you? There are probably more moments of *unlove* we could count, but these are depressing enough. From November 2009 when I received divorce papers to November 2010, five hundred twenty five thousand six hundred minutes passed, and for many of those minutes I was sleeping, writing, eating, working in a fog, trying to just make it to the next day.

After many months, I finally started waking up to the reality of my life and finding some moments worth counting, professional accomplishments, time with my children, fun with friends, a desire to date again, and so on. And as unbelievable as it sounds, in one year my life completely changed. Of course, the post-divorce life is more complicated than one can imagine. Couples from a committed and loving marriage which has stood the test of time are so blessed; those couples can't even really imagine the intense pain of divorce. So that explains why your happily married friends just do not understand. And while our bodies can separate and live in different houses, our emotions are still intertwined. Because married couples shared moments of love which measured out the years together, divorced couples share moments of *unlove* which measure out the coming apart little by little, more and more, as each minute passes, as each day passes, as each year passes. It is almost like a cosmic crowbar pries in between the tiny crack caused by this issue or that issue and forces the two apart forever. And just when you think enough time has passed that there's no way anything your ex does or anything that happens to your ex will affect you or matter to you at all, then out of the blue, something happens and you realize you're not completely over your failed relationship yet. It feels like someone has ripped the bandage off, poured salt into your open wound, and the pain from whatever just happened unexpectedly brings with it a torrent of all of the pain of all of the other moments of *unlove*.

And it hurts. Haven't you felt this way? Don't you wonder why is it that your heart races and your voice becomes shaky and agitated when you speak to your ex on the phone? It's just not simple to divide what was put together. Married couples are not supposed to come apart. You shared your life with this person, and now you don't share your life with this person. Divorce is really the craziest thing ever. And so, of course, you are going to have moments where you feel like your life is crazy and upside down and abnormal. I have felt that way. If you were committed to your marriage and expected your marriage to last five hundred twenty five thousand six hundred minutes multiplied by sixty, then what you are feeling during those moments of *unlove* is absolutely normal. Take a deep breath, and put whatever is happening into perspective. Because for whatever the reason was, you are divorced now. You're not married any more. Your relationship is over. And that's your past. You'll just have to let it go. It won't be easy to let go, but you can do it. I am doing it, and it's not easy. But I'm ready to start measuring my years in love. I have begun a new year and a new relationship, and so I'm looking forward to measuring this year with the sunrise and sunset at the beach, with midnight walks so we can see the stars, with cups of coffee in my K & A mugs, with moments of laughter we share, with unconditional love and support when one of us is having one of those "yes, I really am divorced" moments, with all of the moments of love which will come each day.

Find a way to measure your year after your failed relationship which doesn't focus on your ex. It may not be the right time for you to be in a new relationship yet. God knew I needed true love and companionship, and so did my man who is also divorced, and so that's why God brought us together now instead of later. Maybe you need to measure your year in moments of beauty treatments, shopping for shoes, or finishing your college education. Maybe you need to measure your year in moments of playing with your children or catching up with friends you haven't talked to in a long time. But whatever you do, measure this year with moments which make you smile. Five hundred twenty five thousand six hundred minutes, how do you measure, measure a year? How about love?

Sunday, February 27, 2011

Have you noticed the daffodils with their sunshiny faces looking up into the Spring sunshine? Have you noticed the sprigs of green grass poking through the dry winter Bermuda? Have you seen the new budding leaves on the tips of the trees? This morning, I decided I'd rather spend time enjoying God's creation than going to church. Of course, I believe going to church is important, but I really wanted to have some quiet time to reflect on the blessings in my life and to relax by the creek in the woods. Psalm 46:10 states *"Be still and know that I am God."* And that's what I needed this morning, time to be still and know that God is God, that God has plan for my life, that God provides all that I need, that God has blessings in store for me, that God created the woods, the creek, the birds, and the sky, that God answers prayers, and that God sent me a man with whom I can share my thoughts, my heart, and my hope. And being in a crowded church surrounded by lots of people listening to praise music was just not what I needed this morning.

So instead of going to church as we typically do, we hopped on the four-wheeler and went down to the creek in the woods. Listening to the sound of the water trickling past oh, so softly, while looking up through the sparse tree branches into the pale blue morning sky, is a little bit of heaven on earth. The tiny finches flitted back and forth on the tiny branches above. A woodpecker steadily tapped on a tree in the distance. We could even hear a squirrel scratching on the tree bark. Every so often a cool breeze would tickle my cheek. Talking would only disturbed nature's serenity, so instead we just listened to the woods. When we did talk, we whispered. We laughed. We kissed. It was pure joy. It was like time didn't exist. It was like being in another world far away from the disappointments of our past lives or dealing with post-divorce issues or worries about work. Nothing else existed in this eternal moment by the creek except for the two of us and the glory of God revealed in nature. As we drew closer to mid-day the sun peeked into our scattered view of the sky. A dry leaf or two floated down in between us. A bee buzzed past quickly going on his way without any regard for us. Pure joy. I was blessed with a moment of pure joy this morning. And I was even more blessed to share the moment with someone special to me. Have you ever experienced pure joy? Have you ever really been still, stopped doing everything that you need to do, and found a spot where you can just be still?

To really be still, you have to let it all go. You have to let go of not just the work and the chores and busy-ness of your daily life, but also the pain and the heartache and bitterness of your failed relationship. You must clear your mind of every thought, let go of your troubles, and just feel the moment of pure joy. If you can just choose to let go and have this moment, to be still and allow God to be God in your life, and to accept peace in your heart for just one moment, then you will receive a blessing so sweet that you will want to choose to let all of your past go. There's a song I remember from church as a little girl, "cast all of your cares on Jesus and leave them there." I don't remember the real name of the song or all of the lyrics of the song, but I do remember the message. And this is the emotional struggle I, and probably you too, wrestle with over and over again. Once you find a moment of pure joy, like I did this morning; a moment where peace and love reside in my heart and the bitterness and anger is gone, the struggle is to remain. You see, we can put aside our problems for a moment, we can allow God to give us peace, and then we pick our problems back up again later. We forget that we found pure joy. We forget the serenity of nature. We forget that we are blessed beyond measure with love, and happiness, and joy.

And even though we move forward into our new life after our failed relationships, often we fall back into our old life just a little. We don't really want to be back in our old lives, but it's just so much easier to hold onto the pain than it is to let it go. And so when you catch yourself slipping into

154

anger, into bitterness, into pain, take a deep breath, close your eyes, and remember your moment of pure joy. I will close my eyes and remember the moss growing on the side of the fallen tree lying just beside me. I will remember the trees swaying casually in the wind. I will remember watching how my man smiled as the sun warmed his face when he felt at peace, and he didn't know I was watching him. I will remember every detail of this morning, and I will carry my moment of pure joy with me, so that when something happens to which I react instinctively in anger or aggravation, I will be able to choose joy over pain. And my prayer for my life, and for your life, is that one day there will be only joy, no pain, no matter the circumstances. You too can have a moment of pure joy. Your moment may not come by the creek as mine did, but your moment will come if you believe.

Tuesday, March 1, 2011

This has been a really great day, a really great day, and all the way until this evening, when we realized we had a missing pet. So the search has been on, and the crying children are finally tucked into bed asleep, and I'm taking a few minutes to breathe. We have done everything we can do, and now it is just time to wait to see if he will turn up on his own. But finding a tiny black and white California King snake is like trying to find a needle in a haystack. Yes, you read that right; our missing pet is a snake. We also have cats, bunnies, fish, horses, and in just a few weeks, we'll add a hamster in celebration of my daughter's birthday. Yes, I'm the cool Mom who will allow my children to have any type of pet they want to have. Taking care of animals instructs children in both science and ethics. Owning pets is a part of my life, and I don't know, as much as I love animals, I don't think I'd own pets if I didn't have children. I mostly put up with the

155

inconvenience, the germy messes, and the extra expenses of pet ownership to make my children happy. I even helped my goddaughter catch a frog, make it a habitat, and bought crickets for it until she decided it was time to let him back into the wild.

It's time to pray and wait. Being patient in a time of crisis is one of the most difficult things to do. Being able to go to sleep believing that all will be well tomorrow is nearly impossible. My children probably feel this way. Do you have pets? Did you have a pet as a child? If so, you've dealt with a lost pet, an injured pet, or a sick and dying pet. I love animals, and I could tell many sad stories about this pet or that pet from over the years. But owning pets is not just about fun. Owning pets is work. Owning pets requires dedication and honoring your commitment to your pet. If you're not willing to meet your pet's physical needs, to provide your pet with affection and attention, and to be committed to loving your pet for as long as your pet lives, then you should never own a pet.

The same thing could be said for marriage. If you're not willing to meet the physical needs of your partner, to be affectionate and attentive to his/her emotional needs, to be committed to loving him/her for the rest of your life, then you shouldn't enter into the relationship. The same thing could be said for being a parent. Life demands the best of us. Romans 12:9-12 states *"Don't pretend to love others. Really love them. Hate what is wrong. Hold tightly to what is good. Love each other with genuine affection, and take delight in honoring each other. Never be lazy, but work hard and serve the Lord enthusiastically. Rejoice in our confident hope. Be patient in trouble, and keep on praying."* When I came across this scripture in my reading, I thought, this sums everything up about what I need to do in a relationship. And when I reflect on my life and my

156

relationships with others (spouse, children, parents, friends, pets, extended family, just everybody), I've really tried my best to do all of these. I really love when I love someone. I'm just not the kind of person who can fake emotions. Doing the right thing is always the right thing to do, and I've always tried to do what I thought was right in every situation. This reminds me of something my grandfather used to say, "You can do what you want to do, but this is what you should do, and that's all I'm going to say about it." With genuine affection, with delight, and honoring the other, love the other person.

And when you are in a relationship where both persons are love each other like this, both of you are blessed. I hope that my man always feels like I love him with genuine affection, with delight, and honoring him as my best friend. This is more than romantic, euphoric love; this is friendship too. Having a good work ethic is not just about work for which you get paid. Doing chores around the house, preparing meals, taking care of children, putting together your taxes, putting effort into showing your mate that he/she is special, and doing all of these things and more with enthusiasm. Keeping God first in your life will enable you to be confident in your hope rather than afraid or cynical, and to enable you to handle the next crisis or disappointment. And when that crisis occurs, like tonight when we lost a pet, pray. And I am praying for our pet to return, and if our pet does not return, for our children to have the strength to handle the loss. And I am praying not only for miracles today and strength to endure the hardships today, but also for miracles and love and happiness and strength for tomorrow. Be confident in your hope and believe that tomorrow all will be well.

Wednesday, March 2, 2011

A kind heart…
A kind word…
An act of kindness…

Have you ever been told "you're a wonderful woman, but…? "You really were a good wife, but...?" "You really are nice, but…?" Don't you just hate those compliments which are immediately followed by "but…?" Like somehow the person giving you the bad news believes the bad news will sound better if started with a compliment. The reality is that not everyone appreciates a kind person. No matter how kind you are to someone will not guarantee kindness in return. Be kind anyway. Being kind is not something you do, because you expect a return. Have you seen that commercial, I think it's an insurance commercial, where one person holds a door for someone who has their hands full, and then that person helps someone else, and so on? And sometimes that happens. Like when the real estate agent gave me a list of repairs and tasks to do before we listed my house on the market last year, I just couldn't possibly do it all by myself. But I had to get it all done nonetheless. And so I put out a request for volunteers to friends and family with the to-do list attached. And one by one, items were crossed off the list. And some volunteers brought additional volunteers along. Not only were their acts of kindness greatly appreciated, but even more so were their kind words. Because…you drove our son to piano lessons all those years. Because…you cooked supper for my family. Because…you babysat for me when I needed you. Because…you always helped me with my homework and gave me advice about college. Because…you helped me move. Because…you have been a good friend. Because…you are always doing things for others, of course, we want to do something for you.

I have always been a girl, a woman, who does things for others with a happy heart. That's just who I am. In high school, I'd help a friend with their chores, so we could go out sooner. I'd drive across town to give a friend a ride to work. One time, my great aunt wanted to visit the grave of one of her relatives, I drove her to three different cemeteries before we found the tombstone, because she couldn't remember exactly which cemetery. And I loved spending the sunny afternoon driving through the countryside and walking through those small, old, country cemeteries with her. In college, if I grabbed a soda from a friend's dorm fridge, I'd clean the fridge if it was messy. As a high school teacher, I took kids on picnics in the park on Saturday mornings and to play basketball in the church gym on Monday nights. As a college professor, one of my former students who never had enough money for lunch would always finish the rest of mine. Was I finished eating? Probably not, but he was hungry; and it wouldn't hurt me to eat a few less calories. I don't share these stories with you to say to boast, but just so that you can see that you're a kind person too. You've probably done all sorts of kind things for others too. Why don't you make a list and remind yourself just how kind you are to others? Galatians 5:22-23 states *the Holy Spirit produces these fruits in our lives: love, joy, peace, patience, kindness, goodness, faithfulness, gentleness, and self-control.* This is so amazing if you stop and think about it. Aren't these the things we want in our lives? And don't we want them even more so after we have experienced the trauma of a failed relationship? But more than wanting to receive these things, we should want to give or be these things. I want to show love to others. I want to be joyful, and so I seek out ways to have fun. I want to have peace in my life, instead of chaos and drama, and so I am slow to speak in anger, and I am patient with others when they are having a bad day. I enjoy being kind and gentle with others. Being faithful and trustworthy in the commitments and promises I have made is of utmost importance to me, and so I choose to act in ways that demonstrate that. And doing all of these takes self-control. Because the easier thing is to act annoyed when you are annoyed, but the right thing is to be loving, kind, gentle, and patient. I may mess up occasionally, and to be totally honest, sometimes I really do lose control and say things I probably shouldn't say. But what I really want is to be blessed with all of these fruits of the Spirit, so that I can be a blessing to others. Not only that, but so I'll be able to handle the changes which come.

Yeah, spring is here! Oh no, spring is here, and it's time to mow the grass! Time just passes so quickly. This entire change in attitude from despair to positive hope about my life started with the first time I mowed the grass, and now it's time to start mowing the grass again. A year has passed; in fact, in just a few more days it will be exactly a year when the judge signed the final divorce papers and my divorce became final. How long has it been since your divorce was final? Or are you still waiting for it to be finalized? I have some friends for whom it has taken years for their divorce process to finish. I think I got one of the fastest divorces in Georgia, because my divorce was finalized within four months of being served with the petition for divorce. In my case, the legal process of getting divorced was much quicker than the emotional process of getting divorced. Divorce, whatever the circumstances, is never easy. It's not fun. And you will not get what you want out of the deal. This morning, on the radio, the DJ was responding to a caller who asked for advice about not being sure if they should get married or call off the wedding. And the advice was "Just go for it. What's the worst that can happen? If it doesn't work out, you can just get divorced." Wrong answer! You should never approach getting married with the philosophy "if we don't like it, we can just get divorced."

I never thought I'd get a divorce. I imagine that most of you never thought you'd get a divorce either. Children never think their parents will get a divorce. So if the caller would have been asking my advice, I would have said, "If you're not 100% sure you're making the right decision to marry this person, don't get married. Relationships require total commitment. Your partner deserves your whole heart. The worst thing you can do is promise to love him or her, and then later, change your mind." I almost think it is easier to recover from triple bypass cardiovascular surgery than an emotionally broken heart. Yes, you can recover. That's really the entire point of my story is that no matter what devastating losses you've experienced, you can make it through the trial, recover your strength and zest for life, and be restored with a greater love and better relationship than you've ever had before. Do you know the story of Job? Job is the man in the Bible who lost everything. He lost his property and sources of revenue. He lost his children. He lost his wife. He was afflicted with physical sickness. He was totally devastated. Before I got divorced, I never really thought the story of Job had anything to do with divorce. But yeah, there's a great analogy. Job was faithful. Job trusted God.

And all of the problems which Job experienced divorced people also experience. Divorced persons suffer financial losses. Divorced persons lose their homes. Do you know that a great many of the foreclosed homes on the real estate market today are due to divorce situations? Divorced persons lose time with their children. Divorced persons lose their spouse. Do you know that the person who loses their spouse to divorce grieves in the same way that a person who loses their spouse to death grieves? Divorced persons suffer physical ailments due to stress, depression, and fatigue. Job had it so bad that his friends actually said, "Job, why don't you just curse God and die?" And sometimes when going through the pain of divorce, some people feel like just cursing God and giving up. The pain is just so great. The despair feels like it will never end. But Job didn't give up. And Job lost everything. I'm divorced. Maybe you're reading this book because you're divorced. And you've lost everything, or nearly everything. Don't give up. Have faith in God that He will provide what you need and restore you. And Job's story is so miraculous, because even though the circumstances were as bad as they could possibly be, Job believed in God. And in time, Job had twice as much financial wealth and property, Job had more children, Job gained a new wife with whom he had greater love than his first wife. Job had good health and lived a long life. So all we need to do is give it time. I think about this all the time; if I have lost so much, and God will renew and restore me, then how better is my future going to be than my present is now?

You will have a better life. You will. Do you believe? A little, but you're just not sure? Give it a year, and then see where you are. I am much, much, better off now than I was a year ago. I can see my restoration unfolding. I wonder, how did Job feel when he saw God putting his life back together better than it was before? The Bible doesn't really talk about that, but did Job feel the way that I feel today? I am so happy, because my restoration is tangible. "Believing things that you can see and touch means you don't believe at all," said Abraham Lincoln, "but to believe in what you cannot see is a victory and a blessing." Like Job, I believed in God, even when everything was going wrong. And I believed that love could be real and everlasting between a man and a woman, even when I didn't see evidence in my life. But the victory of actually receiving blessings after the losses and being loved unconditionally and completely and forever after a failed relationship feels so wonderful I could never, ever, express the awesomeness of how it feels in words. You'll just have to feel it to know how it feels. And until you feel it, then you'll have to believe that you will feel it one day. Just take it one day at a time. You will keep on going even when you think you can't. The grass will grow a little taller each day. Wow, I just looked out the window at the yard, and it really is time to mow the grass.

Recovering from divorce is extremely difficult, no more and no less difficult than recovering from a debilitating illness. And if you've ever been really, really sick or recovering from surgery, then you know that the rehabilitation and recovery process is a long journey. Often you look back at your old life, your old marriage, and question your actions, both good and bad. Could you have done anything differently that would have made a difference? Have you done something so wrong, sinned, or created bad karma, that your divorce is some sort of punishment? I'm a good person. You're a good person. But neither one of us is a perfect person. But looking back will weigh you down and keep you from moving forward. Hebrews 12:2 *"let us strip off every weight that slows us down, especially the sin that so easily trips us up. And let us run with endurance the race God has set before us."* Your life did not end when your relationship ended. But did you feel like your life was ending? I couldn't hardly get out of bed for 3 months or stop crying, I was so depressed. I wasn't depressed because I missed my husband as a companion. I was grieving my marital status. I didn't want my life to change. Are you still suffering from depression? You know what? The race is not over; in fact, you are probably only rounded the first bend and jumped over the first set of hurdles. Even though it felt like my life was ending when my divorce first occurred, I know now that was only a phase in my life.

And to be successful in the next phase of my life, I've got to let my past go. I've got to let it all go. The most important point for you to have a full emotional recovery is you've got to let it all go. The pain, the bitterness, the anger, the fear, the regrets, all of it, is weighing you down and keeping you from moving forward. When you put it down, and stand up on your own two feet, determined to run the race with endurance, without giving up, then you will be renewed in your spirit with peace, with strength, with joy, with belief in yourself that you can do it. You can be happy. You can get past this thing. But you need to run with endurance; you cannot give up. In your past relationship, did you give up? Maybe you weren't the one who quit and walked out, but did you ever have doubts and started to believe having a good relationship was impossible? Or maybe you had every intention of staying faithful to your partner and finishing the race you started. That was my intention. Were you running, and your partner dropped out of the race? Did your partner give up on you, on your marriage, and decide to run a different direction? No matter what happened, or who did what, that relationship is over. That relationship is behind you in your race, and your race is not over.

Your race today is just different than your race on the day you got married however many years ago it was. Keep running. Keep going. Don't ever quit. Don't ever stop. Keep believing in yourself. And when you have the opportunity to have a new running partner in a new relationship, don't pick up all of your baggage from your past failed relationship and let it weigh you down and hold you back. I am so fortunate to have found a man with whom I want to team up; our paths were meant to cross. I have no doubt that it was divine intervention for us to meet after each of us experienced devastating failed marriages. Both of us spent many hours and nights in prayer asking for God to deliver us and to bring us hope and to show us that love is real. And God answered our prayers, and then we were introduced by friends. But there are days when we struggle, not with each other, but with the divorce recovery process. But I am so thankful that he supports me when I am feeling weary from the race, and I am so glad that he can lean on me when he feels discouraged. Together we will win the race. Some people can win the race alone, so enduring through the struggles and running the race with hope and confidence is not dependent on finding a new relationship. You have the strength in you to run the race. But I don't think it's God's plan for my life for me to run the race without a partner. But if I was supposed to spend the rest of my life alone, I know I could do it.

In the book "The Lone Survivor" by Marcus Luttrell, he tells his story about being the Navy Seal who was the only one in his unit who survived an attack in Afghanistan. Luttrell explains how life is during Navy Seals training which is so extremely tough that of the 150 candidates that begin, only 1/3 actually finish the training. Some don't have the abilities. Some give up. And when a soldier wants to give up, there's a bell he/she can ring to signify that he/she wants to exercise the quit option. Luttrell writes about how he wanted to talk a soldier out of ringing the bell when he saw him walking towards it, but the trainer wouldn't let him. He said that if you talk someone out of ringing the bell today, he will ring the bell later, because if you have it in your mind that quitting is an option, it's only a matter of time before you'll quit. If you enter into marriage thinking there is a quit option, then you've already quit. You cannot win a race you don't even believe you can finish. Too many people today are entering into marriage thinking I can just get out if I don't like it later.

When you do decide to date again, don't commit for today if you can't see yourself committing every day for the rest of your life. Just as the soldier has to be 100% committed to the cause, even to the point of dying for the cause, I have to be committed to my relationship, to finishing the race I started, so I'm never going to ring the bell. The decision was already made to enter into the race, to run the race, to be victorious in the race, and so I'm going to keep going forward. I've been forgiven for my sins; they are behind me. I've let go of the pain of my past, it's behind me. And I'm so excited! I wish you could really see my face and hear my voice and know how excited I really am! I had a revelation this weekend that I am not a failure just because I had a failed relationship (or failed relationships). I can, and I will have a stable and loving relationship with a good man which will last forever. Maybe one day, when we are ready, my man and I will get married. And so okay, the statistics about the likelihood of second or third marriages lasting are really bad. And yes, if you're counting, if and when I get married again, this will be my third. But my faith is not in statistics. God has a plan for my life and for our life together, and my faith is in Him. I'm not a quitter. I don't think my man is a quitter. And God is not a quitter. And so I'm excited, because this is going to be a fun and thrilling race with joy, happiness, peace, love, kindness, endurance, patience, gentleness, and more. And if tomorrow is going to be even better than today, I can't wait! Just keep running. You're going to make it across the finish line, and you're going to be so happy you didn't give up.

Tuesday, March 8, 2011

There is a saying back home in Louisiana, *laissez le bon temps rouler*; let the good times roll. In other words, it's time to party, to enjoy life, to have fun. Definitely, it's time. Today is Fat Tuesday -- this Louisiana tradition -- the last night to party before one starts observing Lent. Today is also my first *Annidivorcery.* If you're wondering what that word is, it's not French; I made it up. I've developed a whole new vocabulary post-divorce. My divorce was finalized one year ago today. Back then, my friends said, hey, let's throw you a divorce reception. And a party celebrating a divorce I didn't really want sounded like such a great idea in a weird sort of way; after all, I'd had baby showers, funerals, and wedding receptions to celebrate other significant life events. How did you celebrate getting a divorce? Did you have a party? Did you just go out with friends? Did you stay in and watch old movies until you finished a bottle of wine all by yourself?

Really, I was too busy to do anything special to mark the occasion, and before I knew it, an entire year passed. And before you get all excited that I'm about to share with you some big first *annidivorcery* celebration plans with you for Fat Tuesday (a.k.a. Mardi Gras), I'm just stopping off to visit my parents for a few minutes en route as the Mom Taxi Driver before watching Glee with my kids tonight. And we'll probably eat some brownies before fasting begins tomorrow. But I don't really need or want a big celebration. A typical home-cooked family dinner with everyone around the table laughing and having a good time together is the best kind of party to me. Have you seen the movie "Blind Side" with Sandra Bullock and Tim McGraw? If not, you should. If you have, do you know the scene where the homeless boy sits at their dining room table with his plate while the rest of the family is scattered here and there watching TV, and the mom (Bullock) realizes that their family is missing it? Family togetherness is the most important thing in life. Being able to be together as a family; and maybe with a few close friends around the table too, is all I want. That is the greatest celebration on earth to me (Sorry, Ringling and Brothers circus)!

I'm reminded of one of Aesop's Fables -- the Bundle of Sticks. The father on his deathbed calls his sons together, gives each one a stick, and instructs them to break the stick. Of course, the sticks break easily. Then the father takes all of the sticks and bundles them together, and none of the sons can break the bundle of sticks. The moral of the fable is this -- together as a family, as a team, we are unbreakable; we can do anything; but as individuals we are weak and vulnerable. Before your failed relationship, you were a team, a family; but post-divorce, you find yourself alone, weak, and vulnerable. But one cannot survive life alone. And what really happens post-divorce is that your definition of family must be altered. What once was the traditional, nuclear, family with a Mom, Dad, two kids, and a dog is no longer your life. Are you still grieving the change to your family? Do you feel alone without your spouse? Your post-divorce family will evolve over time; but no matter what happens, you are not alone. And you are not going to break under the strain. And the more time passes between the moment of separation and this moment now, the more your post-divorce family will change. And you'll have to adapt and cling to the other sticks to find strength. Love your family as it is now, not as it could or should have been.

Let your fixation on the traditional family go, and celebrate the family you have now. You will draw closer to some of your friends, and they will share in your holiday celebrations; these friends will become sticks in your bundle. My family is much larger today than it was a year ago or two years ago. Now there are seven children and more grandparents in my bundle of sticks. Now I have a man who brings a lot of strength and stability to my bundle. There is more love in my life today, and more chairs are needed at the party table. I have many friends who are sticks in my bundle; I couldn't make it through life without them. Some of my friends are closer to me than my siblings. A simple, home-cooked family meal looks like I'm throwing a party when you start counting the number of people - and it's just family. You don't have to be biologically related and share the same genes to be family. Together we are stronger; together we have more fun; together we are more blessed. Before I could really accept the blessing of my post-divorce family, I had to let go of the pain and regrets over the family I lost. I had to accept the change which took place in my family. It took time, but I'm so glad I had the courage to put myself out there, to start dating again, to make friends, to keep on loving my kids, to love again, because each day is bringing a new blessing. Each day, some little something happens that is a cause for celebration of life and love and new beginnings. I don't have time to celebrate my divorce; I'm too busy celebrating the life I have.

I'm really excited about the opportunity I was given yesterday to share my message of hope, happiness, and having a positive attitude on a radio interview. Not because I'm someone extraordinary, but because I'm just like you, an ordinary woman who has had some ups and downs in life and desires to find the way to be happy despite my circumstances. And being happy is a choice each of us makes as an individual. Aristotle, a Greek philosopher, who is commonly referred to in my professional field as the Father of Rhetoric said *"Happiness is the meaning and the purpose of life, the whole aim and end of human existence."*

And I really do believe that a large part of what every person wants in life is to be happy. We enter into relationships in the search to be happy. That's why I got married. And that's why I committed to a new relationship post-divorce. And some people leave their marriage in the search to be happy. That wasn't why my marriage ended for me; I wasn't searching for happiness outside of my marriage.

I've heard people say "I'm just not happy, and so I want a new life." Let's take a moment and think about all of the life decisions we make in the search to be happy. Did you choose your occupation, because doing that job makes you happy? Do you live where you live, and I mean, like the city or the farm or by the beach or wherever you live, because living there makes you happy? What you did this morning when you first woke up, whatever you did, did it make you happy? Is that why you did it? And if you've spent the day with someone, does being with that person make you happy? If you were alone today, were you happy having some quiet time to yourself? Do you own a pet, and does owning that pet make you happy? Some people consider their pets to be family. Oh, that reminds me, a miracle occurred, my daughter's pet snake was found. She went to use the bathroom, and there he was, right there in plain sight after nearly two weeks of being missing. And do you know what she said? I prayed every night, he would come back, and he did. So she's one happy little girl. And not only that, all of her friends who helped her search, are also happy; there was a lot of cheering and giggling on the phone late that night. I know some of you are still a little queasy at the mention of a pet snake hiding somewhere around the house. Allowing my daughter to have a snake has made me a super cool Mom, but I didn't buy her one for that reason. I allowed a snake into my home, because I want to be the kind of Mom who supports my daughters' dreams even when I disagree with her decision. I want everyone, including my children, to figure out what makes them happy and have the courage to find their own way in life.

What makes you happy? Or would you prefer I answer the question first, what makes me happy? I'm really not a complicated person, and I don't spend my life searching for material things, so the answer is really simple. I'm happy when everyone I love is altogether, when they are all happy, and I get to share in their joy, when there's no fussing, and when I know I'm loved. And so I'm really blessed, because most of the time I have exactly what I need to be happy. And in those times when I am by myself, because the children are visiting their other parents or I have a day off and everyone is at school or work, I find happiness in planning for our next togetherness activity. And in those times when everyone is not happy, and the children are fussing with each other as siblings sometimes do, I am patient and I love them just as they are, because I know the grumpiness is temporary and the smiles are coming soon. And now, in my post-divorce, nothing is what I thought it would be like at 41 years of age. My answers to all of the above questions are: I find happiness in being a professor and writer who has been given the opportunity to motivate others to have hope and happiness. I find happiness living here in North Georgia, because I love walking in the woods, living nearby Lake Lanier, and being close to Atlanta to enjoy the city life occasionally. And yes, most definitely, everything I did this morning and throughout the day with my children before school and with my man on our day off made me blissfully happy. I haven't had much time by myself today, and that's the way I like it, so I'm extremely happy about that. I discovered through counseling that one of my dreams in life is to have companionship with my mate.

And now I have someone who just enjoys hanging out with me, and that's exactly what I need. In a little while, we'll go by the nursing home to visit his mother, so his father can go to mass, and I'll enjoy being there just as much as I'll enjoy our supper out later. The purpose of my existence is to find happiness in my daily life doing ordinary stuff, and it is my pursuit to learn how to find happiness in parts of my life which cause me pain or grief. Ecclesiastes 3:12 says *"I know that there is nothing better for men (and women) than to be happy and do good while they live."* And it is my sincere hope that I will be happy every day for the rest of my life and that every choice I make from this day forward will do good for both myself and others in my life. And it is my prayer that it will be the same for you - that you will be happy - and that you will do good. And if everyone went through life with that prayer and purpose, then this world would be a much happier place for everyone.

Tuesday, March 15, 2011

It rained again today. The weather report said it would rain on Tuesday, and in the wee hours of the morning I heard the rain patting against the window pane. It's my turn to feed the horses, and it's raining. In my family, we share our toys, and we share the responsibilities. And because I am thankful to share in the joys of horse ownership, I am more than willing to share in the chores of horse ownership. But why doesn't always rain when it's my turn to feed? When things happen in our lives, it is quite normal to ask why. Why me? Why is this happening to me? When my son was in the PICU (Pediatric Intensive Care Unit) at 3 weeks of age, I didn't understand why he was so sick. I had good prenatal health and care. I did everything an expectant mother is supposed to do. But what made his life threatening illness even more difficult to accept was the 2 week old baby girl in the room next to him. She was in the

PICU, because her mother threw her against the wall because she wouldn't stop crying.

That's when I asked why me, why my baby. Because it just didn't seem fair that babies are born in homes without love. I don't even know her name, but she was okay after a few days. On impulse, I collected up the baby shower gifts intended for a little girl and brought them to the hospital with me the next day, and gave them to the nurse to give to the foster parents. It wasn't much, but a little baby needs a little blessing and a little love from someone. I just wanted to do something, because my situation seemed so hopeless. My baby was dying, and that baby was going to live and be just fine. When my marriage fell apart, I asked why me, why my marriage. I would have done anything to keep my children from being children of divorce, because children suffer the most from the actions of the adults in their lives. And children of divorce suffer emotionally and physically, even if the pain isn't as obvious as abuse. Sometimes the scars are not evident until years later. Most of the bad things that happen in our life are outside of our control. What has happened in your life where you just threw up your hands and shouted "Why me, Lord? Why is this happening to me? I don't understand." Proverbs 3:5-6 says *"Trust in the Lord with all your heart, and lean not on your own understanding; in all your ways acknowledge Him, and He shall direct your paths."*

You don't need to understand why bad things have happened in your past. You just need to trust God to be in control of your present and your future. I don't need to know why my son got sick, and the moment that I stopped questioning why, that's when I felt peace and reassurance that I would make it through. I don't need to know why my marriage failed; the day I stopped crying why me, that's when I had hope for tomorrow. Philippians 4:7 says *"The*

173

peace of God, which passes all understanding, shall guard your hearts and minds" And it's so true, peace is not something which you can rationalize; peace is something you feel. And I want you to have peace despite your circumstances. So I will continue to pray for your healing, your renewal, and your hope. Then you too can have peace.

Tuesday, March 22, 2011

Do you know how to ride a bike, and I mean, a real bike, not the stationary exercise bike at the gym? Do you remember learning to ride a bike? Do you remember the queasy feeling in the pit of your stomach and thinking "oh, no, I don't think I can do this?" Do you remember putting your feet on the pedals; and with a lot of hesitation and anxiety, you pushed the first pedal down and whispered to yourself "I'm gonna fall?" But off you went pedaling without rhythm, wobbly, with little balance, and almost no faith at all. You probably only made two or three rotations of the wheels before you put your feet down on the ground gripping the handle bars more tightly and gave up. Well, almost gave up. You just stood there straddling the bike trying to decide to go again or to get off. And that moment of decision seemed like an eternity. And the fear of falling or getting hurt was the biggest fear you had ever felt in your young life. Fear and faith are like polar opposites; you conquer your fear by acting in faith. John Wayne said "courage is being scared to death and saddling up anyway."

This weekend, I helped my man's youngest child Ellie learn to ride a bike. For thirty minutes, she tried over and over again. She was afraid, but she kept trying anyway. It was difficult for her to balance, so she didn't want me to let go. So I held on and kept giving her words of encouragement. As she took a moment to catch her breath

174

straddling the bike trying to decide to go again, we watched the older kids whizzing all around us. Each of the children went through the same thing she was feeling and experiencing, and each one of them, in their own timeframe, made a decision to saddle up anyway, to shout "let go, I can do it," and they did. Were there scrapes and bruises? Certainly. But they kept on going despite the scrapes and bruises. Not everyone has the same level of fear; my brother just ran into the side of the house or fell over intentionally whenever he wanted to stop. He didn't care if he got hurt. And he lived his life that way, just forging ahead full-speed in whatever direction he wanted to go. I was always more cautious. I had more fear of falling, of getting hurt, of not being successful. Consequently, choosing to have faith and belief that I can make it, that I can love again without being hurt, that I can have a relationship that works requires a lot of willpower. Maybe right now, in your imagination, you're standing there with your bicycle all over again, and this is your moment of decision. You can both give up on finding happiness and let go of your past or you can just go for it with 100% effort. I think it takes even more willpower to let go and move forward with your new life when your past experiences reinforce your fears. But do you remember the first time you fell on your bike and got hurt? Didn't you try again? I'm sure you did, and eventually, you were whizzing up and down the street or on the trail in the woods or even became a BMXer. My cycling skills are pitiful really; thank goodness for the stationary bike at the gym. But I am able to run alongside a child on a bicycle holding onto the seat as she pedals just so she feels safer.

You got hurt in your past relationship. So what? So you're a little banged up and bruised, that doesn't mean your ride is over. Have just a little bit of faith in yourself, and go for it. Put your all into your new life. Let go, find your balance,

175

and pedal your bike with everything you have in you. And one day, you're going to see a miracle happen in your own life. It will happen in one moment of time. Just like that one moment when as a child you realized "I'm really riding a bike." Do you remember that moment? Honestly, I don't remember that moment for myself. But I do remember the moment I saw the look on each of my children's faces when they realized it. And I saw a miracle. Maybe you don't really believe it will happen for you. Maybe you're still a little bit afraid. But it will happen. It will happen. Your old life will pass away, and your new life will have begun, and you'll know it when it really happens. Until then, I'm going to keep praying for you. Will you keep praying for me? Let's pray together for healing, for renewal, and for hope, and for courage to act in faith.

Monday, March 28, 2011

Henry David Thoreau said *"Most men lead lives of quiet desperation and go to the grave with the song still in them."* And I do agree with Thoreau, in part, because when I look back at the last twenty years (my adult years), I was living, but I wasn't LIVING. I guess you could say I was going through the motions of life, doing what needed to be done, taking care of my home, making practical low-risk financial decisions, putting off things I really wanted to do, raising children, and so on. Do you know what I mean? Has your life kind of been like that, where you are somewhat happy, but not completely happy? Where you were somewhat fulfilled, but not totally fulfilled? Where you felt like you couldn't really pinpoint what was lacking in your life or relationships, but you just felt like something was missing? But you so busy living your life of quiet desperation, you never took the time to really reflect until you figured out why you weren't singing about how wonderful and amazing and miraculous your life was.

I didn't really know that my life wasn't wonderful and amazing. I thought my life was normal, like everyone else's; and I didn't really know that more was possible, and so I didn't hope for more. Harry Nilsson reiterated Thoreau's sentiments, *"I do believe that most men live lives of quiet desperation. For despair, optimism is the only practical solution. Hope is practical. Because eliminate that (hope) and it (life) is pretty scary. Hope at least gives you the option of living."* Okay, so you and I, we've lived in quiet desperation. We've kept silent about our suffering and unhappiness and just kept on going. And then one day, something happened that shook you out of your complacency. For me, it was my divorce. Getting a divorce and putting my life back together post-divorce, made me realize how much I had neglected my hopes and dreams out of desperation. And that now I am free to dream, to hope, to do something out of the ordinary, to not be like everybody else, to not settle for a relationship or marriage that doesn't completely make me happy and totally fulfill my needs in every way, I'm learning how to really live. And Nilsson says it perfectly, we need to be optimistic about our future; hope is practical.

So many times, I've made the practical choice, and it's wasn't the right choice. For example, I chose to buy the safe mini-van or sedan, because I had small children. And I spend more time driving my car, than I spend at home, I should drive a car I find pleasure in driving. Or I put off going to graduate school, because it would be too much of a financial struggle for both my ex and I to go to school at the same time. And now I've finally figured out that hope in a better tomorrow; playing it safe and not stepping out in faith is impractical. And it's also not fun. Worry sometimes causes us to pull back on the reigns, "whoa, stop right there; that won't work; you can't do that; be cautious; don't give too much; don't risk your heart; miracles don't happen." I've always kind of seen practical as relating to wise, and impractical as relating to fun. Like buying a knock-off brand shoe just because it costs less rather than the phenomenal designer shoe that makes you all giddy inside like a kid in a candy store. But then when you are walking around in the practical, these will get the job done, and they kind of look okay, shoe, you don't feel good. You don't say, "yeah, I'm so wise, and smart, and practical, look at my wonderful, cheap, shoes; they make me so happy." No, you avoid wearing them, and they join the other sad shoes on the shelf in your closet, because when you do wear them, you feel like you let yourself down. You didn't treat yourself as someone special.

And if you don't feel like you deserve to be treated special, even when you're the one treating yourself, then how can you expect someone else to treat you special. You have to be wise enough to know what you want and need to be happy. You have to be wise enough to know whom to love and how to recognize when someone loves you. You have to wise enough to know that miracles do happen. Proverbs 24:14 states *"know also that wisdom is sweet to your soul; if you find it, there is a future hope for you, and your hope will not be cut off."* So knowing what makes you happy, what decision will cause you to live happily rather than in despair, that is wise and practical. And I'm not sure where you are yet in terms of being ready to really live life to the fullest, but for me, I want hope that lasts forever. I don't want love for just today; I want real, pure, true, faithful, complete, love every day for the rest of my life. I don't want to be happy in just one moment; sure, one moment of real happiness can sustain you for many days of difficult and dark times. But I want happiness at a level that transcends my understanding of happiness and moments of happiness that increase to the frequency that one moment blurs right into the next, so that I never stop smiling or praising God for just how great my life has become. And I pray this for you as well -- for your healing to a new way of thinking which includes the ability to dream about your wonderful future, for the renewal of your mind to have the wisdom to make decisions that bring happiness to your life, and hope overflowing and unending.

Tuesday, March 29, 2011

Today was an extremely busy day at work -- meetings, meetings, and more meetings -- phone calls, phone calls, and more phone calls. I'm a professional in the field of communication, and sometimes my friends who work "real jobs" like to tease me about getting paid for talking. But there is a great amount of skill needed to talk well. But communicating well requires listening as well as talking. And time. To produce the outcome needed in the workplace, I have to devote time and energy to communicating well. And sometimes that means spending two hours in a conversation to finally get to the one little detail which really matters. And when I finally get the person with whom I'm communicating to share that little detail which reveals the true concern, the actual crux of the anxiety, the real need; then we can start moving forward to resolve the concern, reduce the anxiety, and meet the need. Sometimes the person doesn't even know what the one little detail they really want and need is until they finally say it out loud. Details matter. Jean Francois Paul De Gondi, a Cardinal of the Catholic Church in the late 1600's, wrote in his memoirs, *"in a major matter, no details are small."* And when conflict occurs in the workplace, or in our relationships, the details do matter, because people matter. Or maybe I should say people matter to me. But what I learned today as I reflect on the outcomes of those meetings and phone calls is that sometimes people don't believe they matter; and so, they stop sharing the little details which matter. Have you ever done that in your conversations? Have you ever held back what was worrying you? Have you ever felt like you didn't matter, and so you just stopped sharing your thoughts?

I'll admit it; I've felt like I didn't matter. I've felt like my opinion, wants or needs didn't matter. And after years of feeling this way, I stopped sharing the details. But this is the wrong approach to building a relationship. How do I know this wrong? Because it didn't work; I'm divorced now. So obviously, everything wasn't going well in my relationship. Some relationships fail because of really big things; one partner commits some great wrong to the other - like adultery or abuse. But I think most relationships fail because of the little things. And the real tragedy is not that there are problems, but that the little details which become big problems later are not shared, discussed, and resolved. One partner shouldn't have to guess what the other partner is thinking. So take a moment and think about your failed relationship. Why did your relationship end? Was it due to verbal abuse or neglecting to communicate the importance of the relationship to your happiness? Maybe there was adultery; but if there was, I can almost guarantee there was also lying about the little details. Both partners should be sharing every detail of everything with the other partner. Because if you're putting all of your time and energy and effort into sharing every detail - big and small - then you have nothing for outside of the relationship.

I really have learned the importance of sharing the little details -- on the giving and receiving sides. Open and honest communication is essential to building a relationship. And details matter. Every detail matters. Or it should matter. My man is important to me, and so every detail of what happens during the course of his day matters to me. And every detail of what is going on with me matters to him. Every detail of how we feel about our past, present, and future matters. And when we share the little details, we learn what is important to the other and what the other needs. Our children are important, and so every detail of what they are doing matters. Of course, sometimes, the children act like they wish I didn't care so much, but deep down, it matters. My co-workers and having an enjoyable work climate matter to me, and so I care about the details of my job. So, do I focus on details? Certainly, because sharing the little details make a positive impact on the quality of my relationships. Sharing the details of my life, I hope, is making a positive impact on your life. And this is why I decided to write this book. I'm sure I sound a little narcissistic writing an entire book about myself and my life. But maybe, just maybe the details of my life will reflect the details in your life, and you'll find your way to healing, renewal, and hope for a better tomorrow. I'm praying for you in full confidence that you'll begin to see healing take place in the little details of your daily life and that you'll have hope for a full divorce recovery. God bless you today, tomorrow, and always.

Thursday, March 31, 2011

When was the last time you played a game of catch? It has been raining here in Georgia for the last four days, and I am itching to get back outside and play. When the temperature is just right, tossing the football is a great thing to do. My children love to throw the ball. And quite often my man and I will go outside and throw the football around. We have so much fun. I have a business mentor who explained the concept of leadership in terms of playing ball. She would say, you toss the ball to the person you are mentoring. Sometimes you throw the ball, but the other person doesn't throw the ball back. So then you toss the ball to him/her again. And then you wait to see if the ball comes back to you. You can't force anyone to play ball with you. And some people just don't want to play ball. And if someone doesn't want to play ball with you, you just have to accept it and move on. Throw the ball to someone else, and see what happens. For years, I've always thought of this concept within the context of leadership and the workplace. But as I was sitting here relaxing for a few minutes after cleaning the kitchen after supper, waiting for the dryer to stop, and thinking I sure wish we could have played catch for a few minutes tonight, and maybe the weather will be great this weekend so we can play catch some, I realized romantic relationships are kind of like playing catch too.

And in good relationships, the ball goes back and forth, back and forth, back and forth, forever. Not only that the person throwing the ball puts just the right spin on it and sends it at just the right velocity and throws it in just the right direction to make it easy for the other person to catch the ball. And the other person gets it, and immediately responds by returning the ball in the same manner it was thrown. Luke 6:38 states *"Give, and you will receive. Your gift will return to you in full--pressed down, shaken together to make room for more, running over, and poured into your lap. The amount you give will determine the amount you get back."* And this is the way it should be in a relationship; good deeds, kindness, love, respect, and so on, should be reciprocated. Freely. Each action is a gift to the other person. Think of a small gesture someone, anyone, did for you recently. What did they do? Did they open the door for you? Did they take you to supper? Did they smile at you with tender affection? These are all gifts being given to you. And when you do little things for someone else you are giving them a gift. But this doesn't mean we should be keeping a score or making a list of who has done the most. It's not really a gift if one has that attitude. Because if you keep giving, eventually you'll receive gifts in return in equal proportion to what you have given. Maybe not right away. And maybe not as you expect to receive it. Did you give a lot and pour a lot into your past relationship? You did. I know you did. You gave, and ultimately, your partner didn't give back. I know this, because your relationship with that person failed.

Well, guess what? You can throw the ball, but the other person chooses to throw it back. You can throw the ball, and the other person can choose to take the ball and leave, and then you no longer have the ball or the relationship. And when that happens, you just have to accept it and move on. But that doesn't mean you'll never play ball again. You'll get another chance. Someone will come along who wants to play ball with you. So don't lose your desire to play ball. If you have faith, and you believe that God's promises are true, what you give you will receive. If you love, you will be loved in return.

Monday, April 11, 2011

This week I splurged on myself, and I mean, I really treated myself. No, I didn't buy a new pair of shoes. I bought a new car, and not just any car, but the car of my dreams, the car of a lot of people's dreams. I love classic American sports cars. Actually I love just about any kind of sports car – American, Italian, German, whatever country of origin as long as the car is sleek, fast, and pretty. I love how they look. I love how they sound. I love how they sit low on the ground and hug the curves of a mountain road. When I was in graduate school, I put a big poster of a Pontiac Trans Am on the wall over my desk. I promised myself that I would buy that car when I graduated. Each night while I was working late into the night, and when I'd start to get tired, I would look up and see that car, and I would keep on

working. A dream of owning a sports car was my
motivation. Everybody has to have something to motivate
them to work harder, work longer, and to keep on going.
What motivates you? Do you dream of owning a sports
car? Or maybe you dream of buying your first house? Or
maybe you want to go on a vacation like no other in some
secluded spot on white sand beaches and crystal blue
waters?

When I finished my Master's Degree, I bought that car.
And I loved driving it. I loved taking the T-tops off and
cruising down Hwy 316 between Atlanta and Athens. But I
didn't own it for long. My younger brother was stationed
overseas, and he needed our help to take over his Altima
car payment. So I sold my Trans Am and starting driving
his car. After all, family members were fussing at me about
putting the baby seat in the backseat of a sports car. So
another baby came and that was the end of that. No more
sports car -- just practical sedans and mini-vans. Last time I
bought a car, in 2008, I had driven my Mazda Protégé
forever, and it was time for something new. The kids were
older, no more car seats and strollers, and I thought maybe
now it's time. I test drove a few, but I couldn't make up my
mind. Even the sales guy said, you don't need that sports
car, be practical. It is kind of ironic that a sales guy would
talk someone out of buying a more expensive car for a less
expensive car, but that's the way it was. And I didn't have
someone encouraging me to buy a car that made me happy.
And so I settled for the practical car – a car identical to the
old car I had – even the same color – just only five years
newer. A week later I thought to myself, that was so stupid,
you can't even tell you bought a new car, why didn't you at
least buy a different color. It looked exactly the same. Even
though it was a really nice car, and I should have been
thankful that I had a car to drive at all, I wasn't happy with
my decision. And really, I should have been happy, because
I've had times in my life where I didn't have a car to drive

at all, and I walked to work, to school, and the daycare center. Thankfully, all of those places were just a few blocks from each other. But walking as my main mode of transportation was many years ago; and now, I spend quite a bit of time each day driving. And so, I'm very excited to drive to work this morning. And I'm even more excited to have someone special in my life who reminds me to do what makes me happy. When I was trying to decide if I should or shouldn't buy a new car, my man said something like this, "You're 41 years old; you're a professional who has worked very hard, a doctor even; and you've put up with a lot in your lifetime, and it's about time. It's your time, Allison, buy a car which gives you pleasure."

But I was scared. When the dealership called to say it just rolled off the truck from the factory, and I could come see it, I was so excited. But the closer I got to the dealership, the more scared I got. I almost turned around three times. My man had to give me a pep talk to just go see it. I have a hard time believing that I really deserve to have my dreams. But he just talked to me all the way there, and then once I saw it, I knew it was mine. And so I bought it. The seats were still wrapped in plastic, and I only could only drive it in the parking lot, because it hadn't really been made street ready. The salesman parked it behind the custom body work shop, so none of the other salesmen could sell my car to anyone else. I love my Camaro. I had to go back the next day to pick it up, so they could check all the systems to be sure the car was just as it was supposed to be. And now I'm in love. And this doesn't have anything to do with a man. I'm in love with my car.

I love how the bright Victory Red paint explodes in the sunlight just after my man washed the yellow pollen off for me. My Camaro even has the retro black stripes and all of the true classic muscle car detailing inside and out. I love how the engine roars to life like the car has been waiting in anticipation for me to turn the key. I love putting the top down with the wind whipping my hair as I rev around the curve in the road. I love hearing "that's a beautiful car" when I stop at a red light.

One day I drove through Popeye's Fried Chicken, and the clerk at the window commented how she loved my car and that it was her dream to have a car like mine. It's my dream too. I worked hard, I went back to college and finished my doctorate, and I finally was able to by my dream car. She said she had been dreaming about going back to nursing school. She should. If I can be a working single Mom and finish my doctorate, why can't you go to medical school and become a medical doctor? Go all the way with your education. And then, you too can buy the car of your dreams. What else do you dream about?

I'm having a lot of fun in my post-divorce life. It's like I was forced into a mid-life crisis I didn't even want to have. I've been waiting a long time to have this kind of fun. It's time for you to have fun, too. And maybe you haven't been wishing for a sports car, but there's something else you really want. It's time for you to stop telling yourself you can't have it or you don't deserve it or you can just do it later. It's time for you to start figuring out how to fulfill your fantasies and make your life the life you want to have. Your old life is gone; your new life has begun. You're in the process of moving forward into your new life and putting the past behind you. There are going to be days where you feel stuck between making the decision using the rationale of your old life and stepping out in faith to make your new life what you really want it to be. But one day, it's going to happen; you're going to realize at any moment, you've finally made it through, and you'll be smiling. I found the courage to buy the car of my dreams. Now I just need to get the courage to go get everything else I want in life.

Tuesday, April 12, 2011

The other thing I really want is to have a vacation with a companion where I actually enjoy every moment. I've taken lots of vacations over the years. Little weekend getaways with a girlfriend. Beach trips with the kids. Vacations to visit family members who live in other states. Trips to Disney World. Even a cruise or two. But this past weekend, I had a mini-vacation in the Blue Ridge Mountains which surpassed them all. Because on this trip, I felt something I'd never felt before. Contentment. I had to look up the meaning of contentment when I got back to my computer in my office to know how to describe what I felt to you. From the moment we loaded the vehicle and pulled out of the driveway to the moment we unloaded the vehicle back at home, I was happy. There was not one thing I would have changed or wanted to have done differently. My soul was at rest. I was totally at ease. For the first time in my life, I actually felt renewed in my spirit after a vacation rather than exhausted and more stressed. Instead of saying "thank God I get to sleep in my own bed tonight and to be back in my regular routine" I said, "I wish we could leave for vacation again tomorrow."

I finally learned what vacations are supposed to be like and how vacations should be restful, relaxing, and renewing. Think about some of your past vacations. Did you enjoy them? Really enjoy them? Or were you annoyed at this little thing or that little thing your travelling companion did or did not do? Were you frustrated because you spent a lot of money to only find your accommodations or the food or the entertainment unsatisfactory? Did you plan an itinerary which put you at break neck speed to accomplish more activities in a day or week than physically possible? And even if everything went right on your vacation, so much so that you should have had a good time, but inside it just wasn't right and you weren't enjoying yourself, and you didn't know why? I was reading a sermon by Reverend Carl Haak (Yes, I'm always reading something) titled the "The Grace of Contentment" and he said that contentment is not temperament; contentment is a gift from God. And not only that, I discovered when we are discontented with our spouse or partner; we are actually discontented with God. You can't plan or choose to be contented. And I so know this, because I have always tried to be contented, but just didn't feel that way for most of my life. Contentment is an inward reflection of the gratitude you have for what God has given you, not material possessions per se, but more like recognizing that your mate is a gift from God.

While having a sandwich at a little shop in the town of Blue Ridge, at the table next to us, was a man and his wife, and both of them ate their entire meal without saying a word to each other, without looking at each other, without smiling, as if they were two strangers who happened to be seated at

188

the same table, both of them giving their full attention to their cell phones for over an hour without interruption. At our table, we were laughing and talking and holding hands and telling stories, full of gratitude to be in each other's company on a beautiful, sunny day, on vacation in the mountains, eating a sandwich and drinking a diet coke. My man and I are friends, and we actually enjoy each other's company. Maybe that other couple was content with their life together, but I don't believe so. As I watched the two of them, I thought how sad that each of them found whatever was happening on that little 2x4 inch screen more interesting than their mate. And I don't ever want to be that way; I don't ever want anything to be more important or more interesting to me than my mate. Because to me, I believe if something or someone is more important than your mate, then you have a problem in your relationship. My man sometimes teases me, because I hardly ever watch TV, and we have only once finished watching an entire movie. Why? Because there are so much more interesting things happening in real life with our children, or his story about an event from his day, or my story about something I read. And when we are together, we pay attention to each other. When I am with my children, I pay attention to them. This weekend, we were unplugged at the mountains. We played board games with the kids. We went for walks in the woods. We built a fire in the fireplace, roasted marshmallows, and just talked late into the night. We slept late. We rocked on the porch watching the sun rise over the neighboring mountaintop. We hiked on a hidden trail to find the swinging bring over the Toccoa River which was really and truly one of the prettiest places I have ever seen on this earth. No stress. No whining. No complaining. Just peace and joy and happiness. His hand in mine and my hand in his. Even the kids were happy, so if you're a parent, then you know it must be really good if even the kids aren't fussing with each other. Laughter and silly jokes. Quiet when quiet was needed. The right words when talking was wanted. Affectionate gestures expressing sincere emotions. No five star restaurants, but the best food one can get in a little country Mom and Pop place in a trailer on the side of road.

This weekend I received a glimpse of the life I have always dreamed of having, and I know it sounds too romantic to be true, but it is true. And if the next vacation will be better than this last vacation just as tomorrow is always better than today, then I'm ready to pack my bags and go. But the best part of this vacation was coming home with each other and knowing more is coming, more healing, more renewal, and more hope. Are you ready to become contented? Because your new life, the life you've always dreamed of living, is coming soon. Please write me the moment you feel true contentment; I'd really like to hear about how you are doing on your journey. You'll know it when you feel it. I just felt it. It was the moment I was struggling to find a place to plant my feet to climb up the steep mountain path when I glanced up and his hand was there outstretched waiting to help me. Just as God's hand is always there; my man's hand was there. Rev. Haak also said "contentment is a gracious work in the heart. It is a giving all things over to the hand of God. It is submitting to the hand of the Lord and believing that what He does He does well." I submit my life to the hand of God, and I rest contented in His perfect will, and I am grateful for the gift of the partner He has given me and for the new life He has given me, has given us. I'm praying God will do a gracious work in your heart, that you'll find contentment – either on vacation or at home, alone or with a special someone.

Springtime is one of my most favorite times of the year. It is the time of renewal. All of the trees which lost their leaves in the fall and were exposed to the winter elements without protection begin leafing out again. And it happens so quickly. One week the branches are bare. The second week there are tiny buds that you can barely see them. The third week the tree looks a different color from a distance because the buds are bigger, but still no leaves. And then almost like it happened overnight, the tree is bursting green. The mountainside is completely changed -- from gray and brown and dreary -- to bright and green and new. Just like your life will be if you are patient and give yourself some time. Your renewal will happen little bit by little bit, and one day you'll be completely restored. Some trees put on blossoms. Like the Dogwood. All over North Georgia, the dogwood trees are displaying their message of healing, renewal, and hope in their blossoms. Have you ever stopped to notice the dogwood blossom? Do you know it only has four petals and is in the shape of a cross?

The dogwood blooms just before Easter to remind us of Christ. Dogwood blossoms are tinged with drops of red to remind us how we are healed through the blood of Christ. Dogwood blossoms are a message for you now that your healing is coming. Other trees bear fruit. Like the apple. Apple trees in North Georgia are just now putting on their leaves and their blossoms, but the fruit won't arrive until the autumn harvest. The apple tree reminds us to be patient and to wait for good things to come. The apple tree reminds of to hope in the future. And just like the apple tree, your life will bear fruit. Do you still feel like you're in the winter of your depression over your situation? Maybe you don't believe that good things are coming. Hebrews 11:1 states that "faith is being sure of what we hope for and certain of what we do not see". Before your healing over your failed relationship will occur, before your dreams of your new life will come to be, you must believe. You must believe that you will have a good life long before you see or experience your good life. Just as you must believe when walking through that wintry wood that the trees will leaf and bloom and bear fruit again, you must believe in yourself.

It's a beautiful, sunny, spring day; perfect for going outside and listening to a message from nature. Let's go for a walk today. Put the past behind you and put your hope in the days that are coming. I have moments when my faith is shaky. When something happens, like when someone says something to me that upsets me, or when I have to consult my lawyer for advice when I really wish legal issues were behind me, or when the change from an upside-down life is taking too long to right itself again, I forget that God already has a plan of healing and renewal for me. I don't need to worry; I just need to trust. I need to have faith. I need to believe. And seeing the leaves and blossoms on the trees in the woods reminds me that things will be okay. Everything really will be okay. I pray that when we forget that our healing, our renewal, and our hope will be truly great and miraculous, some little something, like a dogwood blossom, will remind us to hold on to God's promise. Good things are coming.

Tuesday, April 19, 2011

It was a glorious 89 degrees in North Georgia today, and I just had to get in the backyard after work and see to my flowers. The jasmine has exploded tiny yellow blossoms over the arbor. The knock-out roses are a knock-out of reds and dark pinks. In nearly every yard, azaleas are ablaze in various colors. A sure sign that you are looking at a Southern garden is to see bright pink azalea blossoms in great masses under the shade of an old oak tree. But my favorite has to be the iris in purple and yellow. I have iris in several flower beds around my yard, and the original iris was a transplant from my grandmother's garden back in Louisiana. I have dug up and moved these irises with every house. Not only does the iris remind me of my grandmother; the iris is the fleur-de-lis which is a symbol of my Louisiana heritage, and another reminder of the glory of Christ. The fleur-de-lis is the French version of the cross. Nature will remind you of the most important things in life. But what the iris reminds me the most is the importance of sharing in the joy. I was happy to see the iris in bloom, so I texted a photo of the iris standing proudly atop its stalk to my man, and he replied that it made him happy just to see it, and he thanked me for sharing. He shared in my joy, and then my joy was multiplied. I felt even more joyful.

Do you have friends or family members who share in your joy? When you are happy about something, are they happy just because you are happy? Or do other people bring you down? In other words, when you are happy about something, they reply with negativity, so then you lose your joy? You are rebuilding your life, and it is important to your happiness that you surround yourself with friends and family who will share in your joy; people who make you feel better about yourself, not worse. Joy should be contagious. Sharing your joy over a flower, or anything else for that matter, should make you happy. One of the main reasons I love my flower garden is so many of my plants are there because a friend or family member shared with me. The iris and the vinca came from my grandmother's garden. The daylilies were gifts from the gardens of Tammy and Debbie and my mother. The cannas came from Tammy as well. The angel trumpets came from Ray and Syd. The Wisconsin spruce came from my great uncle and his wife. The hostas and phlox and black-eyed Susans were dug up and transplanted from the yards of co-workers. And many of the other flowers, trees, and shrubs were planted in honor of a special occasion, and so when I look at them, the joy of that event springs to my mind. But do you know what is even more wonderful than receiving all of these gifts which grow and prosper in my yard? That I can share the joy that these bring to me.

Every three years, bulbous plants, like daylilies, iris, cannas must be divided to thrive. If you don't dig some of them up and move them to another location, then they cease to bloom. And no blooms means no joy at seeing the blooms. So it is essential for a gardener to share in order to have a beautiful garden. It is essential for you to share your joy in order to have more joy. If you are without joy today, I pray that you will find someone who has a little joy to share with you. Grab hold of it. Share in their joy; smile because they are smiling. Be thankful for the blessings you see unfolding in their life instead of envious or raining negativity on their parade. If you share in their joy, I promise, joy will multiply in your life, and you too will find yourself standing outside on a beautiful day smiling at the beauty of a single bloom. And then one day soon after that, you too will find yourself smiling with gratitude at the abundance of joy and blessings you've received in your new life. Until that day, I'll keep praying for your healing, your renewal, and your hope. And if you ever stop by my garden, bring a shovel and an empty pail, and I'll share some flowers with you for your garden.

Many people don't like raising rosebushes, because they can be so labor intensive. But I don't mind working hard. And for me, looking after my roses is therapeutic. Pruning my rosebushes gives me a kind of Zen-like calm; compare it to trimming a Bonsai tree or raking grains of sand just right in a little tray. Pruning roses is necessary to the health and vitality of the bush. Gardeners call it deadheading. And as a side note, I really don't consider myself a gardener. The flowers that do best in my garden are the ones which can survive through periods of neglect when I'm too busy to work in the yard. But I do manage to find the time to tend to my roses at least once a week, mainly because I enjoy the work. When the rose bloom is spent, that means it has fully opened and started to drop its petals and wither, the gardener must cut it off the branch. If the gardener doesn't do this, the rosebush will not have the energy to produce more blooms. So as strange as it may sound, if you don't cut your roses, you won't have more roses.

Yesterday I was pruning my rosebushes and this parable of the vine and the branches came to my mind. Of course, I had to go look it up, but I remembered the essence of the parable, because years and years ago, I coached a middle school drama group on Wednesday evenings, and we did a little skit based on this parable. In John 15:1-2, *"I am the true vine, and my Father is the gardener. He cuts off every branch in me that bears no fruit, while every branch that does bear fruit he prunes so that it will be even more fruitful."* Ouch! This means that no matter what, we are going to get pruned. So you and I have both had disappointments and painful experiences in our lives. We've been bruised and broken. But that is something different than what this scripture is talking about. The ultimate goal is for the vine or the rosebush to produce a better harvest – more good fruit – an abundance of roses. The ultimate goal for our lives is to live abundantly with mercy and grace and goodness, and when we do, then we produce a better harvest – more good fruit (kindness, love, generosity, compassion, patience, etc, etc, etc). That means we must be pruned. There are parts of our lives which are not bearing fruit. Can you identify them? What about your failed relationship? Was it bearing fruit – was your past relationship creating good for yourself and for others? That's tough to think about.

Maybe, and I don't know if this is really true, but maybe that person was cut out of your life, because they weren't good for you, for your life. Just maybe, as painful as it was to go through the separation and divorce, maybe it was necessary for you to grow into the person you are supposed to be. I think that if we are really honest with ourselves we can look back at our old life and see the branches that needed to be pruned -- the parts of our life that were not good. But this scripture also says that some branches bear fruit, and those get pruned so that they bear even more fruit. There are parts of our lives which are bearing fruit. Can you identify them? What are the areas of your life which are good? And can't the good get even better? Isn't this really what hope in the future is? We don't want good; we want great! If we are truly honest with ourselves, we don't want a good marriage; we want a phenomenal, better than we can imagine, a storybook romance, happily ever after, a partner who is our best friend, constantly compatible companion, amazing lover, and more. So maybe you didn't want your relationship to end. Pruning is painful at the moment of being cut and during the time of healing.

I didn't want my marriage to end. And the moment the marriage ended was extremely painful and the months of healing post-divorce were too. But I have the courage to admit that my life is better than it was before. And I am really thankful that God has a plan for my life and that He prunes me, as painful as the process is sometimes, to be the woman I should be. Please don't think I'm saying divorce is the best path for a better life; because I really do believe that divorce is the wrong choice. It is so much better if we are willing to be pruned to become the mate we need to be to the mate we already have been blessed to have. But many of us in the world today are divorced; sometimes due to our own actions and mistakes; sometimes due to the choice of our partner to have a different life. Either way, single or married, married to our first spouse or divorced or remarried, we are continually being shaped over the course of our lifetime to be the kind of person who bears good fruit – the kind of person who makes a difference in the lives of others – the kind of person who is a blessing to those who are fortunate to know him/her. Right now, your wounds may be fresh and hurting, but your harvest is coming. You will blossom and grow and bear good fruit. I'm right here, in the same garden of life, growing, being pruned, and growing some more, right along with you. I'm praying for you. I'm praying for your healing *(Yes, your wounds will heal in time)*, your renewal *(Yes, you too will bear more fruit than you had before)*, and your hope *(Yes, you too will have your heart's desire)*. And just as my rosebushes have bounced back after the grueling winter that nearly killed them, you too will bounce back. And you will be a more beautiful person after the pruning. Pain is part of the growing process.

Thursday, April 21, 2011

I love, love, love my new car! Not only is it bringing me pleasure to drive my rally sport bright red coupe with a ragtop and black stripes, I absolutely love seeing other people get happy seeing me drive it! Yesterday when parking my car on the way to get a mammogram *(Ladies, please get your mammogram on a regular basis. The new digital machines don't squish your girls that badly. Your health is very important.)* I noticed a pharmaceutical rep watching me put the top up. As I stepped out of the car, he said "excuse me, but when did they come out with a convertible Camaro? That's a beautiful car!" And then when I pulled into my driveway, several of the neighborhood kids on their bicycles were waiting for me just to ask to look at my car. And this afternoon when I

197

drove through McDonald's, the guy taking the money, just started beaming when I pulled around, and he was so excited talking about my car, he even said, "Seeing your car has made my day. I'm in such a good mood now!" I could go on and on with examples of people who stop and stare, or whom I catch taking photos with their cell phones of my car, or who roll down their windows to shout "That's a sweet ride!"

People just get so excited seeing my car, like we are all still kids at heart standing in the Toys R Us aisle with our mouths gaping open and our eyes wide as saucers just staring at the best toy ever and dreaming we could actually get it. I love seeing the excitement in their eyes, and the smiles on their faces. I'm having fun, because I bought the car of my dreams, my big girl toy; I get excited every time I get behind the wheel, and I get like triple excited when it's super sunny afternoon and I'm pushing the button for the top to come down. I'm having fun, because I get the added bonus of seeing other people get excited at seeing me driving this beautiful car. What gets you excited? What excites you? If you were to stop what you are doing, stop reading this book at this moment, and do something that makes you excited about life, what would you do? Why don't you just go do it, and come back and finish reading this book later? There's really no words I could write here that would be more valuable to your happiness than you doing something that brings you joy. Unless, of course, you get really excited every time you turn the page! That gets me excited just thinking that you could actually be having fun reading my book! Now, you have put me in a good mood! Thank you for buying my book! I really do hope these words help you find happiness. Life is good, really good! John 10:10 explains that Jesus said *"I came to give you life more abundantly."* God wants you to have good things in abundance.

Now really, our focus is not on material possessions. I love my car, but it is just a toy. And God has blessed me with a good job which I enjoy which has enabled me to pay for my car. But the abundance has more to do with the intangible things of your heart and soul rather than the tangible things like cars or whatever your favorite toy is. So I do have an abundant life, not because I drive a wonderful car, but because I have a wonderful man in my life; he is my best friend, he makes me laugh, he is fun to be around, he truly cares about my happiness, he shares in my joy. Who knows? Maybe one day I'll marry him; but if not, we'll always be friends. And I have an abundant life, because I have wonderful children with whom I enjoy playing and for whom I enjoy nurturing. And I have an abundant life, because I have wonderful parents and friends who just make my life better because they are in it. The people in my life are the blessing in my life; they are my abundant life, and I have hope in my future, because I know I they will be a part of my future. I love seeing smiles on faces today, and I look forward to seeing smiles on faces tomorrow. I really am happy! And I want you to be happy too! Tonight, I'm praying for your healing, your renewal, your hope, and your happiness, and I'm looking forward to seeing the smile on your face when you receive your abundant life. Why do you have an abundant life? Who or what brings you joy?

Thursday, April 28, 2011

We had horrific storms in North Georgia last night which was making the internet go in and out. I couldn't do any work. I couldn't write to you. I couldn't do much of anything which required electricity. So I just decided to enjoy the beautiful storm and relax. Are you wondering why is she calling this a beautiful storm? A storm is nearly always a negative metaphor for the problems we experience in life. And I'm sure somewhere in North Georgia, someone experienced the negative side effects of the storm, and so they won't agree with me that it was beautiful. But I really enjoyed the storm last night. I am not afraid of a thunderstorm. I grew up with thunderstorms in the country in Louisiana. I remember working jigsaw puzzles with my grandparents by the light of a kerosene lamp listening to the thunderclap in the distance and the pounding rain on the rooftop. Sometimes I would sit for hours with my grandmother on the screened porch and watch the rain illuminated by an occasional pop of lightning. Sometimes I would fall asleep in the chaise on the porch listening to the rain and the rumble. So, I guess you could say, I have a fondness for thunderstorms.

Do you like to listen to the rain? Or are you afraid of a thunderstorm? Louisa May Alcott said *"I am not afraid of storms for I am learning how to sail my ship."* And if a storm is a negative metaphor for the problems we've experienced in our past life, through the conflict of our failed relationships, hopefully we have learned how to sail rather than sink. Finding happiness in the moment is one way I've learned to sail successfully through the storms of life. And yes, sometimes, it's been a rough haul, and I've gotten tangled up in the rigging, and my boat has taken on a little water. But I learned to use a pail to scoop out the excess water. I learned to solve problems a little bit at a time by concentrating on what I can do instead of worrying about what I can't do. And one scoop of water after another scoop of water will eventually remove all of the water with threatens to sink your boat. I've learned to appreciate the storm and to learn from the storm. Last night, my man and I sat on the screened porch at his house listening to the thunderstorms in the distance waiting for the rains to come. The younger children played under the dining room table with their Breyer horses, and the teenagers were all hanging

out upstairs listening to music and doing homework.
Together we sat watching the lightning strike above the
mountains northwest of us. At first, there was an occasional
strike. And then several bolts of lightning almost in the
same spot over and over again. The air was unusually warm
and still before the rain came. But it was still so pleasant. In
a short period of time there was a multitude of lightning
strikes at various intervals all across the Blue Ridge
Mountains.

Never in my life have I ever seen that much lightning. It
really was a beautiful storm. I was in awe and quiet
reverence at the firework display God was sharing with us.
The lightning danced from cloud to mountaintop; the
myriad lightning bolts were like a group of line dancers
moving quickly here and there across the dance floor. Of
course, the lightning was so far away in the distance, it was
easy to feel safe and protected from the storm. But the
storm was moving our direction. I was not afraid of the
torrential rains which poured down upon us a short time
later. I was not afraid of the tornado warning on the
emergency weather radio which broadcast how the storm
was moving from the mountains in the distance to our
mountain. Very soon, within just a few hours, the entire
storm passed over us and was gone. Very soon, the storms
of your life will pass over you and be gone. Are you afraid
that the storm won't end? But the storm always ends; it
doesn't last forever. Today, the sun shone brightly; so
brightly it was if last night's storm never was. One day, in
the very near future, sooner than you think, your new life is
going to be so good, so wonderful, so full of happiness and
love, it will be as if your past life never was. I am thankful
for the thunderstorm last night which reminded me of God's
presence in my life. I am thankful for the sunny skies today
which reminded me that my life can only get better. The
healing begins during the storm and continues every day

for the rest of your life. Without the storm, there would be no need for renewal. And without renewal, how will you learn that miracles are real? Facing the storm strengthens your hope. We can wish away the storms, but we shouldn't. I do not regret my stormy past. Have no regrets. Live each day realizing the happiness in the moment. Appreciate life just as it comes. I will continue to pray for you, for your healing, for your renewal, and for you to have hope for a wonderful future after the storm passes.

Monday, May 2, 2011

Saturday we drove up to North Carolina to go to the mountains for the day, and we were invited to do a little trout fishing. And yes, we had our fishing poles sticking out the back of the Lexus all the way there and back. You know you are comfortable with who you are as a person when you can ride around with fishing poles. I'm sure some of you are reading this and thinking, "I couldn't do that". And maybe a couple of people are saying "I've done that before", or "maybe I should go fishing; it's been awhile" or "where do you buy fishing poles anyway?" Fishing, most of the time, is an exercise in patience. But these trout were an exercise in frustration. We actually could see the speckled trout and the bait on the hook an inch in front of their mouth, and they wouldn't bite. For over two hours, we had a battle of wills with the trout. No matter what bait or tackle we used, they did not care. The kids really, really, wanted to catch a fish. Another guy who was fishing in the same place gave up his pole and just caught one with his bare hands. For the first time ever, and mind you I don't go fishing very often, I went home without any fish. But that's okay; I still have the nearly 5 pound catfish I caught last summer in the freezer waiting for the next fish fry with friends. Have you ever been fishing? When was the last time you went fishing? When you were a kid? Oh, I have many great memories of going fishing on the houseboat on the Bayou D'Arbonne in north Louisiana with my grandparents, parents, aunts, uncles, brothers, and cousins. As kids, we played more than we were allowed to fish. But I could just sit there forever watching that little red and white round plastic bobber bob on the water waiting for a bite. My grandparents had a pond in their yard, and one year, Granddaddy decided to build a little pier to the middle of the pond. He had the intention to put a gazebo out there, but that never happened, so it was a little pier to nowhere on a little tiny pond with more turtles than fish. But we'd take a stool out there with our little fishing poles and pieces of bread or bacon and see if we could catch something. All the fish were too little to do anything but catch and release. Fishing on the pond sure was fun. And oh, if it happened to be a summer day where my grandfather just cut a watermelon in half, that was near about close to heaven.

As I got older, and as my grandfather got older, I enjoyed watching him sit on the stool and fish. Knowing that there wouldn't be any fish worth keeping, he fished anyway. Just for the enjoyment of watching and waiting for the fish to bite. You can either be frustrated that you aren't getting what you want, or you can just enjoy waiting for something to happen, anything to happen, nothing to happen. But when you try to make something happen, it's no good. I think a lot of couples who end up divorced tried to make something happen, when deep down they probably knew it wasn't going to happen. When you look back on your failed relationship, did you know? Did you get married because the other person wanted to and you sacrificed your single life for him/her? Did you get married because you were afraid to not be married? Did you get married because that's what people are supposed to do? Did you have doubts that maybe this person I'm marrying is not the one for me, but I just can't back out, maybe it will get better in time? There are lots of reasons why people get married, and when it's truly the right decision, the vows made on your wedding day are not just words that people say. Maybe you said them because your heart already felt all of those promises. Maybe you said them because you knew you had to, but you really didn't mean them. I don't know what was in your heart when you got married. I know what was in my heart, and I also know that I was really scared.

The first time I got married, I was too young to know what love and commitment really were, but I was willing to learn as I life went on and to honor my promises. The second time I got married, I cried on my wedding day, not tears of joy, but out of fear. I didn't feel like everything was going to be okay. And with the confidence I have now about my life and how my heart feels when I feel like everything will be okay, now I know the difference. And I knew looking at those trout swimming idly in that cold North Carolina mountain stream; I wasn't going to catch one. So I had a choice, I could enjoy the beautiful afternoon, laugh with the kids, study the speckled pattern on one trout compared to another, count them, look at tadpoles, or I could get mad about not getting my way. For a brief moment, I wanted to just reach in to the stream, grab a trout, and cram the hook into its mouth. But then I laughed at myself. You can't force a fish to bite your hook, and thinking even for a moment that I could was really funny. So instead I chose joy. I chose to be happy. And I was really happy. I had a really good time Saturday afternoon not catching any fish. And I am really happy with my life as it is now. I never know exactly what will happen each day or who will do what or even what I will do, but am enjoying watching and waiting to see what will happen. Everything will be okay in my life, so I don't have to try so hard to make anything happen, I just enjoy whatever happens. I'm finally free to love, to be myself, to live life to the fullest, to make decisions without worrying about what other people think is the right or wrong thing to do, to be happy whatever the day brings. So what if I didn't catch any fish, let's go get ice cream? Enjoy your life just as it is, just as it comes, and in time, you will find healing, renewal, and hope. That is my prayer for you each and every day.

Tuesday, May 3, 2011

I have always liked my name. I was named after my maternal grandmother, sort of. My mother made her first name a little longer and her middle name a little shorter and derived at Allison Joy. Tonight I am puppy sitting the most spoiled, pampered, little princess you can imagine. She has to have her blankie, her stuffed animal, her special bowls, her freshly boiled chicken breast, her organic yogurt, her bed, and more. Earlier this evening as my mother was packing up all her playpen and essentials, she tells her in a little squeaky voice "you're going to have fun with Auntie Allison" like I'm somehow related to the little fuzzy ball of fluff. Her name is Alice. And every time I see her I just have to say the line from the Johnny Depp version of the "Alice in Wonderland" film in that delightful British voice "Are you the right Alice? You don't look like Alice. Are you sure you're the right Alice?" Yes, my mother named her Yorkie after her mother, and I'm named after her mother as well. So this means my mother's dog and I basically have the same name. And my grandmother has the honor of having her firstborn granddaughter and a dog named after her. I laugh inside my head every time I think about it. Speaking of thinking in your head, have you ever wondered: Why do dogs have to turn around several times before they lay down? Why do the horses roll in the dirt immediately after you bathe them? Why do cats think they are doing you a favor by letting you pet them? Why do hamsters only run in the wheel in the middle of the night?

Of course, there are obvious animal instinctual behaviors which answer all those questions. Even so, sometimes it makes no sense why things are the way they are. You ask the question, and even though the answer apparent is logical, you still wonder why it is the way that is. Sometimes you see something that looks great, like an awesome stiletto heel, and so you just have to buy these gorgeous shoes. You wear them for the first time; and then ouch, they aren't so great after walking 26 city blocks. You loved the shoes in the store, and you loved the shoes when you first started out, but then the shoes just don't fit right. You love how the shoes look on your feet, and you're happy to be wearing them. But they hurt your feet and rub a blister. And that's when you realize that these shoes just weren't meant for your feet. I have shoes like that; I can take them for a short period of time. But I have other fantastic drop-dead sexy heels I can wear all day and walk forever in them. And like Cinderella's glass slipper, these shoes fit perfectly. I don't know why that is. And I don't know why one pair of shoes feels comfortable when you try them on in the store, but they aren't comfortable once you put them in your closet, match them to your outfit, and wear them around for awhile.

You know the saying if the shoe fits wear it? Well, if the shoe doesn't fit, take it off. Stop wearing the shoes that hurt your feet. Go buy a new pair. DSW has hundreds of diva-licious shoes. You've got to be wise enough to wear the right shoes - and shoes should look great, feel great, and make you feel great about yourself when you're wearing them. But if they look great, feel uncomfortable, and make you question your sanity, then they are not the shoes for you. I don't know how I got from puppy sitting to shoes, but here we are. I'm glad my mother's puppy will only be here for a couple of days. She's cute, but puppies just aren't really for me. Shoes, on the other hand, are definitely for me. And I'm so glad I have my fantastic Michael Kors ankle boots or my Guess leopard print heels or my oh-so-unbelievably comfortable 4 inch black Ralph Lauren strappy sandals to wear tomorrow. Which pair will I wear? Well, that all depends on the rain and the temperature in the morning. But I'm so glad I have choices. And the name I go by is my choice too. And I love my name – my first name and my middle name. But my last name, that one I'm not so sure about. And often I've been asked to take on a nickname, but I have never liked a nickname, only my real name, until now. Now my man and his children call me by an affectionate shorter version of my name, and they are the only ones with that privilege so I'm not even going to tell you what it is, because it is an ho nor for them alone. My children have always called me Mommy. However, my oldest daughter in her teen years prefers to call me Mom now. And that is an honor for them alone. And I feel very blessed and special and loved when I hear these names. Do you have a nickname? Or do you only liked to be called by your birth name? Do you like your name?

Names are very important to me, and naming one's children is of utmost importance, a task which I took very seriously. The names of my children tell the story of my life as a mother. I was a very young mother. I found out that I was going to have a son very unexpectedly. And like a gift is both unexpected and loved, he was. My son's name means "gift from God" and through his life and his life-threatening viral encephalitis and coma as an infant, God saved mine. He wasn't planned; in fact, I didn't really want to become a mother. I wanted to be a writer who travelled the world; getting married and having babies was not a part of my plan. But becoming a mother of a special needs child was a turning point in my life. I had already lost a second child, and I was so afraid. After marrying the second time, I really wanted to have another baby. The doctors warned me that it was not wise and that I was risking having another child with medical problems. Even the prenatal tests pointed to possible birth defects, but I prayed and felt assured that the baby would be healthy. And my daughter was born healthy and is extremely gifted and intelligent. Her name means "God's promises are fulfilled." And two years later, I gave birth to another daughter, and I thought to myself "I've received a gift from God, and I've learned that God's promises are real, and so now all I need is to be reminded of God's grace in my life." And so, I named her Grace. I wrote a poem about my children, and I'm a little bit afraid to share it with you. You're probably thinking, "Girl, you've written a whole book about your life story and the crazy things that have happened to you and the stupid mistakes you've made in relationships, and you've afraid to share a poem." You're right; I need to have a little more confidence in myself, and I need to be a little more open. How can I expect anyone else to accept the real me, if I don't share the real me with anyone else. I'm willing to share most anything but my poetry is sacred and special and secret between me and God somehow. My poetry hides in a special spiral bound notebook on my nightstand, but in the hopes of giving you confidence and helping you to look deeply into your soul to find yourself, I am taking a chance and sharing this with you.

Some Fruit Withers

Winter – comatose
Gray and cold
Sweet breath lose
Three weeks old

Lacking harvest bed
Sucked and squished
Blood running red
Lost – dismissed

Spring promise sing
Prayer and chance
Cut out – screaming
Child of substance

Early summer rain
Tiny and sweet
Mother in pain
No father to meet

My son died nine years ago, I lost one in between out of fear, and my daughters are really not little babies any more. Sooner than I am ready, my daughters will be charting their own course in life away from home, and I pray they will be smarter, stronger, and better women than I am. When I think of the names of my children, I am reminded of how good God is, how He loves me and sends me gifts, how He keeps His promises, and how His grace sustains me every day. So the names of my children are very important.

And my name is important to me as well. Did you notice that my middle name is Joy? And for what are we seeking - joy, right? Even my name reminds me to have joy, to be joyful, to bring joy to others. But there is one part of my name I don't like, and that's the part of it that is always changing. My first name and my middle name are mine, but my last name is always someone else's. My last name began as my biological father's name; then my last name changed when my mother married again, and I was legally adopted by the man who is the only father I have ever known. My last name changed when I got married. My last name changed back to my maiden name when I divorced. My last name changed again when I got married again. And mostly because I was tired of changing my name, I just kept that name when I divorced again. So far I have had five last names, and really none of them are mine at all.

The requirement for women to change their name to reflect their familial or marital connection is one social norm which I find extremely annoying and unfair. I really don't whine and complain very often, because I don't like whining and complaining. But men can get married and divorced as many times as they please, and they are not inconvenienced by changing their name. Part of me wishes I could just make up a last name and claim it and that name will be mine forever and ever. You know, how celebrities sometimes make up their names? A name is a big issue for divorced women - to change or not to change your name back. What did you choose to do? Many women choose to keep their married name, so that their last name matches the last name of their children. The irony for me is that I have daughters, and so they will probably have new last names, and I'll still have this one. So at that point, keeping my married name after my divorce becomes moot. But I've had this one for so long now, I've kind of adopted it as my own, and I've been addressed as such for so many years, I probably wouldn't know people were speaking to me if I had a different last name. But it does hurt my heart a little every time someone addresses me formally by my last name. Not because I wish I was still married; I've come to realize that my new life is the better life for me. But because it reminds me that my life was not a fairy tale, that I didn't have the "happily ever after - until death do you part" normal life. My past life is what it is, and I cannot control much of what happens in my life, but for what I can control, I choose joy. I choose love. I choose happiness. My prayer for you is that you will come to a place of peace where you can let what is unimportant go and live life to the fullest today. My prayer for you is that you will experience healing, find renewal, and have hope. And no matter what problems and pain your old life has created for you, God has a plan for your future, God has promised you a good life and God keeps His promises, and we all need more grace.

Monday, May 9, 2011

Tonight after I cooked supper of grilled chicken and sausage, sautéed zucchini and onions, green peas, I sat outside in the backyard. First I sat in the swing, and while I sat in the swing I felt calm and at peace and happy. The various wild birds flitted from branch to branch and from tree to tree as they composed a symphony of tweets and twirps and whistles. Off in the distance, I could hear the cows lowing at the sale barn just a few miles up the road. Now, whenever I hear cows, I think of this silly song my daughter taught us "cows, cows, cows, they make the world go round, they make a funny sound, they go moo, moo, moo, moo, moo, moo, moo, moo, moo, moo." It's probably not as funny to you since you can't hear the tune. But just imagine two hundred six graders singing "moo, moo, moo, moo" impromptu while waiting in the gym. Fun is contagious. One boy who obviously was in a really fun mood started this silly song, and moments later everyone was singing it. At least, that's how the story goes. And now the cow song has worked its way into this book. I wish I had been there to see the fun; I would have sung along. Would you have joined in? Or would you have tried to "shush" everyone?

The timer went off in the kitchen, and I had to take the cookies out of the oven. I was so enjoying watching and listening to the sunset, I went back outside to sit on the porch so I could face the sunset. And partly, that was a mistake. As darkness fell, my mood shifted. It really was a shame, because the colors of the dusky sky were immensely gorgeous with the soft grays and pinks and lavender and creamy clouds. I couldn't see the sun go down, because it was already behind the treetops, but as the sky darkened I knew the sun had disappeared for the night. The air grew chilly without the sun, and my mood saddened as well. You see, I had sat in that porch chair many a time reflecting on my life and what to do with it when my marriage started falling apart. And those feelings came back in the dim light and chill. I should have pushed them aside and found something else to do, but instead I nursed the despair and despondency and thought only of what I have lost and what was wrong in my life instead of what I have found and what is right in my life. One sad thought led to another and then a tear fell. And once a tear falls, others come. I don't know why I kept sitting there. Do you have times like that where you just kind of wallow in self-pity? Where you know you should find something better to do than feel badly about yourself and your life, but you just have lost the willpower to shake the sadness off and choose happiness?

Well, you just gotta. You gotta choose happiness. Somehow, someway, just reach down inside of yourself and find the courage and the faith to choose to be happy even when you don't feel that way. My man called, and he knew within a second of hearing my voice, that I wasn't my positive self, and so he questioned me. He said how you can say "everything will be okay, if you don't believe everything will be okay?" Or he said something like that. And I had to agree, because I do believe everything will be okay. And sometimes I want to hear someone tell me that everything will be okay. Because sometimes sitting in the dark, I'm afraid. I don't like being alone in the dark. I don't like coming home to a dark house, so if I know I'm coming home from work or a social activity late at night, I will always leave lights on. I don't like coming home to an empty house, and having the lights on, makes me feel like it's not so empty. There's a saying, "things don't happen the same way twice," and thank God. I have to believe that the things which happened to me in my past won't happen to me again. I have to believe that everything will be okay. Because I came home once two decades ago to a dark house, and I was beaten when I entered it. I came home 18 months ago to an empty house to the reality that my husband had really left me. Even though I despaired tonight and had a little pity party about the bad turns in my life, I rejoice, because that's my past. And the past is the past. I'm living a new life full of hope and happiness. My heart is still healing; if it were completely healed, I'd never have moments of sadness as I did tonight watching darkness fall over my backyard. There is no timetable for healing. You are going to have some days where you feel sad and where you doubt. And when you have those days, it will be your turn to choose. Will you put your past behind you and move forward? Will you let go of the pain or will you hold onto it? Will you believe that God will change, and has changed, your life for the better? Please keep praying for me. I will keep praying for you, for your healing, your renewal, and your hope. Everything will be okay.

Tuesday, May 10, 2011

One thing is certain, or I'd say 99.9% of the time, if you were married and your marriage failed, then someone wasn't being honest about something. I had to give the .1% to those few couples out of the thousands upon thousands of divorced couples who were totally honest with each other about every little detail of their lives, but just decided together it was the best decision for the both of them to not be married. Maybe it's romantic and insensible of me to believe, but I believe that if a couple was completely honest with each other 100% of the time, they would be able to resolve any issue and be able to find happiness together and they'd have no reason to divorce. The dictionary defines honesty as...

- the quality or fact of being honest; uprightness and fairness or truthfulness, sincerity, or frankness or
- freedom from deceit or fraud.

214

Leviticus 19:11 states *"do not steal, do not lie, do not deceive one another."* Matthew 7:12 and Luke 6:31 say *"do to others as you would have them do to you."* And we commonly refer to this as the golden rule, "treat others as you would like to be treated." Have you ever deceived someone? Did you discover through the process of your divorce that you had been deceived? Or maybe you didn't really lie, but you withheld information which caused unfair treatment to the other person? There really is never a fair settlement agreement in the event of divorce. Neither party is in their right state of mind and rationally making decisions. And when one partner divorces the other partner, they are not treating the other person the way they would want to be treated.

No one wants to be abandoned. No one wants to be lied to. No one wants to be unloved. And as much as I desire to be loved for myself, I want honesty. I want to know without any doubts that a promise is a promise, not a false promise masquerading as a real promise. I want to be treated fairly, sincerely, honestly, and forthrightly, and I am so blessed to know without any doubts that I am in a relationship with a man who values honesty as much as I do. And I know, some of you cynics out there are laughing at me, but if you knew what I knew, then you'd know that I can be totally confident. Have you ever heard the saying "you can lie to your Momma, but you can't lie to God"? In other words, God knows your heart. And your mate, should you ever be blessed enough to find one, should know your heart too. And he/she should know yours. And then, you can have real love, because it will be honest and pure. If a relationship is built on lies and fraud and selfishness, it will not last. But maybe you're not ready for a new relationship. I'm not sure if I'm ready for a committed, exclusive, it's time to get married again, relationship. And that's okay. But you and I both still need honesty. With honesty comes healing. And while you can't go back to your old life, you can look back at your old life and be honest with yourself about what happened and how you contributed to the failing of your relationship. Learn from your mistakes. And honesty is sometimes painful, and deception sometimes feels so much better, but it's not real. And you deserve real. Real love is worth it. Doing the right thing is worth it. Putting others before you is worth it. As you struggle through opening your heart to look honestly at yourself and your life, I'll keep praying for you, for your healing, your renewal, and your hope. And I honestly believe if you do the right thing, everything really will be okay.

Friday, May 13, 2011

I am, and always have been, a voracious reader. When I want to know something, I investigate every detail, research every possible definition, cause, or consequence, and read from the great philosophers and authors to discover their perspectives. And not only do I want happiness for myself, I want real happiness, I don't want to just be happy some of the time, but all of the time. And if there's a secret to finding happiness out there, I'm going to find out the secret. And you're so lucky, because I'm going to share the secret to happiness with you. Yesterday, I came across this article by Aristotle titled *Virtue, Function, and Happiness* in the book *Social and Personal Ethics*. I know, the title has grabbed your attention, because you want happiness too. I don't want to just feel a little better about my situation; I want to be better. Is that what you want? Are you going through your process of divorce recovery to just feel a little better? Or are you willing to dig a little deeper into your psyche and uncover the good and bad of your past behaviors in order to be healed from the pain of your divorce? In other words, are you willing to do what it takes to not just find out the secret to a happy life, but to implement changes in order to have a happy life?

Aristotle said *"no happy man (or woman) can become miserable, for he (or she) will never do what is hateful and mean."* Who am I to pick apart anything that Aristotle says? But this sentence speaks to me, especially since he asserts that one can be a happy person as in a constant state of being IF one will be loving and kind. So much so, Aristotle says, that person cannot become miserable. And weren't we just feeling miserable or sad? Aren't we looking at the devastation of our divorce and wondering why there are still moments when we feel depressed and burdened? So if what Aristotle says is true, then we shouldn't be miserable if our actions have been loving and kind; we should be happy. And when I reflect on that, how I've been loving and kind to others, like my family, my students, and random strangers who cross my path during the course of a normal day of business, I do feel a warm and fuzzy feeling creep into my heart and the sadness melts away. One day, when we were visiting my man's mother, who has, I guess one could call it, later stages of Alzheimer's; I'm not really sure of the actual diagnosis, but she sometimes knows who she is and who you are and sometimes she doesn't. Anyway, I noticed that always happened when she recognized his father walking into the room; her eyes sparkle with adoration, love, and respect at him. Every time. Every single time. Even the times when she can't think of how to pronounce his name, her eyes love. There is no speck of meanness or hatred, only love. I want love like that. I want happiness that transcends my circumstances.

Aristotle said that *"nobility shines out when a person bears with calmness the weight of accumulated misfortunes, not from insensibility, but from dignity and greatness of spirit."*

217

I believe Aristotle was defining nobility here, not as a reference to royalty of a king or queen, but as goodness of character. So your goodness, your kindness, the love you have for others, shines out, becomes visible to others when you remain calm and gentle during the crisis of your life. And we have had crisis in our lives. I have endured many misfortunes – death of a child, physical abuse, death of a brother, financial difficulties, divorce, and so on. And I have learned how to remain calm, to have faith that God will sustain me through the storm, to have hope in a new beginning. This hasn't come because I'm foolish, but because I have been willing to yield to the Holy Spirit, to allow God to work through me and on my behalf. As I came out of the grief of my divorce, I became determined in my spirit to be a happy person, to be kind even when I am wronged, to do the right thing, and to love with my whole heart. The closer I come to a continual state of being happy, the more mean-spirited others become; others try to steal my joy. But I refuse to be miserable. And I refuse to be unkind. I have learned the secret to happiness and that is to be kind to others, to love others the way Christ loves me, and to act with dignity. And even when the present situation presses on me so strongly I feel like I will break and just want to crumble under the pressure, I close my eyes, take a deep breath, and allow the calm to wash over me. I remember the love I have been blessed to receive and to give, and I let go of the pain. I think of the cards our children have drawn me, the most recent ones, and the ones from all of the years prior, and I hug each of our children in my imagination. And I remember how I feel when I make eye contact with my man and how the corner of his eyes crinkle when he sees my smiling eyes sparkle back at him. I am happy. And I want you to be happy as well. You deserve happiness. Misfortune doesn't make you unhappy unless you choose to react with anger and meanness. You can be happy no matter what has happened in your past life.

You too can be happy no matter what is happening in your life today. I am praying for you to accept happiness over heartache, for your healing, your renewal, and your hope.

Sunday, May 15, 2011

When your life goes through a dramatic change in circumstances, such as a death of a loved one or divorce, it is very typical to feel lost and without a purpose. I can remember, after my son died in 2002, that I couldn't even remember how old I was. I was so lost, and I wandered aimlessly through day to day tasks, and I struggled with knowing my purpose. I know several women who have also buried sons, and we share the knowledge and pain of that maternal experience. And really if you are not a parent, or you are a parent who has never lost a child, then you really cannot comprehend the magnitude of the void left in one's heart when you bury a child. And it is my prayer that you never will know.

And after divorce, you also feel a similar void. It really doesn't matter what the reason why you divorced nor does it matter what type of relationship you had with your ex-spouse. Your life changed in a moment. And if you were living your life trying to fulfill the needs of your spouse and your family, then when you lose that sense of purpose, there is a void. Selfish people don't feel the void, except maybe they miss what other people do for them, but they don't feel a loss of purpose. And I don't really know what other people feel, but I do know what I felt, and I felt lost. Especially the first few days my children went to spend time with their dad, and I was all alone. When you're the kind of person who doesn't eat until you've fixed a plate for everyone else first, you don't really know how to go about fixing a meal. But you have to learn to exist in your new life. And you have to find a purpose for your new life.

Romans 8:28-29 says *"And we know that in all things God works for the good of those who love him, who have been called according to His purpose."* So okay, there is a purpose for my life, and when I am doing something which fulfills my purpose, I am happy. And I am happiest when I am doing things for others which meet their basic needs or make them feel special. For example, it gives me great pleasure to do something as simple as make a sandwich for someone. And I've really always been this kind of person who does little things for other people. Because I'm not a millionaire, I really can't do big things. But even so, after my divorce, and really for many months after my divorce, even though I still had suppers to fix, laundry to wash, and kids to chauffeur, I still was without a real purpose. But then one day, I prayed and asked God to tell me what He really wanted me to do with my life, why was I here on earth, and why had I had the life I have had. In other words, what was my purpose? What is your purpose? Do you already know what your purpose is? Are you living your life in a way which fulfills your purpose? Are you still lost and don't know your purpose? Pray. The scripture in Romans above says that we are called to a purpose, and all things, even things like death or divorce, work for good. And when you find your real purpose in life, your calling, which may not be anything like what you are doing now, God will take everything that you are and everything you have ever experienced and bring about good. I have found my purpose. Writing this book is part of that purpose. Standing up for myself is another part. Discovering how to find happiness is another. I have no doubts about what I have been called to do. But what I lack sometimes is the courage and faith to do what I've been called to do. And so I pray and ask for help. I'm praying that you'll find the purpose for your new life, that you'll find healing from the pain of your old life, for renewal to live strong in faith, and for hope that all things will become good.

Monday, May 16, 2011

The weekends seem to just fly by as if I barely have time to eat a cookie on Friday afternoon before the alarm announces it's time to get ready for work. Yes, it's Monday. And I really wish it was Saturday or Sunday afternoon again. It really was a wonderful weekend. My man and I went for a four-wheeler ride down by the creek to see how much more the leaves have popped out and the grass has grown. The woods were so thick, I felt like we were inside a leafy-woodsy cabin that sprung up overnight beside the rushing creek. The dog insisted on riding on the four-wheeler with us, and so I had a large fluffy backrest. There's a first time for everything, and so, it was the first time I'd ever ridden on a four-wheeler with a dog. But I did draw the line at letting him ride back with us after he had rolled around in the creek and gotten all muddy. I'm just too much of a neat freak for that. I don't mind tracking through the mud in my hiking boots, and I don't mind digging a hole in the yard for bushes, but I don't like mud on my clothes at all. So when I am outside in nature, which is as often as I possibly can be, I look cute and am as clean as possible. That was just one of the many fun activities we did this weekend. What did you do this weekend? What do you do for fun? I hope you have some fun. Just as much as the weekend was jam-packed with fun; Monday, the beginning of the work week was jam-packed with work. Work at work. Work at home. Work in the yard. And now that it's time for the kids to find their pajamas, I'm the one really getting sleepy.

221

But I like this time of the evening. I like unwinding and relaxing and writing after I've had a busy and productive day. I supervised my daughter mixing up some fresh guacamole. I baked some chocolate chip cookies. Maybe we'll have cookies for breakfast. Cookies and a cup of coffee. I gave a speech at a local middle school where some of my daughters' friends attend, and I asked the audience members what they had for breakfast. Cheerios. Donuts. Scrambled eggs. Toast. And then one young man raised his hand and asked me what I had for breakfast. Cookies and a cup of coffee. And then he asked me a second question, "can I come live with you?" And that evening when I got home, my daughters told me their friends were driving them crazy about wanting to come live with us and eat cookies and drink coffee for breakfast. What do you eat for breakfast? You do eat breakfast, don't you? Well, maybe that's one reason why you don't look forward to starting your day. If you had a fresh baked chocolate chip waiting for you, maybe you'd be glad the alarm is going off.

This was a really good weekend. Monday turned out to be a really great day. And I'm really looking forward to tomorrow. I hope you have a great week. I'm praying that you will have some fun. I'm praying that you will get a little bit closer to total healing. I'm praying that you will be renewed and have more hope. You too can eat a cookie for breakfast. It's okay, really. Enjoy! A cookie is not any less nutritious than the bowl of oatmeal with the butter, milk, and sugar you're eating.

Tuesday, May 17, 2011

I achieved a milestone today... really it feels more like a million milestones. Today, I held my finished bound copy of my dissertation in my hand. It represents years of dreaming and years of hard work. Besides the copies to keep, one copy will go on the library shelf at the university. I am the first person in my immediate family line to complete a doctorate. And to think I almost didn't graduate  with my first college degree, but I persevered. I was determined to not let any obstacles stand in my way. When my son had colic and couldn't sleep without being propped on my shoulder, I held him in one arm and my Biology notes in the other. To be able to afford the medical expenses, the living expenses, and the college tuition, I waited tables. I copied all of my notes onto index cards because they would fit into my pocket, and I would memorize definitions while I fixed drinks.

I didn't have the greatest G.P.A. After living with the domestic violence and managing the medical problems my son had, I considered it a miracle that I graduated at all. It was a miracle that I lived through it all to graduate. How did I do it? I just did. I handled everything day to day as it came. I made some mistakes. I adapted to the circumstances and worked hard at what I could control and prayed over what I couldn't control. And I'm a control freak, so taking things as they come is not so easy for me. I work hard to make things happen. It's how I survive and thrive through tough times.

And then I received the opportunity to go to graduate school to complete my Master's degree with an assistantship which included tuition. In 1992, I was now divorced from my abusive first marriage and a single parent of a medically fragile special needs child. Dating as a single mother of a special needs child wasn't easy.

Most men didn't want to go on a second date after I told them about Matthew. And some men just wanted to take advantage of a beautiful girl with no thought about my single motherhood. I waited tables to make ends meet, and occasionally, I made some extra money doing runway modeling for local stores. After some not so good relationships for me, I met my future second husband. A week after I graduated with my Master's degree, I married again. I had intended to immediately start on my doctorate, but that just didn't happen. His career came before mine. My career went on hold for my children. Sure, I had jobs, but just jobs to pay the bills and to have insurance benefits; nothing which developed me into becoming the professional I wanted to be. Ten years passed by before I started my doctoral studies. I worked full-time. I took care of my family. And in the midst of the toughest part of completing a doctorate, conducting research and writing the dissertation, the last year which determined whether I passed or failed at my lifelong pursuit of higher education, my fourteen year marriage ended, and I became a single parent again. And today, I held my dissertation in my hand. An inch and half thick, 181 pages plus 11 pre-pages, 9 x 12, pale blue with gold lettering book. I did it. I technically finished months ago, but it didn't seem real until today. I sat in my car for several minutes with my hand pressed against the cover. I did it. All that I went through no longer matters, because I accomplished my dream.

I could have given up. I had plenty of good excuses over the years which would justify giving up. But I didn't give up. I kept on going. I let go of what I couldn't control. I did what I needed to do. And I didn't worry about what other people thought I should do. It wasn't easy. But I did it anyway. Are you struggling with wanting to give up on your dreams? Does it seem like it's just too hard, too much, too emotionally draining? You can do it. If I can do it, you can too. You too can achieve your dreams. I don't know what you are really working towards, but I do know that you can make it across the finish line if you just don't give up. You have to let some things go -- like your past. You will make some mistakes, so you'll just have to forgive yourself and keep on going. You can't let the obstacles control your outcome. With a vision for a future, believing that your dream will come to fruition, move forward. Press on towards your goal one day at a time. And one day, you'll get there. It may take years, but you'll get there. You really can do it. I'm praying for your success, for your healing, your renewal, and your hope.

Monday, May 23, 2011

I wish you could have seen the view we saw sitting in our brightly striped beach chairs facing the mountain ridges in North Carolina just west of Pilot's Knob as the sunset about 9 p.m. Saturday night. No words could do justice to describing the beauty. No photo could completely capture all of the wonder. Our mountain's majesty was made even more grand and wondrous because we shared it together. For the most part, we spent the weekend in quiet solitude without hardly any technology at all -- no TV, no movies, no computers, almost no cell phones. We were able to check messages and return phone calls once per day when we ventured off the mountain and headed into town for supplies. Can you imagine going all weekend without checking your Facebook, your email, or watching TV? Would you love being unplugged? Or would it drive you crazy? Well, for me, I loved it. I could have stayed out in the woods with our tent, our 4x4, our ice chest, and my man. For me, our mini (way too short) camping trip was a dream come true.

It wasn't just the quiet, or the mountain views, or the wild chipmunks that zipped past, or the glistening water of Lake Glenville, or the blooms of mountain laurel bursting forth like fireworks in the underbrush, or happening upon the rushing mountain stream when hiking, or the majestic rock face of the Knob that greeted me first thing in the morning when I opened the tent flap, which manifested my dream come true. It was also having the perfect companion. It takes a very special person to facilitate this kind of peaceful serenity on a camping trip. We brought very little with us, and we had everything we needed, because we had each other. I have never known anyone like him; I've never believed in those corny, overly romantic, soul mate claims, but we have an undeniable special connection. There is no fussing. Just contentment we found in a quiet moment. Conversation ebbed and flowed like that mountain stream just as it was supposed to be. Every detail of the environment shared and appreciated. Every detail of our present thoughts and future hopes shared and appreciated. Here's a question we posed each other, and I'd like you to reflect on it and answer it as well. Where do you see yourself in one year? In five years? And where would you like to be?

For me, this was both easy and difficult to answer. My life has changed so much in the past two years. And I finally can see myself able to be where I would like to be in the future. I never really thought about how little hope I had for my dreams to come true just before my marriage ended. I couldn't figure out what was going to happen tomorrow, much less a year from now, when I was in the middle of my divorce. But now, I have hope for a future again. And you will too. You may not feel so now, but you too can dream and believe that dreams come true. My dream of being in contented companionship with another human being doing anything and everything and nothing anywhere at any time came true. It really is possible. I never knew that it was possible to get along so effortlessly, so naturally, until now. And while I can answer the question of where I see myself and where I want to be, I'm no longer worried about what's going to happen. Because I'm enjoying, really enjoying, what's happening right now in my life. The future will be as it should be. God knows what will be. I can't wait to go camping again. But not just that, I can't wait to experience whatever is next. Because I know everything is going to better than okay. I'm still praying for your healing, your renewal, and your hope. I wish you could have seen the sunset over Pilot's Knob. Maybe you will one day.

Sunday, June 5, 2011

Summer is here. And that means I am on the go, in and out of town, and in general so busy living life that I don't stay connected to the computer very much. Today, I am struggling with my whole message -- being positive and happy post-divorce (and being positive and happy in any situation, not just post-divorce). In other words, there are four reasons why I've been finding it difficult to be positive and happy, and I'd like to share them with you, because maybe, just maybe, you struggle with these same reasons too.

1. all available energy is spent on surviving the crisis du jour
2. feeling too weak and lacking faith to keep moving forward when my path isn't easy
3. "wearing rose-colored glasses" is not seeing life as it really is
4. other people won't let you put the past in the past and keep reminding you of past failures, faults, and faux pas.

So, do any of these struggles strike a chord in your heart? Do you see yourself in any of these situations? Is it right, appropriate, just, and healthy for me to choose to be optimistic about the future, full of hope, and refusing to focus on the negatives of life in order to cultivate a positive attitude no matter what the situation? For the past week, I've been totally absorbed with reflecting on this question. All relationships have their ups and downs, good days and bad days, and moments of conflict. But how do you know this time will be okay, that this relationship is the right one for you and not another mistake? Over and over again, throughout my life, I have been criticized as being too positive, as living life wearing rose-colored glasses, for not seeing the world as it really is. And this morning, finally, after a really difficult series of events in all four of the above reasons have challenged me, I found my answer. To be blunt, life sucks, and I can't survive if I take off my rose-colored glasses. Having faith that everything will be okay in time, in the future, that God will give me the strength to endure, that this hardship will pass, is what has gotten me through every crisis, struggle, and impossibility in my life. In short, I believe. And I refuse to stop believing. Healing is possible. Renewal will happen. Hope is everlasting. Christ is love. And through Christ all things are possible.

Yes, even when tears are streaming down my face and my heart is so burdened it feels like a heavy stone sinking in the marsh and my stomach is lurching due to the anxiety over the crisis, I believe that I will be happy one day. I believe that miracles happen. I believe in things hoped for, but not seen. Other people may call me a fool, irrational, silly, unrealistic, but I will just pray for them. Because they lack faith -- not faith in me -- but faith in God and the wonders that God can do for our hearts, for our needs, for our future. I am just a woman like so many other women out there. I'm really not any more special than you or anyone else. I'm not perfect. I make mistakes. But no matter what, I will be positive and happy. And you can too. And choosing to have a positive attitude is essential to living a happy life. I will keep praying for you, for your healing, your renewal, your hope, and for you to find your steely resolve to be positive and happy no matter what tries to steal your joy. If you hold on to your joy, no one can take it from you. You too can be happy. Please just hold on.

Encouragement defined....

- the action of giving someone support, confidence, or hope
- persuasion to do or to continue something
- the act of trying to stimulate the development of an activity, state, or belief
- the expression of approval and support
- boost: the act of giving hope or support to someone
- the feeling of being encouraged
- giving courage through words of comfort

No matter what is happening to you in your life, or what has happened to you in the past, you need encouragement. I need encouragement. And people come into our lives, cross our path, to fulfill this need. Have you ever stopped and wondered why do you know the people you know who encourage you? Was it random chance that you met? Or was it part of a divine plan? Or is it your fate? Is it your destiny? I happen to believe that everyone who comes in and out of my life is all a part of God's plan for my life. And sometimes I pray for God to help me, and then in what would seem like a strange coincidence, someone enters my life and through them I find encouragement which meets my needs. Meeting my man was like that -- I have come to discover that we know hundreds of the same people, and we lived in close proximity for over a decade, and yet, we did not know the other existed on the planet. But after he prayed for God to send him a woman to encourage him, and I prayed for a man to encourage me, we were introduced. He supports me to follow my dreams, to write this book, to do what makes me happy, like no one has ever before done in my life. He is the first person, besides my parents, to tell me that he was proud of me. And I support him unconditionally. I want him to find happiness in his life even if happiness is not found with me. I want you to find happiness in your life.

One week a short while ago, when he and I were both feeling weak, discouraged, and without hope that total healing can occur post-divorce, through what seemed like random chance, a person shared her story of physical healing and the encouragement found through friendship with a missionary couple, and consequently, he told me about them, we were introduced, and now, another prayer has been answered. I have new friends who want nothing more than to provide encouragement. And when I need it, they are there. Not every day, but just at the moment of need. And just last night when I spoke with them, the first question asked was "do you believe that goodness and mercy shall follow you all the days of your life?" and the second question asked was "do you believe God has a plan?" And the answer to both is, yes, without hesitation or reservation, yes. No matter what the circumstances or troubles of the moment, I believe God has a plan, and I have evidence to substantiate this belief, because when I need help, He sends it. When I was in my first marriage during which I suffered physical and emotional abuse, through what seemed like random chance, I was assigned to do my student teaching with the wife of the local police chief. And with me only asking in prayer, not to any person directly, they helped me escape that life. God sent them. I could list multiple examples, but I won't, because the bottom line is that I believe in goodness, in mercy, in God's plan for my life, in answered prayers. Perhaps for you, this book is providing you with words of encouragement. I want to encourage you, to give you hope that you can make it through today, tomorrow, and every day to come. Very soon, your healing, your renewal, and your hope will be evident in your life. I believe. If you are finding it difficult to believe, then today, you should pray. Even I have moments where I find it difficult to believe that goodness and mercy and happiness and love will be with me every day of the rest of my life. But I just believe anyway. I'll pray with you for your healing, your renewal, your hope, and for God to send you an encouraging word.

Wednesday, June 8, 2011

One thing I have discovered living this post-divorce existence and being a parent is that divorce undermines the authority of the parent. As a parent, you have no one to back you up. No one steps in and says "It is inappropriate for you to speak to your mother that way" or "You should speak to your father with more respect". All teenagers struggle with the "you're not the boss of me" attitude. But I've noticed that teenagers adapting to their new divorced family try to take on an authoritative parental role and boss their parent. "Go here." "Do this. Don't do that". "You've been on the phone too long". "You can't invite so and so to go with us." Younger children adapting to their new divorced family sometimes try to take on a nurturing parental role and take care of the physical and emotional needs of their parent by cleaning, cooking, or "dating" their parent. By "dating" I don't mean anything weird by that, just so you know, I'm talking about how it's easy for a divorced parent to have only their children for social company, in the same way that mothers of small children who choose to stay home during the early years feel isolated and without adult conversation. Just as it is not natural and healthy in a two-parent, intact (not divorced) family for one parent to put the children's wants above the needs of his/her spouse, a divorced parent cannot allow the child to feel like an equal, an adult, an emotional partner.

Children should be encouraged to be children. Teenagers should be going to the movies with their friends, not their parent just because the parent doesn't have a spouse to date anymore. The divorced parent still needs to set boundaries and expect appropriate attitudes and behaviors just as any other parent does. If you have children, have you noticed some of these things happening to you with your children? Have you felt helpless when your child rolled their eyes when you spoke? Maybe you don't have children, and so you may wonder what does this have to do with me? The same thing happens with you as the child. Some parents of divorced children, and realize if you're in the age bracket I am, you have children and parents involved in your life. And many divorced women revert to being child-like, instead of grown-up, real women, or their parents start treating them like they are little girls again because they are no longer married. When you are an older, professional woman, you are no longer a child. Your children shouldn't treat you like a child, and your parents shouldn't treat you like a child. If you allow either of these parent-child relationships to get off balance, your healing will be delayed. Does this make for interpersonal conflict between you and the family members you love? Of course it does. And it's up to you to monitor the appropriateness of your relationships and your role and status within them.
There will be times when you find yourself annoyed and frustrated. Like yesterday, when I stopped to visit a friend on the way to take my children to the bookstore and a movie. One daughter kept interrupting me with a condescending tone saying "It's time to go. I'm ready to

leave. You've talked long enough." It was embarrassing, and when we did leave when I was ready to go, I had to call her out on her rude and disrespectful behavior. Or the time when my parents wanted to tell me that I shouldn't go to dinner on a holiday with anyone not related to me or queried me about how late was it when I came home from a date. You know, my parents haven't asked me that since I was in high school and broke curfew which was over 25 years ago. But I so recognized the same tone of voice. Unfortunately divorce is difficult for everyone, the couple, the children, the extended family, and your friends. And to be happy post-divorce, you're going to have to develop some conflict management skills. And you'll learn as you go along, and you'll make mistakes. I'm still learning how to deal with the relational tensions, and so the other thing I've realized I need is a sense of humor. Deal with it when it happens, and then laugh it off. Put it behind you. Let it go. Just as I had to learn to let the pain go, I have to learn to let the conflict go. No grudges. Be patient if others are slow to adapt to your divorce. I'm praying for you to find yourself, to keep life in perspective, to keep your relationships in order. You're going to have a great life! I just know it.

Sunday, June 26, 2011

Last week I went to the beach – a much needed family vacation – a chance to get away from the hectic world of work and chores and stress. My man and I rented a house on the beach in the hopes we could persuade all of our children and our parents to share in our vacation. Seven children ranging from 21 to 8 years of age, the two of us, and my parents shacked up for a week of sun and surf. It was our first attempt at merging our families together under one roof. Every day the ocean waves were a different color, and the further one looked out to the horizon, the ocean waters changed again. Sea foam green with white caps crashed onto the crystal white beach. Pale aqua when the water became deeper. Bright turquoise – almost clear like aquamarine – rolled over the sandbar. Deep cobalt melted into the horizon. And that was just in the morning! As the day progressed the water colors changed again. And at night we watched the moonlight move and spotlight a different area of dark violet waves. I wish I could say that every moment was perfect. We had tensions with putting so many people who weren't accustomed to each other in the same house. We had some moments that were almost like you just need to pack your bags and go home early. But some moments were like heaven – like the perfect moment when my man cut up my watermelon for me – or the perfect moment when we were all piled up on the bed laughing and telling jokes for hours – or the perfect moment when we sat on the deck gazing out at the amazing colors of the ocean in the distance.

I was amazed to see my toes through water that was so clear! We could see algae, fish, and different sea crabs. The very first day, my daughter found a perfectly intact starfish. The last day, one of the boys found several sand dollars out on the sandbar. And the temperature of the water changed from day to day. The first day it was warm like bath water; and then after the rains one evening, the water was refreshingly cool, almost too cool. I went kayaking for the first time when we were at the beach. Was I scared? No, not at all, well, not until after we capsized multiple times in the surf. And even then, I wasn't as much scared, as really tired. It's exhausting climbing back into the kayak, especially after you've just been conked on the head. We just couldn't seem to get into the kayak for longer than 30 seconds. The kids sitting on the beach said they wished they had a video camera and could post on YouTube their Dad and me flipping and flipping and flipping again out of the kayak. It really was ridiculous. But I was determined. I was going kayaking. I had made up my mind, and it was going to happen. I had never kayaked before, but I was kayaking today. Part of me wanted to give up, but I was determined to not give up. And finally, there I was, paddling my kayak out to sea, over the sandbar, and into the crystal waters. It was a wonderful feeling – like I was free for the first time.

Have you ever felt free? And I don't mean free like you just escaped from jail, but free like you can do anything. Have you ever really felt like anything was possible? I have really felt this way very few times in my life. I've said this phrase many times however. And the scripture, "In Christ, all things are possible." Or sometimes the scripture is translated as "I can do all things in Christ who strengthens me." I don't remember the chapter name and number right now, but I remember the words.

Well, as I was paddling out to the middle of the ocean after getting all beat up by the kayak in the surf, not really believing I could do it, but I was doing it, these words came to me again. For all of the things in life for which I don't think I can do on my own, God provides me the strength. He gives me the strength to love again, the strength to conquer my fears, the strength to smile in the time of grief, the strength to hope and believe in a good life for myself, the strength to not give up. And really, this kayaking experience became another metaphor for my life experience. I put myself out there, I attempted to live life, the surf was brutal, I struggled with just getting into the kayak, the kayak beat me up, literally, you should see the bruises on my arm, my knee, my head, but I persevered with a positive attitude and determination, and then I was paddling over the waves, I was soaring like the brown pelicans who flew past our house every night, I found another moment of happiness, I found freedom. My past was behind me, totally forgotten. I was free. You're going to find your moment. It will happen. Don't give up. I'll keep praying for your healing, your renewal, and your hope, and that if you ever try to find your moment of happiness in a kayak on the ocean that you will have an easier time than me.

I have never enjoyed a vacation as much as this time at the beach. I have never been as happy, even in the midst of sad news, I was happy. My brother Ricky died from terminal cancer while I was enjoying another perfect moment of happiness. We received the news halfway through the vacation, and as the waters changed, so did my life. I am now the only surviving sibling in my family. I am the only child. I am alone. But one is never really alone. Friends and family love you and are with you in thought and prayer if not in person. God is with you. But I still feel alone. And driving from the beach to the funeral in Louisiana, I was in total despair. And I bore the weight of my grief alone, as I always have. I have buried more loved ones than most. I can plan the details of a funeral easier than I can plan a backyard BBQ. Because I seem to take it all in stride, only out of familiarity mind you, some people think I don't grieve and suffer. Do you know the saying "still waters run deep?" Even if I say nothing, I am deeply affected. Even if I smile on the outside, my heart is crying on the inside. I wish I could go back to the beach, back to the day before my brother died, back to the bliss of companionship with my man, the joy of watching the children build sandcastles and complete abandon in the perfect moments. If I could, I would close my eyes and just feel the wonder of it all, just take it all in, the smell of the salt air, the softness of the water, the comfort of my man's hand and mine intertwined. That was a moment of pure joy. I could live in that moment forever, and that moment sustains me in my grief, even now. The loss of my brother is moment of pure pain. I wandered for days in shock not really believing he was gone. There wouldn't be another day to talk to him or to get one of his funny text messages. My brother Ricky and I weren't close, but he was always there. And now he's not. I feel alone, but I'm not alone. God will never leave you or forsake you. That's a promise you can always trust in no matter how you are feeling.

I stand in the cemetery of my ancestors in a royal blue sundress and sandals because I didn't pack a funeral outfit in my beach bag. I stand staring at the coffin of my brother. The bodies of both of my brothers are now in the ground and their souls are in heaven. I walked from his graveside and stand in front of the tombstone of my son. I had forgotten the color of the granite, the vines and flowers along the side, and how I had chosen to write his name. Each time I have made the trip back to Louisiana in the past several years, it has been for a funeral. I have watched more coffins lowered into the ground than I ever wish to see. It is the greatest juxtaposition of emotions for a believer than one can imagine – extreme grief over what you have lost in losing an earthly relationship with this person – extreme gratitude in knowing that their pain and suffering is over and their bodies are whole and immortal and glorying in the presence of the Lord. I do not reveal the overwhelming emotions I feel at the church or the cemetery; I wear a mask as if I am a spirit myself. I smile. I greet others. I am numb. But later, when I am alone in the dim light of my room, I feel it all. I release the myriad emotions that are tugging at my heart. In all of my life there has been only one person I feel safe enough to share the depth of my grief openly; with everyone else I have been and am guarded. And unfortunately, my man does not understand the honor I have bestowed upon him or the desperate need I have to share the depth of my grief with him. He is the only person with whom I have felt safe to say anything too. I pray he will always be there for me, and I am overcome with fear that he will not be. I am smothered by my own desperation and despair. I cry out to God, and say, why not me? Why is it their time to pass from this earthly existence to the heavenly one, but not mine? Why I am I still here? What is my purpose for living? Can I do this alone?

Do you ever ask yourself these questions? Have you ever buried someone you love? If you haven't, I really hope you never do experience the grief I have experienced. However, out of grief comes inexplicable joy. They are polar opposites. I believe for you to know joy, you must have already known grief. As horrible as that sounds, only those of you who have suffered bitter disappointment and loss and hurt and shame will really be able to find joy. There are some people who go through life with relatively little problems and no loss; they marry young, all goes well, they die old together. But for most of us, we have lived complicated lives. And we are still living complicated lives. We are still learning our purpose for existing here on earth. I know my purpose; my purpose is to love others the way God loves. My struggle is not being able to love, but being able to bear the weight of the burdens I take on when I truly love. Please don't think I'm being sacrilegious. I'm not at all claiming to be God or like God; I'm just saying that I know God has called me to love others more than myself. Have you ever heard the saying "it is more blessed to give than to receive?" I am more blessed when I give love, but my heart cries out to receive love. And when I receive love, I can give more love away exponentially. And when I am free to love and to give my love without holding back without conditions, then I am truly happy. And when my love is constrained, held captive to either the rules of society or the demands of another, then it is like my love is being buried in a coffin. And I watch my love go down into the grave just as I watched their bodies go down to be seen again no more. I refuse to bury my love. I have no control over terminal illnesses that claim the lives of those I love.

But I do have control over how I demonstrate my love. And my love is free, not contained in a box, but shines forth from my heart into the lives of my family and friends. Many people do not understand me, and that's okay. Many people probably think I should do things differently than the way I do them. But I am me. I do not act out of anger or to harm. I want to do my best, to do the will of God, and to do the right thing. I do hope my words resonate with some part of your past experiences and your dreams, your grief and your joy, your giving and your receiving. I am praying for you. Even though there are days I don't find time to write, I never stop praying for you, for me, for God's will to be done. Although the depths of my grief are great, the amount of my hope is equally great. I believe that goodness and mercy will follow me all the days of my life, and this day of sorrow is now a part of my past, and the days to come will be ones of happiness.

Wednesday, June 29, 2011

I am writing today from Koenigswinter, Germany. That's right, Germany. For years and years I have wanted to travel back to Europe, and finally, through a European Council fellowship, I received the opportunity to go. But going did not come at an easy time. As you know from reading the last few pages, Ricky died a little over a week ago. And because of this, and other reasons, I have been heavy-laden, without hope, and unable to rest. Even as I was getting on the plane, I was reticent about going. All my life I had wanted to travel; I thought seeing the world was my heart's desire, and a month ago, I finally realized what I wanted

239

more than anything. And the day I left the beach to go to my brother's funeral, my heart's desire was affirmed. I know where I'm meant to be. And it's not across the Atlantic Ocean. My heart is back in Georgia. But I was committed to making this journey. I needed time for reflection; time alone, time to evaluate my life and to affirm or negate what I thought was my heart's desire. I've flown many times in my life, and I've crossed the Atlantic more than once, and I am totally comfortable traveling. But when I boarded the plane, I was hurt and broken. And I was doing it to myself, because I was going in the opposite direction of where my heart wanted me to go. And I was keeping silent about what my heart was demanding me to say. But I had hoped that God would give me answers to the questions I had.

On the second day, I awoke refreshed and renewed. God restored my joy that I thought was lost to me. I knew what I needed to do to be where I needed to be. And I found happiness in knowing that this week in Germany would provide me the time away for God to renew my strength. And I read the following verses:

Psalm 16:9-11 "my heart is glad...I rest in hope...God will not leave me...He will show me the path of life, give me joy and happiness always"

My faith is restored, because I know the path I must take. It will not be an easy path, but it's the right path for me. Have you ever lost your way? Have you ever not known what direction to go? What do you do? I wait. I speak very little. I pray. When I get back to the States, I'm going to visit friends who are missionaries, so that I can spend more time in prayer and reflection. Maybe that wouldn't help you, but it will help me. You'll have to figure out what helps you to know the will of God and to give you the strength to do it wholeheartedly.

To celebrate the return of my joy, I bought some flowers for my hotel room, some sweet dark purple violets with lush dark green leaves, and some tiny lavender forget-me-knots with a dot of yellow for the center, both placed in bright yellow containers. When I wake up and when I go to sleep and every time I enter my room, their purple and gold remind me of God's glory and my love. Flowers bring me great joy – the shapes, the colors, the textures, the fragrance, everything. My heart smiles when I see them. In a single moment of seeing the flowers on the table, I remember every other single moment of joy involving flowers. I remember the flowers given to me by friends. I remember the flowers blooming in my yard. I remember the flowers I've given to friends. I remember how my grandmother appreciated flowers growing in her yard. I remember the overflowing giant flowerpots on my mother's deck. I remember the vase of irises on my man's desk and the vase of daylilies on the kitchen counter. I remember the flowers at the funeral. I remember the wildflowers we saw across the field. I remember the mountain irises outside our cabin. I remember the tiny flowers picked by tiny hands and presented to me with love. Every memory is good and right and beautiful.

There's another scripture in the book of Matthew, and I'll have to look the number up for you later, but it's something like this *"if God cares for the lilies in the field and feeds and waters them, how much more does He care for you."* That is why I feel renewed. My hope is not in people or things; my hope is in God that no matter what happens in the future, God will provide for me. Take time to look at a flower, really look at it. You too can find joy. I'm praying for your healing, your renewal, and your hope.

Thursday, June 30, 2011

As I have written about many times before, I love to walk.
And Germany is a country where folks walk. Each day –
usually once in the morning and again in the evening – I
walk along the Rhein River. For those of you unfamiliar
with your geography, the Rhein is not a creek; it is a major
waterway through the country with barges, pleasure boats,
and ferries. Seeing the rushing currents and hearing them
crash against the rocks restores my soul. Wherever I go, I
want to be near water, a mountain stream, a river, a bayou,
an ocean, any water. I have been thinking about being
baptized again. Almost did so in the ocean, but the time
wasn't right. I don't when the right time will be, but one
day, I'm going to be baptized again. I think when my old
life has really passed away, and I feel like I am whole
again, then it will happen. But I don't know when that will
be.

Have you ever been baptized? Maybe you're not a
Christian believer. And that's okay. Each person must
decide for his/herself. But if you have, think back to when
it happened? How were you baptized? What did you feel?
Did you feel like your old self, your old life died, and you
were reborn? For some people, it's only symbolic. Others
really feel changed in an instant. I don't think there's one
right way to be baptized or one right way to feel. I just want
you to reflect on that experience in your life and think
about where you are in your life today. And if you've never
been baptized, maybe think about if it's for you.

As I lean against the rail watching a small log float along in
the currents of the Rhein, I imagine that I'm that log,
pushed along however the currents of life take me, with
little control of my destiny, accepting whatever happens to
me as what is supposed to happen to me. I don't try to

swim against the currents, just like the log doesn't float against the currents. Sometimes I'm flipped over and under and this way and that. I smile when the log flips over, goes under, and pops back up a little ways downstream. Sometimes you're not going to be strong enough for the river currents and you'll go under. Sometimes the surf will knock you out of the kayak, and you'll shockingly swallow salty water and come up sputtering. Sometimes it rains, like today, and I walked carrying my umbrella. I have had a lifetime of sorrows and painful experiences; I've gone under the water's surface many times, but every time I have resurfaced. I think of that little blue fish from the Pixar film *Finding Nemo*, "just keep swimming, swimming, swimming…" I don't know why that popped into my head; I haven't watched that film with my children in years. But that's what I've always done, I've just kept going.

You can't give up on life when you don't like what's happening in your life at that moment. You just have to keep swimming. At some point, somewhere on the river, that log will find a resting place. It won't float forever. There's a reason the log is floating down the river, and when enough time has passed and the log has gone the distance intended, whoever happens to be walking along the river at that spot will know why. There's a reason why my life is the way it is, and one day, after I've gone the distance, I'll know why. And I believe that the journey is not in vain. I don't understand why everything happens the way it does. But I do have hope that tomorrow will be better than today. I have hope, that in time, all will be well with me, and with you. I'm praying for you, for your healing, your renewal, and your hope. You too will find your new life after the strong currents have taken you to where you are meant to be.

Friday, July 1, 2011

As I prepared to leave Germany to go back home, I thought about my children. I have really missed them this week. There's just something about being away on a trip which makes you miss your loved ones more. When I am at home, the children are always coming and going, in and out, visiting the other parent, hanging out with their friends, or doing some activity which doesn't include me. Text messaging has been a blessing to me. And I can't believe I just said that. But seriously, text messaging keeps my children and I connected. Children of this generation seem to be always on the go, and children of divorce are even more so. Children of divorce have multiple homes. When I say "I'm coming home" I know where I'm going, and it's the same house. Children of divorce are "coming home" every day or week, and it's never the same house. Daily life is really confusing. I have an extensive and detailed agenda like you wouldn't believe. My iPhone calendar maintains my personal schedule and business commitments, but my Vera Bradley "Night and Day" pattern binder agenda keeps up with everybody and every detail. Imagine what all I have recorded for this year – the personal schedules of 2 adults, 3 divorce visitation schedules, 7 different activity schedules for children, doctor/dental appointments, plus the grandparents, important contact info for everybody, and more. And friends get frustrated when the automatic response to any invitation is "Maybe. I think I can. I'll have to let you know when the date gets closer." Maybe I can't handle the schedules of a family this size with all these complications.

How do you manage your schedule and the chaotic schedules of your children if you have them? How do you maintain the lines of communication when you are apart? If you're not an organized person, and you've recently found yourself in a divorce situation, or other change of life situation, and you have children or are an instant parent to new children, because your new partner is a parent, then you need an agenda. Get one ASAP. Fill it out. Take it with you everywhere.

I'm not complaining. I love every minute of organizing my crew. Catching chickens is what I sometimes call it. And after our recent trip to the beach and learning to catch sand crabs – keeping up with our children is as easy as netting a sand crab. Netting a sand crab is really not that easy. I love receiving a text message that says tells me not only the details of where they are, but also, the "miss u" and "luv u 2" and "c u soon" and the even just the plain and simple "k" which translated means "I got it. I'll do it. Thank you very much. I love you, but I'm a teenager or young adult, and I'm not going to stress myself out typing a long text to you, but that doesn't mean I'm didn't want you to text me, Mom." Maybe I should ask them, but I think my children like getting a text when they are away. I try to text them every day, especially when I don't see them that day. I reply to every text they send me. This has really helped me to form close relationships with my new children, because we don't have years of history, and they need little encouragements that I do care about them and their daily lives. This has really helped me keep in touch with my children when they are visiting their Dad, or while I've been on this trip, and being able to text has served as a good surrogate for the breakfast table talk, the after school talk, and the bedtime good night which we had their entire lives prior to the divorce. I think texting makes them feel more comfortable, because they don't have to talk to one parent when the other parent can hear them. They also don't have to say a lot when they don't feel like it, but yet, they know you're still there.

245

Ironically, I'm coming home, and even though I'm desperately missing my children, I won't see them all right away. My biological children will be home with me tonight, and then they leave for vacation with their Dad tomorrow. Two of my man's girls are at the beach with their Mom. His boys are working or doing activities with friends. And the youngest has visitation with her Mom this weekend, and I won't see her until later in the week. So I'm coming home, and even though I have 7 children in my life, I will be childless for the most part this week. That's another strange thing about life post-divorce; your family bonds are maintained across distances, not across the dinner table. In the past eight months the week we were on vacation at the beach, and only two of those meals, all of us were together at the table. But it really is okay, because although divorced and blended families are not traditional, or nuclear, or "normal" -- to not have this chaotic, disjointed lifestyle would mean not having the children, and that would be a lot worse. I love my life. I love my family. It isn't easy making the transition to this new family structure, but every day is better than the day before. I'm not sure how I will really handle having a family this large and chaotic, but I love them all enough to try. As long as there is love, children will be happy.

Saturday, July 2, 2011

Somewhere over the Atlantic Ocean, a weight that has been crushing my heart simply evaporated. For the past several weeks, I have felt like my heart was being squeezed in a vise grip, and I've been unable to breathe. Grief has ups and downs. Feelings are like that too. No matter what your life circumstances, you'll have days where you feel like everything will be okay, and you'll have days where you feel like you just can't do it. And that's where faith comes in. I just wanted to point that out, because I'm not super human. I have emotions just like you do. And I choose to have a positive attitude and a happy life. I just felt like you needed to know that it is okay if you feel depressed sometimes.

So anyway, all of a sudden, in a moment, the tightness in my chest I'd had for weeks just went away. My heart expanded in my chest, I took a deep breath as if I had been dead and was alive again. I am smiling from the inside out, bursting forth; my eyes are sparkling reflecting the love in my heart. I am free. I am a shining star; I am a pearl of great price; I am a strong woman. I can do anything. My happiness rests inside of me. My happiness is not found in others. Sure, my man can do something or say something that makes me happier, but I am the one who makes me happy. Do you get what I'm saying? Do you feel happy? Or are you depressed right now? Is there something going on currently in your life that is upsetting you? Are you wishing someone would do something differently so you can be happy? Well, this is my point. It doesn't matter what anyone else does or doesn't do. If you want to be happy, you, and you alone, are in charge of your happiness.

You see, I was burdened, because I was afraid. I had already lost so much in the past. I had failed at marriage before. Family members have died. And I became so afraid that my new life, my new, wonderful life with the happy stories of fun and love were just going to go away. I was afraid of losing all that I hold dear. Fear is not rational, so if you're looking for a rational explanation as to why I'd be afraid, you won't find one. My fear of losing the man I adore, my children, my extended family, my friends, was holding me captive. My fear was crushing me and stealing my joy. John 10:10 says *"the thief comes to steal, kill, and destroy, but I (that would be Jesus Christ) have come that you may have life and life more abundantly."* The thief was in my house, and the thief was trying to steal my joy. And what I realized that my faith was like a security system on my house keeping me safe, and that the thief cannot steal my joy if I don't let him in the door.

And so, the thief has to flee. I'm not giving into fear. I love with my whole heart -- truly, purely, and holy -- and if I let fear take hold in my heart, then I can't do that. I can't be the woman I am destined to be. I can't love my man and my family the way I they need me too. And I hurt myself, because I forget how to be happy. I realized in that moment, flying somewhere over the Atlantic, flying home, that I am free. Free from fear. I've been saved. God has a plan for my life, and God is going to help me see it through to the end of my life. And I'm going to be happy living the life God has for me, no matter what the conditions, the issues, the problems, the tragedies, the struggles, no matter what happens, I will be happy. I am determined to be happy.

I am glad to be home, and not just to my physical home. When my children hugged me last night, I was home. When my man hugged me last night, I was home. And when I woke up this morning and fed all the pets, I was home. When I remembered that God cares for me and will provide for me, I was home. When I realized that I haven't lost my joy, I was home. I'm so glad to be home. May God bless you and keep you. Please keep praying for me, because I know the thief will try to steal my joy again when I am feeling weak. But I'm not afraid any longer. I'll keep praying for you, for your healing, your renewal, and your hope. Live in hope.

Tuesday, July 5, 2011

I can't even describe how happy I am right now. I am beaming from ear to ear. I am so blessed. This has been a wonderful day. I have received so many words of encouragement from so many different sources. I'm so giddy, I can't even think of how to describe what has happened to you. Deep breath, Allison, take a deep breath. How are you doing today? Stop reading right now, close this book, take a deep breath, and answer that question. How are you doing today?

Yesterday morning, I woke up really early. Now, I wake up around 5:30 every morning, but usually for a different reason. Yesterday morning, I woke up just really wanting to talk to God. I prayed and gave everything in my life over to God. I decided to stop trying so hard to make things happen, and to just let God be in charge. I decided that instead of telling God what I wanted him to do for me; I only wanted what God wanted for me. And I felt stronger and less anxious and more at peace after I did that. God laid it on my heart to visit 3 people, to write a letter, and to not call one person I always call. And I was obedient.

This morning I was struggling, because while I felt good about doing some of those things, I felt sad about one of them. Have you had mornings like that where you knew you were doing the right thing, but you just felt so discouraged because the right thing wasn't what you wanted to do, but you chose to do the right thing anyway? Is there something that you just want so much that your heart aches for it, but you know, deep down, that you can't make it happen; you just have to wait for it to happen?

But I was faithful. I began today honoring my promise to God. I felt weak. And every time today I felt sad, I stopped and prayed. All throughout the day, I received comfort and assurance and encouragement. A phone call from my man just to say hi and let me know he was still here for me even though we aren't exclusively dating anymore. I have to say that is weird to go from married to single/divorced to ready-to-date to an exclusive new relationship to almost-ready-to-get-married-again to let's-just-be-friends-for-awhile. But I'm grateful to have him as my friend, because I really do care about him. A card from a former student which reminded me that I am the kind of woman God wants me to be. I had lunch with a friend who always encourages me. A phone call from a friend I haven't spoken to in forever, who is another strong woman, who even in the midst of her illness called to tell me she was praying for me. Supper with my man's eldest daughter, a young woman I see maturing and blossoming before my very eyes. I am so proud of her. And before bed, I received a phone call from my missionary friend to share some more good news - a phone call from a new friend, a woman I've never met in person, who takes care of my man's parents at the nursing home, and who has been praying for me and our family for months and months. She was responding to the letter of encouragement God told me to write yesterday.

All of these things showed me that God really is in control and that He is going to do wonderful things, amazing things, miraculous things in my life, and I am so filled with hope and peace about the future. The other day I was full of fear and anxiety about the future, and now I'm at total peace. So much so, that I am happy. And nothing in my circumstances has changed. My circumstances are exactly the same as they were on last week, yesterday, and today. Nothing is really going the way I want it to. But everything really is okay. I want you to have peace like this. I want you to be happy.

Thursday, July 7, 2011

Today has just been a fantastic day! I have felt renewed in my spirit. I have strength and confidence that I can do anything. And hope that anything is possible. Today, I have been anxious for nothing. I'm not worried about the future. I'm not worried about what is happening in the present. I'm just happy. I'm happy because I know everything is going to be okay. And that doesn't mean that everything is going to be what I want necessarily, just that whatever it is, I will be okay with it. And I just feel free.

Are you worried about anything? Do you feel anxious? Last night, I had the horrible pain in my chest, like my lungs were being crushed, and I couldn't breath. I actually thought I was going to faint. And I've never in my life ever felt this way. Luckily I was having supper with my man, the medical doctor, and he diagnosed me as just having anxiety, not a heart attack. But I tell you, I've never had a heart attack, but my guess would be that's what it would it feel like. Because one minute I was fine, I felt great, I was laughing, I was happy, and then just all of a sudden, like the snap of a finger, I was having an attack, an anxiety attack. I didn't know why right then, because it was just instinctual and uncontrollable. But after I caught my breath, I realized that I was struck with it, because I saw something I never expected to see. I can't explain it, but it wasn't a ghost or anything crazy like that. It actually was the absence of something that was ever-present. I noticed the A was absent from my man's chain, and in that moment I knew that his heart was no longer totally committed to me, and he was stepping back from us. I never would have imagined that something so small, simple, and symbolic would have such a profound impact on my heart. Just maybe you've had an anxiety attack before, and you can relate. Well, anyway, I felt faint and weak and I nearly

251

passed out. I felt like I was having a heart attack.

And I realized I had a choice. I had a choice to give in and just pass out right then and there. Or I had a choice to reach deep down into my spirit and find the source of my strength and be bold. And that's what I did. I chose to be strong even when I didn't feel that way. I chose to be happy even when I was sad. I chose to share loving words about the miraculous power of God. I chose to play with the children and listen to him explain his heart. And I was set free. For the first time in a really long time, I didn't cry. And I'm so excited today, because I am one step closer to being totally healed. My life is not exactly the way I want it to be, but I'm happy anyway. It is miraculous, because it makes no sense. Who could be possibly be happy when you lose the love of your life? How could I be happy when I realized I wasn't going to have the relationship the way I wanted it to be? But what I learned is that I don't to be in control of every detail of my life to be happy. Its okay to just wait and see what happens. I have been so consumed with fear over my future, so worried about my financial security, my emotional well-being, my relationships, etc, etc, etc, that I've had moments of happiness, but I haven't lived in a constant state of happiness.

But right now, I feel great. I'm not waiting for the phone to ring. I don't care to check how much money has accrued in my investment account. I'm not thinking about how I am going to accomplish all of the things on my to-do list that I never get finished. I feel great. And I'm so looking forward to the day you feel this way too. It's going to happen for you too. Oh, this is something you may think is funny. My man's son mowed the grass for me today. And when I came home and saw him mowing the grass, it made the happiness I was already feeling bump up a notch. So I texted my man and said "it made me so glad to see your son mowing the grass when I pulled up in the driveway." And he texted back, "just don't forget you too can mow the grass." He makes me smile the way he subtly shows his support.

Friday, July 8, 2011

It's Friday! Almost the weekend! I really enjoy the weekends, because I'm able to get out of this little concrete block wall office and out from behind of my computer, and get outside and do stuff! I'm actually really shocked at myself, at how good of a mood that I am in, because most people would be feeling depressed if they were facing what I'm facing. What am I facing, you ask? Well, my kids are gone this weekend, and so I don't have them to hang out with. My man is busy, so I don't have him to hang out with. My ex is getting married on Saturday; but that's okay, because I don't want to hang out with him. But it's really not a horrible thing to be footloose and fancy free with no one demanding my time. Of course, I'm always open to invitations. And I am going to go swimming, and maybe hiking, with my friend on Saturday afternoon. Other than that, I'll try to knock some things off that never ending to do list and spend as much time as I possibly can outside in my yard or go for a walk, and of course, go to church on Sunday morning. Maybe I'll go horseback riding this afternoon, but I don't know, we'll just see.

What do you do when you have no plans? I'm a scheduler. I like plans. I like knowing what I'm doing at 2 o'clock, 4 o'clock, 6 o'clock, and so on. I'm really not a "just go with it" kind of person. I like knowing who I'm going to do something with, what that something is, getting my supplies in order to do that something, and exactly when that something will occur. Although I do like not having to know exactly what time it is as if I have to follow the commands of a clock rather than the desires of my heart. So

253

I guess I'm a real contradiction. Gee, no wonder men say women are impossible to figure out what makes them happy. I want a plan, but I don't want to be confined to the plan. I can be both incredibly patient about not getting my way and completely stubborn about wanting my way all at the same time. I am the most frou-frou, fashion conscious, high heel loving woman you'll ever meet; but yet, I can't wait to do guy-things like get out in the woods, play football, or go target shooting. Next week, a friend offered to take me to the target range and let me shoot some of his guns. And I'm really excited about that. Now I just have to figure out what day fits my schedule. And this is what is really great about the invitation; with a day's notice, he said he'll adjust his schedule to fit mine. It's been a long time since anyone has offered to change their schedule to accommodate mine.

I guess I'm just a Southern woman, through and through. I love with my whole heart and give everything I have into a relationship, but am prepared to stand my ground when I need to do so. And that kind of confident and positive attitude is something you have to grow into. And to be honest, if I wouldn't have had all of the pain and suffering for years and years of failed relationships, I probably wouldn't be able to believe in my self-worth as much as I do. When I was married to my first husband, he told me I was ugly and stupid. After our divorce, I became a runway model and a high school English teacher. When I was married to my second husband, I felt like I couldn't accomplish my dreams. I still struggled with issues of self-esteem. I still worried that I wasn't pretty enough or nice enough or good enough. I worried every day that I wasn't perfect enough. I just couldn't let go of my emotional baggage from my first marriage that I couldn't be good enough to be loved. I probably wasn't very easy to live with, because I tried so hard to create a perfect home and perfect life and to be the perfect wife. And so I had high expectations of myself. Then I didn't dress pretty to make myself happy; I dressed pretty trying to be perfect. I finally decided in 2003 to have breast augmentation surgery. No, I don't have implants. I had the opposite problem; my breasts were too big. Since puberty, I developed an hour glass figure with boobs, hips, and a narrow waist, but after having babies my body was out of balance. My mother designed custom made swimsuits for me by sewing in bras to hold my breasts in and taking in the waist. I bought swim suits, dresses, and shirts several sizes bigger than I really wore to just try to hide the size of my breasts. I ordered bras from a company in Oklahoma, because you can't buy a size 34FF off the rack at Victoria's Secrets. And my breasts caused me so much back pain. Bruised indentions were carved into my shoulders. So I just decided I had to do something about my breasts. So I had a breast reduction. And as my physical scars closed, my emotional scars opened. I spent that year facing every fear and emotional hang-up I had about every relationship I had with men and my own body. I confronted my past abuse and came to accept my life as it was. I came to realize what I really wanted. And while I wanted less on my chest, I wanted more for myself.

After I felt better and after we moved into a new house and once the children were settled in elementary school, I decided to go back to college to work towards my doctorate. I didn't need my husband's permission or support. I could do it all. And I did. I kept house, took care of the children, worked, and went to school. I was perfect. I was pretty. I was smart. I was a good mother and a good wife. I was nearly perfect, but my marriage was not. I wanted it to be so badly, but it just wasn't. And the more I improved myself, the more distance grew between my husband and I. Do you question yourself? Do you think you're not pretty or smart? Have you let others lead you to believe that you're not good enough? Well, you are more than enough.

So it really doesn't matter what anyone else thinks or says about you. I have heard so many times, "you're a good woman", "you'll make some man so happy", "you'd be the perfect wife", and look at me, I'm divorced. I'm single and no one is asking to marry me. Another contradiction. The perfect wife isn't married. But that's really okay. I really am okay with that. I'm still proud to be me. I still have hope for the future. And maybe one day, if it's God's will, a good man will want a good woman by his side, and I'll get married again. If he's a good man and he treats me right, and he wants the best for me, but I'm happy either way. I don't need a man to be happy. You too can be happy either way. Enjoy life's contradictions. Be the woman you are, not the woman others try to make you be. And if a man is really the partner God intends for you, he will support your dreams and accept you as the woman you are.

Saturday, July 9, 2011

I've been tossing it back and forth in my mind trying to decide if I should share something with you or not. Last night as I went to bed, don't tell, and then later if everything works out the way you want it, then no one will know there was a bump in the road. This morning when I woke up, I realized that if I really wanted to turn it over to God, that I needed to turn it over to you too. After all, I am writing this book to help you figure out what you need to do to have a happy and positive life. And if I'm struggling with something, you're probably struggling with it too. And I can't pretend that everything is just wonderful, when it's really not. It's time for me to do something different with my life. I am going to be just friends with my man for awhile, maybe forever. Neither he nor I have been totally healed from the pain and damage of our respective divorces, and we just aren't ready to move forward to total commitment.

And one thing I know is that I am a fantastic woman, and I need a man who would move mountains to be with me, to please me, and to prove to me that he loves me. And ironically, my man is the one who taught me I deserve all of that. Until I met him, having all of that seemed like a fairy tale that just doesn't happen. But now I know that it is possible to have a relationship where promises are kept and love is real, honest, and pure. And so, I'm holding out until I can have it all. I don't want a little love and kindness. I don't want a man who isn't prepared to give me his whole heart. And my man just isn't ready for that yet. Maybe he will one day. But it's in God's hands. We aren't broken up, per se, but we're not an exclusive couple anymore. And we won't be an exclusive couple again until he's ready to put a ring on my finger and love, honor, and cherish me every day for the rest of my life. We're still talking to each other. He is the companion I enjoy being with more than anyone else; he has blessed my life, and I have learned so much about myself and what I want and need from being with him. I will always be grateful for the time we had together. I have no regrets about choosing him; and I have a lot of regrets about the choices in men I've made in the past. He is a good man, very special, with a humble spirit, and a good heart. Failed relationships wreak havoc on us all. Sometimes you think you're healed only to be tormented with your past unexpectedly. I'm praying for him just as I pray for you.

We all need healing, renewal, and hope. Only God knows what the future holds. Things are just different now. It's not easy making this change to my life, but I'm okay. There is a time for everything. And right now, this is a time for me to spend some time with God and to make new friends and learn more about myself and get some of my personal goals accomplished. This is a time for him to spend some more time with God and to allow God to heal his broken heart over his ex, and decide with full confidence if I'm the woman for him. And if I'm not, it's okay. God has a plan for me.

Ecclesiastes 3:18
To everything there is a season, and time to every purpose under the heaven: A time to be born, and a time to die; a time to plant, and a time to pluck up that which is planted; A time to kill, and a time to heal; a time to break down, and a time to build up; A time to weep, and a time to laugh; a time to mourn, and a time to dance; A time to cast away stones, and a time to gather stones together; a time to embrace and a time to refrain from embracing; A time to get, and a time to lose; a time to keep, and a time to cast away; A time to rend, and a time to sew; a time to keep silence, and a time to speak; A time to love, and a time to hate; a time of war, and a time of peace.

Please pray for me as I go into this season of something different. Pray that I will have the strength and courage to just trust God and not try to fix things on my own. I'm always praying for you, for your healing, your renewal, and your hope. And I always believe that good things will happen. I believe in miracles. And I believe in peace that passes all understanding. My peace is intermittent right now. Some moments I feel great and happy and full of hope. Other moments I feel lost and alone. So what does one do about that? I'm not sure. Let's just take it one day at a time.

Sunday, July 10, 2011

Crying cleanses your soul. Don't be afraid to cry. I spent my entire life being afraid to cry in front of other people. Did you see the movie Blind Side, how Lee Ann would always go into another room or in the car to cry so no one could see her tears? Well, that's me. I've put up with incredible things where any other person would just break down and cry. I've been cursed and abused, and I didn't cry. I've been lied to, deceived, and mistreated, and I didn't cry. I'm a brave little soldier, I guess you could say. When things are really, really tough, I am resolute. I stand firm. I refuse to give in or give up. But that was me from twenty years ago. That was me from ten years ago. That was the "I'm not going to let you see me cry I will survive" woman. The "I don't care if you see me cry I have survived" woman cries when she feels like crying.

My empathy for others is so great. If I see someone else cry, there I go, tears welling up in my eyes and streaming down my face. I cry at movies. I cry when I see my mother cry. I cry when I'm angry. That's something different about me. I rarely, if ever, get angry about anything, but when I do, I don't shout or curse, I cry. If you ever find me shouting or cursing, then I'm just joking around or trying to give myself a pep talk. Do you know what a pep talk is? That's when you know you should do something a certain way, but it's not what you want to do, but you know you have to, and so you try to build up your strength and courage by coaching yourself through. I'm going to have to give you an example. Let's say, you decide you aren't going to take your ex back under any circumstances, because you know you can't trust him or her.

Side note: Most of the time, the person who leaves will ask to come back at least once. Everyone gets scared to change their life, especially when the reality of the new life sets in, especially when you are fabulous and wonderful, especially when they were stupid to wrong you in the first place. You have to prepare yourself to be strong, to not cave in. It's so easy to cave in and let someone walk all over you. But this is the truth. If he'll hit you once, he'll hit you again. If she cheats on you once, she'll cheat on you again. If he leaves you once, he'll leave you again. So you say to yourself: I'm not the kind of person who puts up with this crap. I deserve better than this – way better – way f****** better!

So you make your decision. No one else can tell you what the right decision is for you. You know what is good for you, and if this person is not it, take control of your emotions. And once you can move emotionally from the place of "he left me" to "I don't want him" then your healing will come. So what if he left you? My ex left me a year and half ago, and he got married yesterday. Do you think I care? No, I don't want him. He's not the man for me. You're not a victim. You're a strong, wonderful, amazing woman. And once you stop crying over how much you've been hurt, then the cleansing tears will come. You're finally ready to let it all go, let go of the emotional pain, let your past go. Then the miracle of your healing will come, and you can move forward with your life. I cry all the time now. And I'm not depressed and nothing is wrong with me. I'm just more in touch with and honest about my emotions. I used to never cry. One time, and this is really so silly, I'm embarrassed to tell you, I cried because my man wanted to buy me a candy bar, and I didn't want one. I just can't stand the thought of spending money just to spend money. And I don't like to be pressured to spend money, especially on something that will make me worry about how I look in my bikini. We all have our emotional hang-ups.

But it really is okay to cry. You're not weak when you cry. Hope can come in the midst of your tears. Don't be afraid to let your emotions show through. You are strong, even when you are crying. I cried three times yesterday. I already cried once this morning. I cried a second time while I was talking on the phone. When was the last time you cried? Right before you picked up this book and started reading? If you don't cry when you are bearing your heart and soul, something is just not right. I'm still a strong, fabulous, wonderful woman who deserves it all, who will have it all. I believe that good things are going to happen for me. I believe good things will happen for you. I'm praying for you, for your healing, your renewal, and for you to find hope in the midst of your tears. Just keep a box of tissue with you. It's okay. I keep one hidden in the trunk of my car, and when I really need a tissue, I pull off the road and take out the box. Of course, I don't want to drive around with tissue in plain sight; someone might think I'm emotional.

Monday, July 11, 2011

My friends continually amaze me with their kindness and concern for my well-being. I cannot possibly deserve such friends. My friends pray for me; my friends protect me; my friends counsel me; my friends remind me who I am and what I deserve; my friends show me over and over again that they care so much for me. I am so grateful to have good friends. Sometimes I get so absorbed in my own life and worries that I cannot possibly be as good a friend to them as they are to me. But I try to be a good friend. And I love my friends just as they are. Each of my friends is different from the other, and each of them brings something different to my life. I am so blessed to have good friends. I am so blessed that my man is my best friend before he is anything else. Friendship is the basis for real love. I don't know how to do this "I only want to be your friend" thing, but all I know is that I love him enough to try to be the friend he needs me to be. I don't know if I can do it.

Think for a moment about your friends. Think about how your friends have loved you and supported you through your trials and struggles. Think about your friends who have celebrated life with you. Think about your friends who have cried with you. You may not have a lot of friends. Some people only have one or two really good friends in their entire lifetime. It doesn't matter how many friends you have. It matters how much you love.

Jesus spoke about love and friendship in John 15:11-13 *"These things have I spoken to you, that my joy might remain in you, and that your joy might be full. This is my commandment; that you love one another as I have loved you. Greater love has no one than this, that a man (or woman) lay down his (or her) life for his (or her) friends."*

If you love your friends (and truly that probably applies to every person, not just your close friends) the way God loves, then your joy will be constant and overflowing. I want joy that is constant and overflowing. Knowing that my friends love me fills my heart with joy. Hearing my man say that he cares about me, and I am his best friend, especially in the middle of our difficult time, fills my heart with hope. It renews my faith that God can do anything, that God can restore my soul, and whatever my present troubles, I have peace about my future. I still don't know what the future holds, but I do know that my friends will be there, and that's great! I am so blessed. To all of my friends: thank you for being my friend.

Wednesday, July 13, 2011

Sometimes a look says a thousand words and a hug says a million words, at least they do when you are connected to the heart of the other person. Have you ever been around someone where you could communicate everything you were thinking and feeling and hear everything that person was thinking and feeling without saying any words at all? If you've never experienced a connection with someone like that, hold out for it, because it is priceless. Too many times I think some relationships are doomed to fail, because there is no real connection. The connection is a facade or a lie or forced to be there when it doesn't it really exist. But sometimes, in very rare cases, the connection is real, so real that it only can be felt, not explained with words. There is nothing more special than really knowing someone and being known by someone and being liked just as you are. I appreciate the times of silence where I have sat for hours next to my man, not talking, but just enjoying looking at the stars, or the view of a foggy blanket covering a distant mountain range, or watching the waves roll onto the sandy shore in the darkness. In those times, a peace found only in quiet companionship, undisturbed by noise and confusion, extinguishes all of my worries and fears. I rediscovered this peace last night, and I awoke with this peace this morning, and I carried this peace with me all through the day. I thank God for peace that passes all understanding. I thank God for giving me the gift of a special relationship that doesn't make sense to anyone else but me and him. It is unique. We are unique. Sometimes you just to be still. You have to stop trying so hard to figure things out. You have to wait for God to perform a miracle in your life. You can't make miracles happen. You just have to dream, hope, believe, and wait.

Each day, I've learned a little bit more how to turn my life over to God. Just because I said I was going to let God take control of what happens in my relationships, doesn't mean I know how to let go. Healing is a process. Healing takes time. But I am so blessed to have found peace in a decision to wait. And waiting feels right and good for me. I had to ask a lot of questions and spend a lot of time in prayer and talk it out with my man before I realized that waiting was right for me. I'm a doer; I like to get things done, and done quickly. But just like the best food cooks slowly, the resolution to emotional turmoil come in the appropriate timing. Healing cannot be rushed. I realized that learning how to wait on God to heal my heart and his heart is the best direction for my life. And now I have perfect peace about my decision. The next thing I need to learn is to not care what other people think and just do what God wants me to do, even if it doesn't seem logical to anyone else. After all, it's not like God is asking me to build a giant boat for all the animals on the planet. All He is asking me to do is to be patient and give Him time to mend broken hearts. I can do that. You too can wait for good things to happen in your life. Be patient.

So I promised to wait. Am I crazy? Would you wait for a man to realize that you were the woman for him? Never before today would I have ever said I would wait for a man. When I was married the first time, I didn't wait for Roger to change from being an abusive alcoholic. I packed my stuff and left as soon as I could figure out where to go. When I was married the second time, when my children were little, my ex-husband went through a phase where he said he wasn't sure if he wanted to be a husband and a father. And I gave him two weeks' notice to figure out if he wanted to stay or go. But no matter what, I wasn't going to wait forever for him to make a decision. Get in or get out. And that has been my philosophy in regards to men –

dating them or marrying them – you're either in or out, but I'm not playing games. For the first time in my life, I am an emotional wreck just imagining tomorrow without my man in my life. What am I going to do? Start over and try again.

Thursday, July 14, 2011

I am so blessed. And I didn't realize I had received this blessing until this morning. I knew that this event had happened, but I just didn't really think about how much this was a blessing to me until today. I know, I know, I'm taking a long time to get into this story. So this is what happened. Today I went to the podiatrist, because I had injured my foot at the beach a few weeks ago. And compared to all of the other patients in wheelchairs, on crunches, and bandaged from hip to ankle, my tiny bump on the heel on my foot was nothing. There I was in my cute sundress and sexy heels, and all these other people were really, really hurt. But my foot was hurting, and my injury needed to be treated before it got worse or infected. It did make me feel a little bit less like a pampered princess when a lady in a wheelchair dropped her purse, and I was able to pick it up for her and talk kindly with her for a few minutes. At least I did some good while I was there feeling guilty about complaining about my tiny, little, injury.

Have you ever guilty for complaining about your problems when you compare your situation to someone else's? If you ever start to think your life is unbearable, I can promise you, if you look around, you'll find someone who is going through something way more horrible than you. But that's not the blessing I realized. The blessing I discovered was that I owed God a huge thank you for a miracle He did through this doctor for the man who has brought so much joy into my life. Several years ago, long before I met him, my man had a waterskiing accident, and then later he had an infection where he almost lost his legs. I didn't know him then, and so I don't really know how much he suffered. I don't really understand what happened. All the details I know second-hand. But when the doctor who performed the multiple surgeries which saved his life and his legs said to hear how well my man was doing today, that my man being able to walk and play with me at the beach was a miracle, that's when I realized how blessed I am. Getting this little injury had the purpose of showing me the glory of God. I have taken for granted just how much God has done for me. I've written all about the walks in the woods, the football playing, the horseback riding, all the fun that my man and I have had together, and I had forgotten just how much a miracle all of the times we spent together is. God didn't just bring him into my life to my friend and companion, but He saved his life so that he could be my friend and companion. And no matter what happens in the future, I am so blessed. And I am so grateful God healed him.

There are so many miracles which happen in our lives every day that we just don't notice. We take these blessings for granted. We are too busy and distracted with our problems to remember how wonderful life really is. Every day is a gift. Every moment of happiness is a gift. Watching the girls play four-square in the driveway and hearing their laughter is what is really important in life. I thank God for all He has done in your life. I thank God for all He has done in my life. And I thank God for the blessings He will do for our future. Take a moment and count your blessings.

Monday, July 18, 2011

Happy Monday!!! Not really. I have been sick and throwing up all weekend. I can't eat. I can't sleep. I can't keep anything down. I've never had the flu in my life. I never even really had morning sickness when I was pregnant. And I am sicker than I have ever been. But I went to work anyway. And I had the joy of going to the doctor for my lunch break, which doesn't really matter since I can't eat anything anyway. The positives of being sick (if there such a thing) is that I've lost several more pounds. I'm not really trying to lose weight. I eat well. I exercise regularly. And except for now, I normally feel great. And that matters to me more than the number on the scale. Plus, most people think I'm a lot younger than I really am. And I don't think they are just trying to be nice, because they usually imply I'm younger in a condescending, you're too young to know anything kind of way. I actually love when people ask me when will I have children, and I say the oldest is 21. One of my colleagues today told me that he was sorry to hear about my brother. And then he said, you're the nicest, kindest person I've ever known. You are always making others feel better, and you light up the room with your positivity. I hope you have lots of children, so there will be more people like you in the world. Isn't that the sweetest thing ever? Of course, I didn't say a peep about not feeling well. And the nurse practitioner and two patients complimented me on my shoes. Of course, I had on cute heels when I went to the doctor. Who dresses up to go to the doctor when they are sick? Me. You just never know where you will meet someone new. A girl has to keep her options open until she's ready to say "I do." And I've already said "I do" twice, so I'm not in a hurry to say it again.

I went to church yesterday. To be honest, I really just wanted to stay in the bed. But the girls wanted to go so badly, I just couldn't let them down. So I took some ibuprofen, drank half a cup of coffee, dressed up, and drove to church. I don't know about you, but I always feel a little better when I look pretty. So I still dressed cute for work and for the doctor's office. Why look like death warmed over, even if you feel that way? So yesterday, I put a smile on my face and went to church. And I'm so glad I did, because the sermon was on commitment - that there will be disappointments and discouragements as you try to stay committed to your goal. And that if your goal is worthwhile, then the commitment is worth the challenges you will face along the way. One has a choice to either give up or renew your commitment. Renewing your commitment means making the choice each day to keep going in that direction. Have you ever been in the situation where you couldn't decide if you should give up or renew? Have you ever wondered if what you had committed to was worthwhile? Maybe this is how you felt before your relationship or marriage ended. Maybe there are other life situations, like staying in school or quitting school, where you have to renew your commitment to keep going. And if that's your situation, keep going. No matter what challenges you face in life, education will help you be better prepared to handle it. I finished my bachelor's degree and completed most of my master's degree as a single parent of a terminally ill child. I finished my doctorate while going through my divorce. And while I regret some things in my life, I do not regret getting an education. It wasn't easy, but it was so worth it!!!

Then after church yesterday, I went to lunch with my parents, because I was just trying to make them happy. I ate a roll and a few bites of salad. But all the kids ate well, so that was good. And then I came home and took a nap. And basically I napped off and on all day and all night, and then lost what I ate yesterday, took a shower, prettied myself, and went to work. Overall, it was a very good day. I would have felt badly whether I was at work or at home, and so at least, I was productive and made a positive impact on some other people's lives. And so I'm happy about that. I'm in pain, and I'm really tired. But my house is clean; the children are happy; and the dryer works now, so I can do laundry again. I'm so excited about that. Really I am. You too can do the laundry when you're sick. That doesn't sound as encouraging as mowing the grass, I know.

We are working a puzzle on the dining room table. I'll do anything to distract myself in between trips to the bathroom. The puzzle is a picture of ducks on a lake with a canoe pulled on the shore by a campfire with tall pine trees in the dusky evening. I wish I was sitting by the campfire right now, listening to stories and jokes, and making s'mores, even if the kids were the only ones to eat them. That would make me feel better. Just thinking about that makes me feel a little better. The song at church yesterday went like this, "storms in the night, but the joy comes in the morning." Happiness comes if you stay committed to finding happiness. I hope this is just a stomach bug, but unfortunately, I feel like this is so much more serious than a stomach bug. I'll know more when the test results come back from the doctor's office.

Thursday, July 21, 2011

In Matthew 17:15-20, a story is told of a boy who is afflicted, and the disciples prayed for his healing, but could not heal him. They asked Jesus to help, and the boy was healed, and they asked Jesus, "Why could we not heal him?" And Jesus said because they didn't believe they could do it. *"If you have the faith as small as a mustard seed, you will say to this mountain, move and it shall be moved, and nothing will be impossible to you."* Now, a mustard seed is extremely tiny, and unless you have no faith at all, then I'm sure you have a tiny, tiny bit of faith. And that, my friends, is all the faith you need to accomplish

269

the impossible. In other words, with a little faith, all things are possible.

I have never been this sick before in my life. I am hurting and so sick, now for over a week, that my faith is really shaken. My faith is really tiny. And yet, I believe. I believe God will not leave me or forsake me. I believe in miracles. I believe that all things are possible. My son was sick all of his life. All of his life, from the time of his infection which caused the brain damage, the paralysis, and the blindness, until the day of his death, I believed he would be healed. I had more faith as his mother looking at his impossible situation than I have for myself. I find that really surprising, because my medical problem is nothing in comparison to his. I can still see. I can still think and function. I can still walk, although sometimes I am dizzy when I stand. In the last year of his life, he needed a feeding tube to be able to have nourishment. And while I can't eat very much, I can still eat a little, enough to sustain my life. I don't know why I had more faith then than I have now. I always believed God will heal him, and even when I sat beside him when he died, I knew God had answered my prayers, and that heaven was my son's real home, and his painful, unfulfilling, life on earth was nothing in comparison to the glory of heaven. After he died, people would ask me if I still believed God can heal, just like in the Bible. And yes, I do. I believe.
But even though I have only a little faith, I have not given up. I believe. What are you going through? Are you in such despair that you are at the point of just giving up? Does your faith feel so tiny that it is almost nonexistent? I know how you feel. But just hold on. Don't give up. I think there's a reason why I'm going through what I'm going through. Like all of the other difficulties in my life, I learned something from those experiences. I learned something that made me a better woman. I learned

something that prepared me to deal with the next difficulty with more grace and dignity. We have the power to move mountains. Think about that. I can move mountains! You can move mountains! Mountains! A mountain is not a tiny little problem. A mountain is huge problem. And you can overcome a huge problem with tiny faith. So whatever you are going through, you can do it. You too can have enough faith to make it through. I believe in miracles. I believe that I am going to get well. I believe that you will be healed, renewed, and have hope everlasting. I'm praying for you.

Sunday, July 24, 2011

I'm still sick, but I'm not contagious. Whatever I have has kept me from eating or sleeping for two weeks. I have lost 16 pounds. I feel horrible constantly. The pain is constant. But I refuse to give up on doing the things which bring me joy. Every week, at least one day a week for an hour or so, I go to the nursing home and visit my man's parents. That's what I did yesterday, just like most Saturdays. His Mom has dementia really badly, and his Dad isn't a patient at the nursing home; he is her caregiver. And being by her side makes him happy. He takes care of her every day, except for when he takes a break on Saturday evenings to go to Mass. Over the last several months, I've gone with my man and sat with her sometimes while he's gone to Mass. But lately, he's been more worried that she's getting worse and that he's going to lose her, and so I've tried to go when I can talk to him some. I can't do anything to change things, but I can sit and listen. Sometimes I read to him a Bible verse which encouraged me that week. Sometimes we talk about their lives when they were younger, their home back in Louisiana, where all they've lived in the world, and politics. Sometimes we talk about gardening, my children, or their grandchildren. Sometimes we talk about livestock – like today, we talked about hay and cows and the drought in Texas. Sometimes we talk about how proud he is of his son and how worried he is about everything. But in general, he's a very positive talking man. He's a Christian believer, and he has lots of faith. A quiet faith he doesn't brag about, but strong and constant. I learn a lot about the kind of life I want to live from talking with him.

But most of all what I like best about visiting them is seeing real love. They have been married for over sixty years, and neither one of them can remember exactly how long. But he can tell me about the day he met her for the first time and how he courted her. And he blushes when he tells the story. It's the sweetest thing ever. When she has good days, she and I talk and talk. She always tells me I'm a pretty girl which I like hearing. And then we talk about makeup or shoes or the color of our nails. She taught middle school English, just like my mother does, and just like I did when I first started out in education. Or we talk about flowers, because she loved her flowers in her yard, and I love the flowers in my yard. Today, she told me I needed to water in the late afternoon when it's not so hot. And it sure is hot here in Georgia. And we talked about why the hydrangeas are blue. And sometimes, when it's just she and I, she'll tell me stories about when they were young and when her son was a small child.

Last Saturday, she was having a bad day, and I held her hand for a long time while she cried in pain. I stayed nearly all day, because she was just having such a bad day. I just couldn't leave her when she was in such a bad way. Thankfully this Saturday, she was having a good day, and we laughed. He cut up a banana for her, and she told him he was a good chef. And I asked her if he was such a good cook, would she keep him around for a little while longer. You know when she's about to make a joke, because she gets this sly expression on her face, a twinkle in her eye, and the corner of her mouth smirks up just slightly. She takes a long pause like you know she's thinking, and then she's says "I'm thinking about it." And she just beams at him like he's the greatest thing since sliced bread and he just melts her butter. And we all laugh. And when she's a playful, lucid mood like this, she loves to joke around. I wish I could have known her when she was a young woman, because I think we would have been great friends. Obviously, I mean if we were both the same age at the same time. So I said, "Yeah, he can cook alright, but maybe you just like having him around because he's handsome, and you just like looking at him." To which he replied, "No, I'm old and ugly." So I asked her, "What do you think about that?" And she smiled and winked at me, "he's handsome." Then she looks at him, and there it is, in the sparkle in her eyes, real love. After all these years, through whatever they've gone through, they have real love. And it makes me happy just to see real love between the two; I don't worry anymore if I ever have it for myself. Real love between these two kind people is precious, priceless, and just plain wonderful. And I walk to my car and drive home humming happily to myself. I believe in real love that lasts a lifetime, and I always will, even if I have been married and divorced more than once.

Monday, July 25, 2011

It is easy to love people who are kind to you, a friend who does something thoughtful for you, your small child who looks at you with adoring eyes, or a lover who loves you with the same intensity. It is so much more difficult to love someone who has hurt you. Forgive, surely. But love? I don't know if I can. I believe that the heart always holds the love that you have for someone even after that person is no longer in your life, but then your heart starts building walls to guard itself. Since I received it last November, I always wear a Tiffany heart necklace. I have only taken it off once in anger to prove a point which was wrong of me and immediately replaced and apology given. Another time I took it off for my mammogram. And I took it off just briefly to add a significant and important charm, the letter K, to the chain. I prefer to even clean it while wearing it, and so really, I never take if off. But last week, I added a shield with a fleur-de-lis next to the heart. It is the shield which guards my heart, because I am afraid of being hurt again. I honor the man who gave it to me and our love we share. I promised to wear it always, and I don't want to ever take it off, no matter what the future holds. This necklace is, without a doubt, my most important possession, and I would be naked without it. In this picture, you can see my Tiffany heart necklace with the letter K and my escutcheon – my fleur-de-lis shield to guard my heart.

I can't really explain why I wear it, but I just don't feel comfortable without it. I just feel naked if I look in the mirror and it's not there. I guess it's kind of like how after you've worn a wedding band for years, your finger feels naked without the circle of gold around it. Some people never stop wearing their rings; I did, because I was never going back. I guess I keep wearing my necklace, because I just don't know what will happen in the future, and my heart isn't ready to give up. I still believe love is real no matter what.

Part of the healing process is learning to love without fear of being hurt, and right now, I worry about being hurt. And so, I am hesitant to love. I gave my heart freely in the past, but now I am captive to fear of being hurt again. Yesterday, the minister spoke in the sermon that God calls us to love others even knowing that by loving as God loves we will be hurt again. Jesus said in Matthew 5:43-48, and I'm going to modernize the language, so please forgive me if you're a scripture purist. *I am to love those who are not part of my family, who have hurt me or betrayed me, or who has caused bad in my life. I am to do good to those persons who have wronged me, and most importantly, I am to pray for those who have taken advantage of me and who have hurt me deeply. God loves everyone, those that have done good, and those that have done bad, equally. That God doesn't love me more than another person just because I am a kind person.* And that if I truly want to love as God loves which I feel strongly God has called me to do just that many months ago. And to be honest, I thought I understood then what that meant, but I have learned in the past few weeks what that really means. Because I love, yes, as a feeling. And I love, yes, as a commitment and keeping a promise to love. But I also loved, because of the reward I received in return. The reward of which I speak isn't a material gift, but being loved in return or doing an act of kindness for someone because you know they'll do an act of kindness for you. Have you ever done a favor for someone? Did you do the favor so you could get a return on that favor later? I have taken my time and energy many times to do little things for others, and I'm sad to say, I've expected to be reimbursed. But that is not really kindness.

And I so easily was able to close off my heart after my divorces in regards to my ex-husbands, because I felt that being wronged justified me to hate them. And I have struggled with hating others who have done some wrong to me. But I want to really know love, not just romantic love between a woman and a man, but real love. I want to know the kind of love that is able to sacrifice one life for another. I want to have the kind of love that is perfect. And I will probably spend my entire life trying to figure out how to love like this, and the Holy Spirit will have to help me, because I am only a woman after all. And I have forgiven them. My general way has always been if someone hurts me to just avoid them, to cut them out of my life, and not to let them get close enough to hurt me again. Once my ex left, he was not coming back, no matter what. And I am stubborn. You must be somewhat like me, because you probably avoid your ex as much as I do. And you probably pat yourself on the back for not saying ugly things about him or taking your revenge on him just as I do. But that's not enough. God wants more from me. He wants me to not just forgive, but to pray, and to love.

Today, I took a small step towards showing this type of love by doing an act of kindness for my man who has hurt me deeply by his behavior. I did this knowing that he would likely not reciprocate the kindness, and that I may even be met with indifference or hostility. But I did it anyway. Not so much for him, but for myself. To show myself that I can, in a small way, do something to represent love without seeking a reward. And I can honestly say that it doesn't matter if nothing changes between him and me, because I did not do this to manipulate the situation, but only to be kind and loving. And for no other reason than to try to discover how God feels when He loves me and blesses me, and I don't respond back, so that I can learn how to love even when I don't feel loved in return. And

276

yes, this also means I have to start praying for my ex, and the people at work who annoy me, and anyone who ever does something which harms me, not just my friends and family. The minister specifically mentioned that ex scenario as being common for many people in the room. But I know I can do it, or at least, I'll try to do it; and every day, I'll get better at it. And if I can do it, then you too can love the jerk that broke your heart. I mean, you too can love as God loves. And yes, you may get hurt again, but love anyway. Don't ever stop loving. Don't ever put your heart inside a stone cold fortress and lock it away never to love again. Learn how to love perfectly by figuring out how to let go of the pain and loving the person who caused your pain. It won't be easy, but you can do it. When you do it, and by the way, you never have to tell the person you love them, just pray for them, you'll find happiness, healing, renewal, and hope. I'm praying for you. I believe that you are strong enough to learn to love as God loves.

Tuesday, July 26, 2011

I'm feeling a little better today. I'm still sick, and I'm still in a lot of pain. But finally I feel like I am getting closer to finding out what is wrong with me. My doctors just weren't listening to me; I couldn't even get one to return my phone call, much less refer me to a specialist.

My man, and even though we are more like friends now than a romantic couple, he will always be my man to me. That's his name to me, and there are various versions of that. Did you ever watch Little House on the Prairie? Do you remember Laura Ingalls calling her beaux, Manley? And that became his name to her. Well, that's how it is with my man. That, and darling, as he is the only man I've ever addressed as such, and that's how it is. Just as he has a nickname for me, and even though it aggravates my parents

277

and my children that he calls me by a nickname (and I'm not telling you what it is, so don't ask), it will always be his privilege to address me as such. But I'm on a tangent of nicknames; it must be the pain medication typing.

Anyway, today he did something he didn't have to do. Today he made my health a priority, and he helped me get into to see specialists and to get tests done. I've been politely asking my regular doctors for a month now to do some scans and tests to see what the reason for my pain is, and nothing. And so, I am extremely grateful, because I needed help. I don't know how to navigate the medical world, and I don't know what to say, what to ask, or what to do. All I know is that I am sick and hurting. I appreciate him so much. Most people can't put their emotional feelings to the side and do an act of kindness for that person. He showed me compassion. And I feel a little better, because he genuinely cared about my well-being today just as he cared about me being cold in my office during the winter and gave me a space heater. It really doesn't matter what happens in the future. It just feels good to know that I have friends that care about me, and he's one of them. And several of my other friends have been so caring towards me. And I appreciate them all so much. My friends help me to remember that I'm not alone.

Do you feel alone? Sometimes after a failed relationship, one feels alone. Abandoned. Lost. It doesn't matter if you left the other person, or he/she left you, or whatever the reason why the relationship failed. Everyone feels lonely sometimes after the relationship ends. But you're not alone. God is always there. And there are people who care about you. Your friends may seem busy and distracted, but that doesn't mean they don't care. Reach out and ask for help. I did, and my friends, my man, they all responded with kindness and compassion. I will be better soon; this pain can't last forever. Pray for me. I'm going to keep praying for you.

I've been sitting here for the past two hours writing in my journal, distracted with my own thoughts and fond memories of some of the best times of my life. I put my journal down on my nightstand. I went to brush my teeth. I read the cards taped to my mirror which I read every morning and night. One says "a new beginning." Another says "your old life is gone and your new life has begun." I smile every time I read them, whether I've a good day or a bad day, whether things have gone my way or if I've been disappointed, I still feel warmth in my heart when I read them. I have favorite pictures on my vanity, and I look at the smiling, happy faces looking back at me, and say a silent prayer of thanks. I will always be grateful for the people I love in those pictures. No matter what happens. And yes, even on the days when one of my children does something which really aggravates me; I still am grateful for my children.

Today was a good day and a bad day. I'm still sick and in a lot of pain, but I finally found a doctor who listens to me so intently I can speak in my soft, polite voice, and he heard me. And he was proactive on addressing my health concerns. And he ruled out some of the really scary things that could be causing my pain. I had several tests for cancer and more. And I'm grateful that my man is my friend before anything else and that even if he doesn't love me as a husband he loves me as a friend. There are more medical exams to come. I'm really not looking forward to the colonoscopy. But at least now I have hope that I will get better soon. Last week I almost felt like giving up and giving in to the pain, because I just thought I would hurt forever until I died and no one would ever listen to me and understand that the pain was real. But this week, so many things have happened to restore my hope. Little things which may seem insignificant, but they really are of major importance to my life. I am a romantic. And I've very sentimental. And so a scrap of paper or a card received from a friend, or a kind word, these all mean very much to me. And I cherish even a five minute phone call from a friend expressing care and concern and a happy thought. I'm learning to be thankful for the little things.

For what are you truly thankful? Stop and think of someone who has done a kindness for you, who is that person? Have you told them? You should. Even if the kindness was a long time ago, and a lot of other things have happened which have disappointed you, remember back to the good that person brought into your life and thank him/her. Maybe if you don't feel like you can tell them to their face or call them on the phone, mail them a card. A good, old-fashioned, stamped letter. You don't have to write many words -- as you can see from my comments above -- just a few words mean more than a novel. I wrote a letter of thanks today. I'm always writing letters.

Thursday, July 28, 2011

I'm really happy. I feel great. I still am in a lot of pain, and my symptoms are still all there. I still can't really eat anything. I've lost another ten pounds. But so far, I've had a really good day. I woke up early, took my medicine, had a cup of coffee, replied to messages from friends across the country and across the street, and then went back to bed until my man called around 10:30 and woke me up. I like getting wake up calls. The first voice I heard this morning was a joy to my soul. It seems like all I really do now is just lay in the bed completely cuddled down under the quilted coverlet with my hair feathered out over the huge pile of down pillows. You can never have too many pillows. My man and I talked about what the kids needed to get ready to go back to school, whether or not I was feeling better, and that his daughter's pet frog had a baby. At first, I thought he was pulling a joke on me. I have been accused more than once of being gullible and believing just about anything. But seriously, somehow the pond water that our daughters put into her frog's habitat the last time they played together came with a tadpole who grew up to be a baby frog. Wonders never cease. I hung up the phone smiling wondering just what does that baby frog look like. I stayed in the bed for many moments longer. I wrote in my journal, and I thanked God for my life, my friends, and all the children I have been given the opportunity to love. It is a very rare morning, indeed, when I am lazy in the bed. Sometimes it's not a bad thing to be sick, because it has given me an excuse to have a lazy morning. Of course, I did a little work on my laptop and emailed some reports and spreadsheets into the office. Even when I'm being lazy, my mind is constantly thinking what I can do next.

Are you a morning person? Do you like getting up early or sleeping late? I'm a morning person. I like getting up early, but I love staying in the bed when I don't have to be somewhere. Even more so with a fresh cup of coffee prepared just the way I like it. I could so easily be spoiled if given the opportunity. I finally crawled out from under the covers, showered, and went to work to finish packing my office to move to my new office. I have another doctor's appointment. Even though I was so tired and hurting from packing the last box and going to the doctor again, I stopped for a few minutes to visit the nursing home. And that visit was the best medicine a person could have. A warm and wrinkled hand envelopes mine and the circle of smiles brighten even this sunny room, and I knew in an instant that I made the right decision stop and say hello. Don't let pain stop you from doing the things you want to do. Coming home, I chatted with my man's oldest daughter about how she wants to decorate her room away at college. And hearing her cheery voice made me so happy. I am giddy with happiness. So many people have told me that I shouldn't be holding on to having a relationship with his family if we're not going to be together, but talking with them and doing little things for them makes me happy. And I'm in such physical pain; I have to do anything which makes me feel a little better. To have friends, to have family, I am so blessed. I may just have to go shoe shopping this weekend to celebrate if I can get up the energy.

But first, I need a nap. I've never slept so much in my life than these past few days. And I can't wait until I feel better, because I want to exercise. Some minor yoga-like stretching is all I've been able to do the last few weeks. And I really wish I could go for a long walk through the woods under the thick green canopy of summer. I want to hear the waters tumbling over the stones in the creek and pretend to fuss at the dog for soaking in the creek and getting me all wet when trying to climb onto the seat of the four-wheeler with me. If I feel even a tiny bit better, I'm going for a walk in the woods this weekend. There's a park with a hiking trail across a covered bridge nearby, and I love bridges hidden in the woods. I think I will walk there. And I'm hoping that in a few weeks, I'll feel so much better that I can go up to the mountains by Pilot's Knob. I just want to live in my folding chair with all of refreshments close at hand in my ice chest and just write. I don't care if I am all by myself; in fact, right now, being alone may be better. I long to be at peace where I can periodically look up from my scribbles on the page to note the changing colors in the evening sky over the mountains in the distance. I long to revel in the relatively silent world with no sounds but the crickets and bullfrogs by the pond. I am content to be alone in such serenity of our mountain. Who am I kidding? I don't want to be alone. I would be even more content to share my peace and perfect contentment with the most compatible companion. I'm really happy, and no present circumstance can steal the joy and hope I feel in my heart.

Friday, July 29, 2011

I forgot to set my alarm on my iPhone for this morning, and I overslept. In part, because I woke up during the night and took another pain pill. I was just too groggy to get out of bed this morning. Thank goodness I didn't have to be anywhere before 11 am. So it really turned out okay. In fact, in turned out better than okay, because I got woken up by some little cheerleaders this morning. Do you have trouble getting going in the morning? Well, you just need to bottle the energy of small children, because at 9:22 my phone rang, with "Good morning, you want to hear my cheers?" And blinking the sleep out of my eyes, I said, "Sure, lay it on me." And 8 minutes later I had heard 5 different cheers to be performed for the last day of camp. How can you not have a wonderful day after being woken up my energetic, happy, sweet little voices?

Today was going to be a great day! And it was. I quickly showered, got dressed, and headed out for my meeting which went fabulous, by the way. I am so excited about the strategic planning work we are doing for expanding college-level education in the local county. And even though I ate just a few bites, I had lunch with two of my girlfriends. I still don't eat much of anything, and I've lost another five pounds. I'm really not trying to lose weight; I just can't do anything about it. I can be in pain at home all alone, or I can be in pain listening to my friend tell stories about her recent trip to Oklahoma with the Pioneer Woman. Friends, no doubt, the better choice.

John 16:33 says "*These things I have spoken to you, that in me you might have peace. In the world you shall have tribulation: but be of good cheer; I have overcome the world.*" And from the beginning my day until now, I am in a good mood; my spirits are cheery. And I have peace over my circumstances and my future. There is no reason to worry; everything will work out as it should in time. So my little cheerleaders woke me up this morning like a bright ray of sunshine. My Mom called to see how I was feeling, but mostly to tell me excitedly that the new Joann's fabrics opened today. Then my friends encouraged me with their pep talks and smiling faces. Of course, one of the things I like about friends is how they can make you laugh at things they say which should actually annoy you. Friends have a way of telling you what you need to hear, without being condescending or judging the choices you've made.

I bought a baby gift for my friend's shower tomorrow, and if thinking about a new baby coming into the world doesn't make you feel joyful, then I don't know what will. And then just as I woke up from my nap a little while ago, my man's Dad called me to see how I was feeling and to share the little details of his day and how good of a day his wife was having. And then one of my former students posted a note of thanks on Facebook for being a great teacher, and another friend tagged me in a post with some kind words about how I'm one of the women who inspire her or something like that.

So even though my day didn't really turn out like I planned, and I didn't receive everything I wanted today, I still feel wonderful. I had a great day. I feel so blessed and so loved. I thank God for every person in my life. I thank God for keeping me here on earth to be a cheerleader for you. And you know what, if tomorrow is going to better than today, I am so excited. Enjoy your Friday night and the rest of your weekend and the rest of your life. I'm praying for your healing, your renewal, and your hope. Please, please, please keep praying for me.

Wednesday, August 3, 2011

I can open jars with tight lids. I can take out the trash. I can trim the shrubbery with the electric trimmer. I can reattach the loose deck board with a few more screws. I can rearrange the furniture in my house with those little slider things and can muscle a chair up the stairs one step at a time. But I cannot change the light bulbs in the light fixtures in the vaulted ceiling. Or anywhere else where a ladder and someone to hold the ladder, and someone to hand you the light bulb so you don't drop it while climbing the ladder are required. Do you hear a bad joke coming on? How many single Moms does it take to change a light bulb?

But seriously, I'm embarrassed to ask friends to come over just to help me change a light bulb. It was okay when I first separated in 2009, but that was nearly two years ago. But sometimes there are just simple things that one is capable of doing, but it's just a two person job, and I'm just one person. The light on the front porch has been burned out for two months now, but I can't reach it. No problem when a visitor comes in the day time, but it's embarrassing when they have to leave in the dark. I think I'm going to get a basket of mini-flashlights and give them away as door prizes. That would solve the problem. But then there's the fancy chandelier over the grand foyer, the halogen light in the vaulted ceiling in the bathroom, and the light bulb in the toilet room. Whose idea was it anyway to start designing houses with a toilet room that is too small to put a ladder in there with a ten foot ceiling? What are those little things you struggle with? For what do you need help and are too embarrassed to ask for help?

I really would just like a like a little more light. I would like little things to not be so hard. If I had known years ago I'd end up in this big house alone, I would have picked out a small cottage with lower ceilings. But it will be okay. One day, and today may be the day, I'll get really frustrated about the lack of light, and I'll come up with some creative acrobatic solution to reach the light fixture and change the light bulb. And if I'm lucky, one of my children won't find me funny enough to tag me in a YouTube video "Mom changes a light bulb." To be safe, I think I'll wait until they've gone over to a friend's house. And after I change all the burned out light bulbs, then I can go into the attic and clean out the dryer lint pipe. It may sound like complaining, but I'm really not complaining. I'm just sharing this illumination issue with you, just in case you've experienced a similar frustration. You are not alone. And just like I can figure out solutions to taking care of my house on my own, you too can change your own light bulb. You too can figure out the solutions to whatever home repair problem you need. So what if you've never held a hammer in your life before? You're smart; you can figure out how to do anything you need to do. I'm praying for your healing, your renewal, your hope, and your resourcefulness.

Sunday, August 7, 2011

It's Sunday night. The weekend is almost over. For many children, tomorrow is the first day of school. The weather forecast is predicting rain all week. And oh my goodness, this evening, the rain came down. I haven't seen the skies this cloudy and stormy and windy since I don't know when.

286

It was one of those rain storms where you look out the window, and say, "It really looks bad out there." And then you say a silent prayer of thanks that you have a warm and safe home. But you know what? No matter how bad the storm looked. No matter how hard the winds blew. No matter that the power went out, and we were in the dark. The storm didn't last.

Storms come, and storms go. The blessing in the storm is that you know the storm won't last. Whatever storms you are going through, whether a storm of nature, or a storm of personal torment, you can rest in the knowledge that the storm will only be for a moment. This too shall pass. Just like how the rain seemed to be upon us all of a sudden, my moments of worry come just as quickly. As a child, we had thunderstorms quite often, and when I was at my grandparents' house, because it was out in the country, we would lose electricity. We would play cards or Scrabble by the light of a kerosene lamp. Sometimes we would just sit on the screen porch out back and watch the rain come down. No matter how hard the storm blew, I always felt safe. I don't always safe anymore. Sometimes I feel so fragile. And then other times I feel like I can handle anything. But mostly, I just pray that the storm will pass, or that the storm is not real, and that I can just revel in the sunshine on the sandy beach. Are you afraid of the storm? Do you worry too much? Do you allow your insecurities to steal your joy?

Have faith. Have courage. The storm will not last forever. Look for the moments of reassurance rather than focusing on the things which distress you. Through a caring comment from a friend or the love of a child or a memory of good times, you will be renewed.

Wednesday, August 10, 2011

Lately there have been so many gloomy, overcast, thunderclaps in the distance days that it made today seem even sunnier, even more beautiful. Today was a beautiful, sunny day. Unfortunately, I spent most of my day in meetings, but walking between buildings, and especially driving home with the top down was wonderful. I love driving with the wind blowing my hair, with fun, upbeat music playing on the radio, and on the curvy road over the bridge where I can see the sun glistening off the lake and envy the boaters down below. Driving past Lake Lanier is one of the best parts of my day. And do you know what the best part is? I get to drive over the lake twice – once in the morning and again in the evening.

We lived in Florida when I was in high school and learned to drive, and so of course, cruising the causeway and Clearwater Beach was a must. And I loved driving anywhere I could see the ocean. And when we lived in Louisiana, I loved seeing the water collect in the ditches beside the road after the rain. And I loved driving past the Bayou D'Arbonne over White's Ferry Road. There used to actually be a ferry from one side of the D'Arbonne to the other that was operated by the White Family. I remember my grandmother telling me how we were related to the folks who ran the ferry, but I don't remember the details. I still think it's neat that before the bridge, there was a ferry. I imagine what it would be like to have to wait for the ferry to come to cross the D'Arbonne.

I think I'd like to be baptized again, and I'd like to be baptized in Lake Lanier or in the ocean, but I'm waiting for now. Now just doesn't seem like the right time, but one day I hope I will. Have you ever been baptized? Maybe you're not a Christian, or maybe you've never had the opportunity.

So just in case you don't know, baptism is symbolic of dying to your old life and being reborn to your new life in Christ. There's a lot more to the theology and the story than that, but that's the basics. Some people choose to get baptized only once, and some religions don't do immersion. And really the way to be baptized is the way that feels right to you. Some people choose to get baptized more than once for various reasons. And the reason why I would like to be baptized again is to symbolize leaving my old life – my divorces, my failures, my pain. So it's not so much, for me, about becoming a Christian, or reinforcing my religious views, but more about being ready to walk in my new life with a new partner. And so, I can't be baptized alone this time. So I don't know when, or if, it will happen. But if I ever am baptized again, that's how I would like to do it. And if I ever marry again, that is all the wedding ceremony I need. Rather than a fancy dress or a big reception, I would just like, in a very simple and subtle and special way, symbolize that his life before our life together and my life before our life together is gone, and when we come up out of the water we enter into our new life together. Healed. Renewed. And full of hope for the future.

Saturday, August 13, 2011

This may sound really strange, but while I was watching TV earlier I just really started missing my football. And so, I got off the couch, went into the garage, opened the trunk of my car, and got my football. I brought it back into the living room and ran around the living room playing football by myself. I tossed my football into the air. It's silly, I know, but I didn't have anyone else to play football with, just myself, and I just really needed to play. Today has been a really serious day. It feels like I spent all day on the phone talking with one friend or the other. I am the go to girl. And I don't mind it at all. In fact, I love talking to my friends and listening to my friends. Every friend has a different issue, a different life situation, a different problem. But they all have one thing in common. Every friend wants to figure out how to get from point A to point B with point A being the mess they are in now and point B being what their heart desires their life to be like. Is that what you want? Are you trying to figure out how to make your dreams come true? Do you need a game plan?

Step One: Figure out what your dreams really are. And your dreams are not what someone else wants for you. They are not what society thinks is right for you. I can't even tell you what you should or should not be doing. I do know what my own heart, and I know what I want. And I am okay with taking life one day at a time and waiting for my dreams to come true.

Step Two: Don't let anyone put you down. Negativity will not get you closer to your dreams. It's okay if others don't understand you or your dreams. You don't need anyone to approve of what you do or don't do. It's okay to be you - the real you - just be you.

Step Three: Surround yourself with people who believe in you, who want you to have your heart's desire, and who unselfishly want the best for you. I think this is why my friends call me. Because I don't want anything from anyone. I'm not friends with my friends, because they do things for me. I'm friends with my friends, because I care about them. For each and every one of my friends, I want their dreams to come true.

Step Four: Believe in the impossible. Dreams do come true. Miracles do happen. Real love exists. You can do anything. Don't give up on your dreams. Don't give up on yourself. Don't give up on love.

The way your life is today is not the way your life will always be. I am happy, because I know what I want, I know who I am, and I have faith that good things will happen. And I don't have to see to believe. Only time will tell what the future holds for you. I own a beautiful white ceramic watch given to me by my man. This was the Christmas gift he gave me on our first Christmas together as an exclusive couple because only time will tell what will happen. I wear it every day to remember that I do not have to anxious about the future; that God knows my heart's desire, and the future will happen just as it is meant to be. I don't know what the future holds exactly, but I do know everything will be okay. In time, you will be healed, you will be renewed, and you will have hope in your weakest moment. I'll always pray for you.

Friday, August 19, 2011

I was so exhausted last night I kept dozing on and off while trying to do things around the house and on the computer. If I sat down, I'd feel myself getting relaxed, and then my eyes would drift shut slowly. I was writing in my journal, and several times I found I was just holding the pen in the air, but I refused to go on to bed. I worried that if I went to bed early, I would wake up way too early. So I forced myself to stay awake until after 11 pm. But I still woke up at the crack of dawn. Go figure. I woke up before my cats started fussing for breakfast. I woke up before the first alarm clock went off. I woke up before the rooster started crowing. I don't have any roosters or chickens; I'm just kidding. But I would have chickens if I didn't live in a subdivision.

We had chickens when I was a kid. Back in Louisiana, my grandparents had farm animals. And we had a few chickens and a rooster so we could have fresh eggs. But my grandfather never let the chickens hatch the eggs. One day I asked to see a baby chick. Matthew 7:7 *"Ask and you shall receive."* A few weeks shortly after, a crate arrived at my house; I came home from school and found a crate full of baby chicks - 103 baby chicks on my doorstep. My grandfather had shipped chicks to my house. My parents were not too happy, but we built an enclosure, and then began my chicken raising days. I had a blast. I named every single one of them. They were all different types of chickens, and it was like a whole bunch of birthday presents seeing how each one transformed from the tiny peeping fluff into its full grown feathered glory. There were white chickens and brown chickens, speckled chickens with feathers flipping out over their toes, red chickens. I didn't even know that chickens came in all those different colors. And then when they started laying eggs, I found out their eggs were different colors as well. We dye eggs at Easter, but nothing is as pretty as all of the different shades of natural egg shells.

But farm life is not always fun and throwing out feed without a care in the world. My 103 chickens grew up, and that was too many fresh eggs for one family, and my parents had no interest in going into the chicken business. So one hot and sticky afternoon, I locked myself in my room and cried myself to sleep as my parents slaughtered all my chickens. They plucked them, they cut them up, and put them in the freezer. I didn't eat chicken for nearly a year, because every time my mother cooked something with chicken, I knew it was one of my babies. I came to accept the realities of farm life, or either that, my appetite for fried chicken won out, because I eat chicken today. Those of you who didn't grow up on a farm probably don't have affection for the animal which ends up as food on your table later, so it may be difficult to understand what it was like to play with your friends in the yard where you

could see the aftermath of the slaughter of your
pets. Maybe you're horrified by a story like this and thank
God you don't live on a farm and that you buy your food
neatly packaged in a grocery store. But you know
something interesting about all of the sorrow and pain I felt
at the death of my chickens; I wouldn't have wanted to have
never received that crate of baby chicks. That was one of
the best days of my childhood and the months of playing
with the chickens were some of the most fun I had growing
up. It was worth it. Looking back on it, it was worth it. I'm
thankful I received the baby chicks. I remember the fun and
joy more than anything else. And that's what I've learned to
do as I've grown up. I remember the fun and joy more than
anything else. Why? Because I'd rather be happy than sad.

Tuesday, August 23, 2011

The past few weeks I have been hurting both physically and
emotionally. I'm tired of not being well; I am exhausted to
the point that the tears of there just waiting for the moment
of release. Yesterday I added a sore foot to my list of
medical ailments, because that tiny little injury I told you
about several weeks back became a serious infection, and
today the doctor injected my heel, and my foot feels like it
is on fire. Last night, it was just almost more than I could
bear. I prayed some, but I was exhausted I didn't even have
the strength to pray any words of substance. But this
morning, I woke up really, really early, with renewed
strength and good humor. Proverbs 17:22 says *"A cheerful
heart is good medicine; a broken spirit saps your
strength."* Maybe what helped was getting a good night's
sleep. Maybe what helped was laughing at me taking a
shower with my bandaged foot sticking out so it wouldn't
get wet. I'm sure I looked ridiculous. By the time I got in
my car to drive to work, I was cheerful. And I realized just
how important my positive attitude is to me. I really can't

allow myself to have a pity party, because feeling sorry for myself and my situation makes me feel worse. And it does me absolutely no good. Have you had a pity party before? Have you cried about your situation? Have you ever whined that life is just not fair, and you don't deserve this?

It's okay if you have had moments of despair and weakness. It's okay if you've shed some tears. It's okay if you've whined, because life isn't fair. And no matter who you are, or what you've done, you don't deserve to be mistreated or neglected or unloved. You deserve to have your heart's desire. I wanted one thing to happen this morning. I wanted this one thing more than anything else that could have happened. I wanted this one thing more than my pain of my throbbing foot to go away, more than anything; I wanted to hear a voice. Not just any voice. I'm not crazy like I hear voices in my head. I mean, I wanted to hear the voice of one particular person, and I didn't expect that I would, but I did. Between my home and my work, my phone rang, and the voice I had been wishing to hear since I woke up was on the other end of the line. And not only was I glad about that, but I was even happier that I had made a decision to be cheerful. That whining about my problems was not going to make things better, but being happy will. So I chose to be happy. And consequently, I really got to enjoy that phone conversation.

I may never have everything that I want, but I appreciate the little things that I do have. I may be really sick, but I'm not as sick as other people. I may have to hobble around for a few days with a sore foot, but I'm not in a wheelchair. My son spent 11 years confined to a wheelchair. I have friends who have had much more severe medical problems than I have. I should be thankful for how great my health really is, and how much I really have. And so the best medicine is not found in the little bottles from the pharmacy. The best medicine is found within your heart. And waking up with the decision to choose to be happy and to go about my day with a positive attitude and a generous spirit allowed many little wonderful things to happen throughout my day. None of these wonderful things were earth-shaking things. Apparently there was an earthquake in my town today, but I guess being on the 4th floor, I wasn't close enough to the ground to feel it. I found happiness in the little things -- like a phone call, a kind word in passing in the hallway at work, the awkward smiles on my student's faces when they had to answer impromptu questions in class, a cup of coffee, a productive meeting, the gift of a lunch, time to write a few thank you cards, and so on. I could keep on with the list, and you would see that any of these things are ordinary day to day happenings, but in them, I found joy. I want you to have joy. I want you to find your strength within, so you too can be happy.

Monday, September 5, 2011

To help you and me both get out of the funky, post divorce dating blues, let's focus on the benefits of post divorce dating. And there are benefits, really. I just want to make a side comment, I do believe in happily ever after, true love, and being with your soul mate for the rest of your life. But that's not where I am in life right now. I don't have all of that, and I don't know if I ever will. So I can whine, complain, and pout about not having that, or I can choose to be happy and embrace my life as it is with a positive attitude. I choose happiness. I choose to enjoy life. So benefits...

The first benefit is that one man doesn't have to be everything. If you're not ready to have a new life partner, well then, you can just have lots of friends. If you like fishing, then you can have a date to go fishing with one man. And if that man doesn't like the theatre, then you can go to the theatre with another man. I think I may just make a list of all of the activities I like, and then just look for a companion for each activity. I can have a bowling partner, a fishing partner, a shooting partner, a movie partner, a symphony partner, and so on. Now, I just need to make a list.

The second benefit is that I can maintain my independence. I can do what I want when I want, and it doesn't matter if no one approves of my decisions. Not that I plan to go wild and crazy. But it's really nice to wake up when you want and to eat when you want or to work late if you want and to decide to stay home or to go out without having to take a vote.

I'm still holding out for real love that lasts a lifetime, but until then I'm going to have some fun and enjoy my life. I'm still waiting. I'm still taking it one day at a time. Whatever you are going through, figure out what you need to have some peace and happiness, and just do that. Don't worry about what other people think you should or shouldn't do. Don't worry about your problems. You too can be happy.

Sunday, September 11, 2011

Everyone has one; a list, I mean. A list of things you really want to do in life. I know, you thought I was talking about my list of men friends. But I sometimes have to strike from that list too. But this time, I'm talking about my wish list. Some people call it a bucket list - things to do before you die. I just call my wish list - my list. I'm not worried about completing my list before I die. In fact, I'm always constantly updating my list when a new idea of something awesome pops into my head. And I don't really want to rush through life. If I miss out on doing one thing because I'm taking my time and really enjoying something else, then I'm okay with it.

Yesterday I crossed one item off my list: see a Broadway show on Broadway. I've seen plenty of Broadway shows which have travelled to other major cities, but I've never actually been to Broadway. And I saw the most fun, most amazing, most entertaining show of my life. We saw the matinee of *Priscilla, Queen of the Desert*; the rest of the day and night, I was singing and dancing. I crossed a second item off my list: to buy a pair of Christian Louboutin shoes in his store in New York or Paris. And since I am in New York, I bought them here. The New Simple. That's the name of the shoe. This shoe is the classic black patent leather 4 inch stiletto pump with the signature red sole. Gorgeous, I can't wait to wear them. No, I didn't wear them traversing the New York City streets for 10 hours. I didn't want to mess them up the first day. Besides I was already wearing my Giana Binis. I'll admit, by dinner time I switched to a pair of flats. My friends were wondering how long I'd last. I wonder if they placed bets. Because people ask me all the time how I walk in my heels. One time when I was meeting friends for drinks after work, a man who was being a little to forward considering that I was with a date, said "I like your shoes; how do you walk in those? I replied, "Well, I have lots of practice." That's how I always answer that question. Then he commented, "I have lots of practice too; just not with shoes." And that, my friends, has to be the worst pickup line I've ever heard.

Let me tell what is at the top of the list is real love that lasts a lifetime. I want to have that more than designer shoes, more than fabulous vacations, more than anything. Everything else on the list is just to entertain me until I find it. I know God has a plan for me. I know He wouldn't have given me a heart like this if there wasn't real love predestined for my life. I'm so excited to be flying home today. And yes, it is 9/11, and flying home from New York today. I'm not superstitious. I'm not afraid because just like every day my life is in God's hands. And this is a beautiful day in a beautiful city. This city mourns the loss of loved ones a decade ago and celebrates life as it is today. We all have loss in our past; live in today; hope for the future.

Monday, September 12, 2011

And now I can't sleep. I have had a wonderful day, and tomorrow I expect to be even better than today. Does this ever happen to you? Like maybe the night before you go on a vacation where you've really been anticipating all the fun stuff you're going to do? Or maybe the night before you have a significant surgery and you're worried? Or maybe the night before a really big date? Or maybe you can't sleep because your relationship issues are causing you anxiety and you just can't turn off your brain from thinking and go to sleep? And there could be other reasons you may have, but whatever the reason, you just can't sleep.

When I can't sleep, I just turn off all the lights except for the lamp beside the bed, and I cuddle down under the covers, and I just take a deep breath, and relax. I allow my mind to wander and reflect over this and that. And I try to focus on the calm, peaceful, happy things of my life. And I just let go of the things that have hurt me or are worrying me. It's not always easy to let go, but I just keep bringing my thoughts back around to the things which make me smile. Things like a kind word. Or a thoughtful gesture. Or the hug from a dear friend. Or the last time my man and I sat and talked. Sometimes my emotions overwhelm me too, and I cry a little over what I've lost, but then I reflect on how much I've gained. I have lived an amazing life where many wonderful people are a part of my life. This past weekend, I had so many friends text me and call me while I was in New York. They were worried about me, and it just felt nice to be worried over. So what if I'm not in a serious and significant relationship? I am loved. My friends love me. My children love me even if we did fuss over homework and messy rooms tonight. My goddaughter called me this after school on her way to cheerleading practice, and I had the joy of hearing the giggles she shared with her friend as they told me stories about their day at school. My life is so full of joy and happiness. I am so grateful for my life just as it is. And I am looking forward to seeing how much more my life becomes. Will I spend my life alone? Will I have a relationship full of real love and companionship? I don't know what's going to happen; but I do know this, I will be happy.

So it's time to turn off the lights, say my prayers, and go to sleep. And the simplest prayer is to say *"our father which art in heaven, hallowed be thy name, thy kingdom come, thy will be done, on earth as it is in heaven, give me this day my daily bread, and forgive me my trespasses as I forgive those who trespass against me, lead me not into temptation, but deliver me from evil, for thine is the kingdom, the power, and the glory, forever, amen."* Anything else that you think up in that moment to add to your prayer will be good too. And then I close my eyes, and go to sleep dreaming of how my sins have been washed away, how God has provided for all my needs, and how He has a plan for my life and I can trust and believe that all will be well in my future. Good night. Pleasant dreams.

Thursday, September 29, 2011

When I returned home this evening, I walked around my yard for a few minutes just to enjoy the cool autumn air and to survey the changes that have taken place so recently. While watering the newly transplanted rosebushes, I realized that sometimes change is needed in your life so that you can grow and blossom. That saying "bloom where you are planted" does not mean that you should be stuck in a flowerbed where you cannot bloom. Maybe at one time you flourished in that flowerbed. You had love. You had warmth. You were watered. You had everything you needed. And time passed. And your relationship changed. What once was a sunny bed is now in shade.

The maple tree grew taller and is now providing too much shade for my knock-out roses. For years, my roses were beautiful and plentiful. I had to trim them back every evening, and the next day, every time, they rewarded my efforts with new red blooms. But this year, this summer, they stopped blooming. My rosebushes were dying. I watched them for months become more and more sickly - unsure of what to do. My heart was broken. I became sick with grief in the coolness and distance of love I had once had. And I tried so hard to keep blooming without warmth, without rain, without sunshine, without fertilizer, without love. But finally I had to accept the inevitable; it was time to move on. It was time to change flowerbeds. One day I made a decision that it was time, because I wasn't going to allow myself to die from a broken heart, any more than I can watch my roses die. If you need to make a change in your life, make it. If you need to move the roses to a sunnier spot, move them. If you need to find love from someone else, search for the man that can love you for you. Just let go of your past and move on. That's what I did. And I'm putting down new roots, and every day, I'm getting stronger. I planted myself in a new spot, and now I'm blooming. Are you blooming? Or have you been watching and waiting for what will not be?

Is it time for you to find courage to move on with your life and leave your past behind?

So I didn't bloom where I was planted before, and that's okay. And I need help to grow, and that's okay too. Next Spring, I am expecting a glorious display of reds and pinks under the dappled sunlight streaming between branches of the river birch. And I am so excited to see next season's blooms and to see where I will be in my life. I could have taken care of my rosebushes by myself, but I am so thankful that I have help from a friend. I can take care of myself, but I am so happy that I can share my life. You too can take care of yourself, and you also have people who love you and with whom you can share your life. If you're not blooming where you are now, then move to a spot where you can bloom. You are too beautiful to wither away. God has a plan for your life. God has healing for your broken heart. I believe. Do you?

Tuesday, October 4, 2011

The telephone has allowed us to connect to friends, family, and loved ones easier, faster, and across long distances. Technology has increased as such that actual miles and miles of cable lines are no longer necessary. Your words are carried through the air on invisible, imperceptible, beams. Like magic, I can log onto my computer and Skype with someone on the other side of the world and see and hear them for free. When I was in Germany this summer I communicated with my children, my parents, my man and his daughter using the computer. As long as I don't mind the buffering or delay, it really is like magic what technology can do. To be able to pick up the phone and call someone when you are thinking about them is a miracle. To be able to type a text message to let someone know that you care or that you are safely arrived is a million times improvement to the slip of paper tied to the messenger pigeon's leg. Before the invention of the telephone, I don't know how people had the patience to wait for weeks for a letter to arrive by the pony express. And I'm someone who loves to write actual letters with paper, pen, and a stamp on the outside of the envelope, and when I, at the moment I am missing someone, desire instant communication, an email, a letter, a Facebook wall post, a text message, a phone call, just is not sufficient. I am thankful for the convenience of the telephone. I am thankful that when time and distance and other obligations prohibit travelling to sit down with someone to converse that we are blessed to be able to "let our fingers do the walking." For those of you who don't remember how to look up numbers in a printed phone book, that's the slogan for the yellow pages directory.

But no matter how thankful I am for technology, the worst torture to me is waiting for the phone to ring. When I want so badly to hear the sound of someone's voice, and it just doesn't happen, I don't know what to do. Do I call, or do I wait? My mother always said girls are not supposed to call boys. But then I read this one post-divorce dating book where the author said to not play games and just call if you want to talk to someone. My ex prefers to email me, even though I ask him to call when he wants to talk about the children. I refuse to call my man, since I called him one time and interrupted a date after we broke up. That was too much. I couldn't handle that. But it is somewhat ironic that he will call me late at night to see how I'm doing, and I think one Friday night we both had just gotten home from our respective dates, and then we talked on the phone about life in general. Neither of us admitted having been on a date prior to the phone conversation. And secretly, I wished I had been on a date with him. I miss him. Since I've been sick, even though we aren't together, he checks on me. I rarely see him; sometimes it's just I bumped into you in town somewhere kind of see you. He is my friend, a real friend. And I've found that other men just don't understand how one can be friends with their ex. But I try really hard not to burn bridges. You never know what is going to happen in the future. And I really don't like being told who I can talk to and who I can't. So ladies, don't put up with jealousy and possessiveness. It's okay for a man to be jealous that you have a date with someone else. I'm jealous that my man is dating someone else. Feeling jealous and acting on that jealousy is too different things. If you really love someone, you want them to be happy, even if their happiness is not found with you. I want him to be happy. And I want to be happy. And you, me, him, and everybody else, needs to take the time to figure out what they want and need and what makes them happy. The biggest mistake I made in my post-divorce life was rushing into a new relationship. I needed this year to find myself. And now it's been nearly two years, and I have found happiness in my life. But I still wait for the phone to ring. Just not for my man to be on the other end of the line.

If your friend or teen forgets the number one safety rule, text to say you made it home safely at night, do you assume all is well, or do you call 911 and file a missing persons report? For dating safety all of my single girlfriends text each other where we are going for the date, with whom, and then when we get home. That's our just in case someone never makes it home, we know what to tell the police. And if you're in a mid-sentence phone conversation with someone, and the cell signal is lost, and the call is disconnected, what happened? Was it really a technical problem outside of human control, or did the other person decide to end the conversation abruptly with no explanation? I can't stand it when I don't get to finish my sentence, and I really can't stand it when the other person hangs up on me on purpose. So as much as I love talking, and for as often as I get as excited as Pavlov's dog to hear the ping of a new text message, voicemail message, or the ring tone for someone special; for this and other reasons, I'd rather take the time, the gas money, and the effort to drive to in the same room with the person with whom I wish to converse.

The main reason why I'd rather hold my conversation in person rather than on the other end of a little plastic box with buttons is that I want to see your face when we are talking. I need the additional meaning added to your words of the paralanguage and nonverbal gestures. I need eye contact. Looking into someone's eyes, or feeling the pressure of their hand in yours, reveals more about what they are thinking than magical, garbled words travelling through space. Also, silence is so awkward and disconfirming on the phone, but can be so pleasant and comforting in person. Sometimes you want to be connected, but you just don't feel like talking. Sometimes you just want to be in proximity to someone, but you don't want to interact with them. That's kind of like when my kids want me to be in the room with them while they watch cartoons and not talk to me. Or when a couple wants to sit on a park bench with their arms around each other and feel the same breeze, sunbeam, and hear the call of the whippoorwill or the song of the mockingbird, and be one without speaking. That's the type of connection you can't get in separate locations holding a phone up to your ear. So while I'm anxiously holding my fingers back from typing out a text message, or when I'm carrying my phone around in my pocket and praying that the cell phone tower keeps transmitting a good 5 bar signal just in case the person I'm waiting to call me calls me, what I really want is to be standing right in front of you.

Have you read Jane Eyre? It's a classic, and if you haven't read it by now, you deserve to have the ending spoiled for you. Due to a crazy plot twist which would make this too long of a story to tell I will abbreviate, Jane and Edward find out at the altar that they cannot wed, and Jane runs away. For a year they live separately from one another; a tragedy befalls Edward as his home is burned to the ground, but in fate, this enables them to now wed. But Edward has no means of informing Jane, and Jane is considering marrying another man and moving with him to become a missionary. And then one night, Edward in his desire to see Jane, calls out his window, "Jane, Jane, Jane" and Jane standing outside her home hears her name on the wind, and replies "Where are you? I am coming." And the next day, without knowing anything more than she is compelled to find Edward, she goes and searches him out. As disconnected as circumstances caused them to be, they are still connected. Love connects them. There's no secret message in this story; my point is very simple, as human beings we desire communication and connection. We want to be able to talk and to listen to our family, friends, and loved ones. The phone is a fabulous invention which makes it easier, but sometimes you do just find yourself sitting behind the steering wheel of your car with tears streaming down your face trying to decide if you really did hear your name on the wind, and there you wait. Or sometimes, in the morning, you just wake up early to pray that your friend is safe, and that all is well, because the phone didn't ring when you wanted it too. That's what I did this morning. I'm praying that all is well; I'm praying for more than one friend, and I'm praying for you, as always.

Thursday, October 6, 2011

After supper tonight I went for a walk for exercise, for fresh air, for just plain fun. And like the miracle of true love, I saw the very first burning flame of the season in my own backyard. It wasn't there yesterday. But tonight, with the sun going down behind it, the maple tree by the wrought iron gate my brother made me was a burning flame, bright red, gorgeous, representing everything I love about this season. I have been waiting since springtime to see the mountains aglow with the reds, oranges, and golds of autumn. I have been wondering what does the land around Pilot's Knob look like now, or what the treetops would look like if I were sitting in the deer stand by the creek just a little bit north of here. But in God's own amazing way, autumn came to my own backyard. I don't need to go find autumn by driving my car through the Blue Ridge Mountains.

Sometimes we search and search for love, for friendship, for companionship, and sometimes all we are wanting is right here in our own backyard. You don't have to try so hard to find your heart's desire. Just as the leaves turn when the nights are cool and the afternoons are still warm, at just the right timing, in God's timing, your life will change into a glorious display of beauty and peace and hope. Love will find you. I promise, you will have everything you want in time. Open your eyes, and see the burning flame of the maple tree right there in front of you. Open your eyes, and see your despair turn to peace. Open your eyes, and see your heart mend and glow from love sent into your life today. I could have so easily walked past that maple tree without looking that direction. I could have missed it. And in just a few short weeks, the branches will be bare, and I, not seeing the burning flame, would have been without knowledge that it happened when I wasn't looking. But I did see it. And my hope is renewed by the intensity. May your hope be renewed as you see the leaves turn from faded green to autumn bright? I'll be praying for you to find healing for your heartache and happiness in the moment.

Friday, October 28, 2011

I received several pieces of good advice yesterday. Yesterday I was feeling a little afraid to move forward completely - 100%. What if I make the wrong decision? What if everything that I want to happen doesn't happen? What if I don't really know how to have a successful relationship? I don't want to be like the marriage counselor who has been divorced 6 times. I don't want to be the writer who can tell all the other women how to survive a broken heart, because my heart keeps getting broken over and over again. What if I put my trust in one person and I am let down again? It's like putting all your eggs in one basket with the last few eggs balanced precariously on the top of the pile, and when you try to catch the one which fell when you stumbled, you lose your balance and drop the entire basket. I want safety and stability and love and peace and companionship and a future. Have you ever been scared to move on with your life? I have a wonderful opportunity for a wonderful life right in front of me. And I choose my new life. I don't want to go back in the past. I want to move forward. But tiny, tiny part of me is a little bit scared. I wish I was completely confident, but yesterday I learned something which helped me feel more confident and sure of myself, and I feel more like I'm standing on solid ground, and I have a good hold on my basket of eggs and none are wobbling.

1. Make a list of all of the good things; I guarantee the list of the good things in your life is longer than the bad. Focus on the good.
2. There will be happy days and sad days, because our emotions as a woman are just like that. Don't make a major,

life altering decision, on a day when you are unsure or sad or angry. Just wait for your emotions to settle out in a day or two. Look at your life when you're steady and calm, and then make a decision.

3. Know where you are going, and move in that direction.

4. If your heart is not completely in it, you will see more flaws in a potential mate. When your heart is completely in, you will love him for his supposed flaws. You will cherish the ways in which he is different from you. So if you're focusing on his idiosyncrasies, examine your own heart. Maybe you like him a whole lot, but you don't feel unconditional love the way you should.

5. Remember the Golden Rule. Treat someone the way you want to be treated. Or in romantic relationship terms: if you wouldn't want your partner to do it to you, don't do it to him or her. If it would hurt your feelings if he or she did that same thing which you are considering, then that is not the right decision to make.

6. Some relationships are never meant to be. Your past relationships are in the past for a reason. Quit worrying about your past, let the pain go, let the tiny sliver of romantic feelings go, pull the thorn out of your side, let the guilt you feel over failing go, and move on to a better tomorrow.

There are probably hundreds of pieces of good advice. But I have only two more pieces of good advice from me for you. First, only you know what will make you happy. And on your journey to real happiness, you will have tears as you go through the renewal process. It's okay to be sad sometimes. It's okay if you feel scared. And everything will be okay in time. I wrote this book to help you see another way of seeing your life and your heart - to offer you a different perspective to examine what you have lost and what you have gained - to give you hope that you will find real love that lasts a lifetime if you just keep moving forward. I am moving forward with my life. Last night I went to sleep knowing I need to change directions, and this morning I woke up with the courage to do just that. I am ready to start shift gears in my heart.

Secondly, do you remember when I said "you don't have to answer the telephone just because it rings?" I also promised to tell you why. When you answer the phone, you bring that person into the present moment. So before you answer the phone, ask yourself, do you want that person on the other end of the line in the room with you - the telemarketer, your nosy friend, your ex, whomever, it doesn't really matter who it is, do you want them in your life today? This is what is important about that; you have to choose to whom you will talk. Do you want to talk to the person beside you or the person calling? Or even worse, do you want to talk to the person to whom you are talking to on the phone already, or the person who is interrupting? Don't let someone interrupt your new life who is just going to weigh you down with the past and bring chaos and confusion into your life after you have moved on. Don't answer the phone if you don't want to be in a relationship with that man. You don't have to talk to anyone you don't want to; you don't have to return the phone call. You don't have to explain your actions to anyone. If you believe what you are doing is right for you, it is. Do you want to move on to a better tomorrow? I do. Let's move on together. Today will be better than yesterday. And tomorrow will be better than today.

Wednesday, November 23, 2011

It doesn't matter that it is November (again) and that tomorrow is Thanksgiving. Today is the day before Thanksgiving, and two years ago, I received divorce papers; one year ago on this day, my man and I had lunch and agreed to be in an exclusive dating relationship; and today, we had lunch as friends. We will always be friends, and for that, I am extremely thankful. I am thankful beyond words, because we have a relationship that no one else outside of the two of us will ever understand. I barely understand, because it just doesn't seem possible to be so connected with another human being. And it's strange to be this connected in my heart and soul, and not be a couple. We are not in a romantic relationship, and we date other people. One of the worst mistakes you can make in this post-divorce world is to rush into a new relationship before you have been healed of the failed one. We made that mistake, and we had to break up to find our individual selves. But he is my best friend, and I am thankful, because even when I forgot how he has always had my best interest in mind, he still was there for me. He has looked over my health issues. He has faithfully called to check on me every so often all these months we've been apart; even if I fussed at him, he still cared about me. He encourages me to accomplish my goals and to find happiness. I don't know what the future holds for me, for any of us, but I know what I want. I want God's will for my life. And I want to be thankful every day for the blessings in my life.

I am thankful for my children who left today to go on vacation with their father. I am thankful for my man's children, because they have a special place in my heart always. I am thankful for my parents, and thankful that they went on vacation with friends instead of feeling like they had to be responsible for me when I am alone this week. I am thankful for my man's parents whom I had the honor and pleasure to visit this afternoon at the nursing home. There is no better story of real love than the two of them, and I pray every day that I will one day have what they have. I am thankful for all of my friends who extended an invitation to me for dinner tomorrow. Thank you very much for inviting me. Divorced and single people rely on their friends to share a seat at the table. And I am so excited to have dinner with a very sweet woman who has become in the past six months one of my closest friends. She has a really good heart, and I am thankful for her. I am thankful for my professional colleagues who have shown me such wonderful support for upcoming projects. Even though I am feeling a little lonely, I am thankful for these few days of solitude to work on my writing projects and to reflect on the stirrings of my heart. I am thankful that I have learned who I am and what I want and what I need. I am thankful that God has a plan for my life, and I just have to keep moving forward into His plan.

For what are you thankful? What has happened in your life in the past year? What do you want to have in the next year? I pray it all comes true. All your hopes and dreams. Be thankful for every day between the day your relationship failed and today. You'll never understand why everything happens the way it did. So don't try to understand. Just live. Everything happens for a reason. And it's okay if you don't really know the reason.

Tuesday, November 29, 2011

We live the consequences of the choices we made in our past. And every day, we have more choices to make. Some choices may seem like minor, inconsequential, trivial details, but you just never know what the long-term impact of even the tiniest of actions has in your life. Choice involves action. You choose to call a friend. You choose to stand up a date. You choose what to wear. You choose what words come out of your mouth when you speak. But you cannot choose to love. You can choose to act on your love. In a way, love is a commitment which involves choices. But in another way, love is a feeling. And feelings you just feel, and sometimes you love someone unconditionally, even if you're not sure you want to feel that way, even if they don't love you back, even when being in a relationship with that person is not where you are at the moment. And in relationships, over time, feelings fluctuate. When you get married - and stay married - you'll have days where you feel more love, or more in love, than other days. That's the honoring your commitment part where you choose to stick with the marriage even on the days when you don't feel like it. Getting divorced is a choice, an action. And you may choose to get divorced because your feelings have changed, or you may choose to get divorced because your feelings are the same but the relationship is just not the right one for you. Choosing to end a relationship is a very complicated and emotional decision.

But what about when you chose to begin a new relationship? Or when a relationship hasn't yet evolved into marriage? What do you do when you know without any doubts that you love someone, but you don't feel ready to get married again? Post-divorce dating is complicated. Part of you wants to just have fun and have no pressures of an exclusive relationship. Part of you wants to move really slowly as you act on your feelings because you are afraid of being hurt again. Part of you wants the stability of a committed relationship. Part of you wants to sit at home and not date at all because that's emotionally easier. I try to think of post-divorce dating as making new friends and building friendships with men, one of which could possibly be the man I would marry in the future, and I just try to enjoy the moment. I have no problem giving out my phone number and making plans for a date with a single, attractive, employed and successful male in my age bracket. After all, it's just dinner and nothing more. My friend says she doesn't need any more friends, and so she doesn't go on a date at all with someone she can't see herself being involved with exclusively and long-term. My other friend says you should keep your options open. But why keep your options open when you already know what your heart wants? For what are you looking? Are you actually looking for someone better to come along? Maybe there is someone better. Or maybe you need to be thankful for the friends or potential life partner you already have in your life.

But whether you choose to keep dating, or you choose to begin a new partnership, ultimately it is your choice. You must choose how to express your love. You must choose your friends. And you are the only person who knows your heart, so no one else can tell you what choices to make. And every choice has a consequence. You'll have to choose whether or not to accept an invitation. You'll have to choose whether or not you want to move forward and accept one relationship has ended and go to the next relationship. And you need to make your choices with confidence, because there will always be critics. There will always be someone who thinks you should do whatever differently. But only you know your heart. Only you know what is right for you. Only you can make the choice. I'm praying that you'll have the courage to make the tough choices, the wisdom to know your heart, and the confidence to stand strong in the face of your critics.

So are you striving to have a positive attitude about the life that you have now? Are you struggling with maintaining your positive attitude? I really, really, really want to just enjoy the life I have and have fun and laugh and play. I want to tell jokes and ride horses and go for walks in the woods and play Monopoly and have tea parties with the little girls and spa parties with the big girls. I want to sing along while my daughter plays Christmas carols on the piano. And I really want to just be amiable and get along with everybody without any drama or chaos. Do you want a happy life like this too? I prefer smiling over crying, although sometimes tears come when I don't want to cry. I sent a link to this Elton John song to my friend today, because we both were feeling a little bit sad.

"Keep smiling, keep shining, knowing you can always count on me, for sure, that's what friends are for, for good times, for bad times..."

When you're feeling sad, you just have to look for something to smile about. Focus on the positive. Look for the good in people. But it's so difficult when you keep getting poked with negative comments from people who for whatever sick reason just don't want you to be happy. Why does someone choose to send a nasty email message when they could just be nice or just ignore you if they don't like you? Why do people go out of their way - like actually put forth effort - to be mean? Sometimes people post negative comments on my blog, and that's okay, because instead of it hurting my feelings, I think, "how sad, this person has nothing better to do than troll the internet poking fun at my positive comments trying to make women feel better about themselves." I'm used to criticism; I work with thousands of students a year and have eighteen co-workers which direct report to me and I have ex-husbands. I'm sure there are lots of people who wish I would do what I do a little bit differently than the way I do it. Too bad, because I do what I need to do, I do the right thing to do, I encourage my children to say and do the appropriate thing, and I do my best to enjoy myself in the process.
Sometimes the veiled sarcastic comment is so vague I don't even know to what the person is referring. But even if I feel like I missed part of the conversation or that I didn't receive some other message in my inbox or voicemail, I know when I'm being poked with a stick. It's like I'm just walking down the street looking cute in my white dress and heels

and smiling and singing a song in my head when for no good reason at all, someone just throws a bucket of muddy water on me. They didn't have to throw that on me. But they did. And I just wish I was the kind of woman who could say "WTF is wrong with you." And if you know what that stands for, then you are the kind of woman who can say it. Good for you! You've got balls! My friends are always telling me I need to stand up for myself. But I just don't want to waste the energy reacting to the crazy things other people do, but I do think things like WTF in my head. Just be nice already. I'll be nice to you. You be nice to me. Or, at the very least, just ignore me or leave me alone if you don't like me. I have found the best approach to dealing with the negativity of others is to ignore them. I just don't respond. So what if I get a hateful email? Delete, delete, delete. Was there some important information in the email after the negative comments? Probably, but I don't care. If you want me to read your email, be nice to me. So what if my date makes a rude comment? Goodbye, I don't have time for you right now, because if you want to be around me, then you're going to play nice. And this is my favorite ugly comment of all time, "Do you really have to have your way all the time?" Because what men mean when they say this is *I'm a spoiled little boy and I just want you to do what I want you to do for me what I want without me doing anything for you in return and if you have a differing opinion, then something is wrong with you.* Well, guess what, nothing is wrong with you. And you do deserve to have your way some of the time. You should be happy. Your man, even your ex, should do things which make you happy. There is nothing wrong with expecting others to be kind, respectful, and considerate. So if someone is not being kind, respectful, and considerate to you, and this upsets you, then ignore the negativity. Just act like it didn't happen and just keep on smiling, keep on shining, keep on loving yourself and your life. That's the pep talk I give to myself each and every time someone does or says something intentionally negative, mean, or hurtful. And it's so hard to ignore them, because your gut reaction is to put up your dukes and fight back, but if you want to be happy and live life with a positive attitude, you just can't react rudely just because someone is rude to you. Anyway, the best revenge is to be beautiful, successful, and happy. Enough said.

Epilogue – One year after starting this book

Each day I kept thinking today will be the last page of this book. So I finally just had to stop and say this is the last page. But the blog keeps on going indefinitely, so if you want to continue with my story, please visit my web site at www.youtoocanmowthegrass.com. But more than encouraging you to read my blog and join in the discussions, I want to encourage you to live your life. Find happiness, because it's really there. Months after finishing this book, I am still sick. The doctors still don't know exactly what is wrong with me – depression, gynecological issues, irritable bowel syndrome, rapid weight loss, constant pain. Who really knows? I think this is just something I have to go through. Not only am I still sick, there has been no resolution in my love life. I still am waiting. I am still hoping to find real love. I still believe that real love that lasts a lifetime is possible. I just don't know what the future holds. Keep your options open. Only time will tell. One year has passed since I started writing this book. I am beginning year three after my divorce. So much has happened, and yet so little has happened. I am happy. I'm excited about what will happen next. I'm excited about what will happen next in your life too. Healing, renewal, and hope as you too can mow the grass. You too can leave an abusive marriage. You too can find real love. You too can complete your college education. You too can enjoy being by yourself. You too can accept that your relationship failed and move on with your life. You too can do anything you want to do. Believe in yourself and just go do it.

Proof

Made in the USA
Charleston, SC
31 December 2011